The American Statehouse

STUDIES IN GOVERNMENT AND PUBLIC POLICY

The American Statehouse

INTERPRETING DEMOCRACY'S TEMPLES

Charles T. Goodsell

 UNIVERSITY PRESS OF KANSAS

Published by the University Press of Kansas (Lawrence, Kansas 66049), which was organized by the Kansas Board of Regents and is operated and funded by Emporia State University, Fort Hays State University, Kansas State University, Pittsburg State University, the University of Kansas, and Wichita State University

Library of Congress Cataloging-in-Publication Data

Goodsell, Charles T.
The American statehouse : interpreting democracy's temples / Charles T. Goodsell.
p. cm. — (Studies in government and public policy)
Includes bibliographical references and index.
ISBN 0-7006-1044-8 (cloth : alk. paper)
1. Capitols—United States.   2. Architecture and state—United States.   3. Architecture and society—United States.   I. Title.   II. Series.
NA4411 .G66 2000
725'.11'0973—dc21   00-009139

British Library Cataloguing in Publication Data is available.

Printed in the United States of America

10 9 8 7 6 5 4 3 2 1

The paper used in this publication meets the minimum requirements of the American National Standard for Permanence of Paper for Printed Library Materials Z39.48-1984.

With love to Barb and John,

two sylvan spirits

Contents

Tables and Figures

TABLES

FIGURES

Preface

This book is about architecture and politics in the state capitols of America. The term "statehouse" refers collectively to these buildings and is used in the singular to impart one of the major themes of the book: that the fifty capitols are usefully studied not just as fifty separate buildings, but as a generic building type.

My analysis of this building type is distinctively political, which makes sense because I am a political scientist, albeit one accustomed to interdisciplinary study. Hence I do not examine these buildings from the standpoint of the architectural historian or the practicing architect concerned with aesthetics and function. Rather, I offer what I call social interpretation of architecture. To make such an interpretation, I utilize three conceptual frameworks or lenses: the first devoted to the search for political values or ideas embedded in the buildings, the second concerned with the effects of the buildings on contemporary political behavior, and the third dedicated to the appraisal of the larger impressions the buildings make on society.

James M. Mayo of the School of Architecture and Urban Design at the University of Kansas initially suggested that I study American state capitols. Good ideas are priceless, and I will always be grateful to Jim for this one. Before getting deeply into the subject, initial guidance was received from William N. Cassella, Jr., of the Institute of Public Administration in New York, who shared with me his rich knowledge and library on the subject.

An opportunity to embark on the study full-time arose when David C. Sweet, dean of the Maxine Goodman Levin College of Urban Affairs at Cleveland State University, invited me to become visiting professor for the 1991/1992 academic year. In addition to providing office space, he made available a substantial research budget that allowed me to begin fieldwork and pay expenses associated with the needed photography.

Later on, assistance was received from other sources. The Graham Foundation for Advanced Studies in the Fine Arts, located in Chicago, provided a generous grant for travel that permitted me to complete most of the remainder of the fieldwork. To assist with the high costs of production of the volume, subvention funding was received from three sources at Virginia Polytechnic Institute and State University: the Center for Public Administration and Policy, the College of Architecture and Urban Studies, and the Faculty Book Publishing Committee. At several points, the Photographic Archives of the National Gallery of Art in Washington, D.C., printed many hundreds of my statehouse photographs for its collection and produced an extra copy of each for my use. Additional printing support was received from the Faculty Small Grants Fund of the College of Architecture and Urban Studies at Virginia Tech. I should note that all the photographs in the book are my own, except the very first, and to reprint it I appreciate receiving permission from the Minnesota Historical Society.

Special thanks go to several individuals. First, looking back several years, my dissertation director in graduate school, Arthur Maass, taught me how to think independently as a scholar and not be content to swim in the mainstream. My former editor for two previous books written some years ago, Max Hall, taught me the craft of writing a scholarly book that is also clear and readable.

Turning to the present day, colleague Humberto L. Rodriguez-Camilloni of the College of Architecture and Urban Studies at Virginia Tech advised me on architectural styles. Cathy Gorman at Virginia Tech's Photographic Services printed photographs. James Dustin of the university's New Media Center assisted with the preparation of the floor plans that appear in chapter 6. At various times, valuable help was received from four graduate assistants: Ronald L. Mahle at

Cleveland State and Martha J. Dede, Vladimir D. Momcilovic, and Percy Luen-Tim Lui at Virginia Tech.

Let me single out another category of people to whom I owe a special debt of thanks: the many individuals who generously permitted themselves to be interviewed in the state capitals around the nation over the seven years of fieldwork. Many of these men and women not only took considerable time to meet with me, but also gave me personal tours of the buildings and rounded up useful documents. The 307 individuals who helped in this way are named at the end of the bibliography.

Finally, I would like to express my deepest gratitude to my wife, Mary Elizabeth Goodsell, for her unfailing moral support over the many years of the project. She accompanied me on many of my research trips around the country and was always a joy to have along.

1 | *Introduction to the Statehouse*

July 27, 1898, was a splendid day in St. Paul, fit for summertime pageantry. A parade of over fifty units filed past the rising walls of the incomplete Minnesota State Capitol, which after two years of off-and-on construction consisted of 400 feet of foundation and subbasement plus elements of the first two floors. Led by the mounted police and culminated by the fire brigade, the parade included the Fifteenth Regiment of the Minnesota Volunteer Infantry, aging veterans of the Grand Army of the Republic, horse-drawn carriages representing the Old Settlers' Association, and no fewer than six marching brass bands, one composed of local newsboys. The headlines that these boys had called out on the streets of the Twin Cities that summer told of stirring American military victories against Spain, with Puerto Rico to fall into American hands the very next day.[1]

The reason for the great occasion was the laying of the cornerstone of the new capitol. A derrick held the heavy piece of granite aloft above its final resting place, in front of a flag-bedecked reviewing stand (Figure 1.1). Standing by to wield the ceremonial trowel was the venerable Alexander Ramsey, who at eighty-three had been, incredibly, the first territorial governor as well as the second state governor of Minnesota. The silver tool's handle was fashioned of wood saved from the territorial capitol, which—from 1849 until it burned in 1881—had stood lower down on Wabasha Hill, a few blocks closer to downtown and the Mississippi River. A replacement building had been built on the same site, but its size and design did not comport with a growing desire within the legislature to portray Minnesota as an urbanizing, modern state rather than a frontier outpost. The new capitol was sited closer to the top of Wabasha Hill, where it would be clearly visible on the skyline along with the fu-

ture St. Paul Cathedral, which was then being planned.

The first of several speeches to be endured under that July sun was delivered by Charles H. Graves, a wealthy shipping magnate and former mayor of Duluth. Graves was one of eleven members of the Board of State Capitol Commissioners, a body formed five years earlier to direct the new capitol project. He noted that the building was rising from land homesteaded by pioneers in 1847. The commissioner said that its shape and approaches reflect familiarity with the Capitol in Washington, D.C.

Graves's speech went beyond rhetoric, however. In remarks that pointedly referred to one of several controversies that had surrounded the project, he warned that unless added appropriations were forthcoming from the Minnesota legislature, the public rooms of its future home would have to be completed with ordinary woodwork and plain walls, not to mention an absence of artwork and statuary. "The interior of such a building," he implored, "ought to be finished with the most beautiful of native and foreign stone, and made an object of art, educative of the taste of our people and inspiring their pride."[2]

A cost limit of $2 million was set for the project, an amount considered prudent in view of poor economic conditions created by the depression of 1893. This sum was considered by the project's partisans as not enough for the job, however. Coupled with the cost issue was another pressing question: where the building's stone was to be quarried. Granite from Minnesota, rather than stone from outside the state, was greatly preferred by vocal regional interests, even though the costs would be greater. After considerable turmoil and publicity, a compromise was struck: granite from St. Cloud was to be used for the foundation, terraces, and steps, while white

Figure 1.1. Laying the cornerstone of the Minnesota State Capitol, July 27, 1898. Ground had been broken two years earlier. The statehouse, designed by Cass Gilbert, was first occupied in 1905 and completed in 1907.

marble from Georgia was to be applied to the exterior walls and dome.

Remaining in the background during the ceremonies was Cass Gilbert, also a source of controversy. Gilbert was the building's architect. Only thirty-four years old when he sought this commission, Gilbert was out to make a name for himself in his chosen profession. A local boy, he had lived in St. Paul for most of his life, although by the time this opportunity arose he had been well exposed to the international architectural scene. Gilbert had studied architecture at the Massachusetts Institute of Technology, spent an obligatory year in Europe sketching buildings, and then taken an entry-level job in New York at McKim, Mead and White, one of the country's leading architectural firms. By 1893, Gilbert had opened an office in his hometown, designed a few local residences, and become involved in design work for the World's Columbian Exposition, which opened that year in Chicago.

When the new Minnesota State Capitol began to unfold as a potential project, Gilbert sprang into action. He wangled an introduction to the governor through a local newspaper editor. He then became president of the state chapter of the American Institute of Architects and persuaded this group to protest the $2 million limit on the project. Most important, Gilbert was able to develop a close personal relationship with the presiding officer of the Board of State Capitol Commissioners, Channing Seabury. He successfully urged Seabury to lobby the legislature for a higher architectural fee than the 2.5 percent alloted, and he persuaded the board to abort the results of an initial design competition in which members of the Minnesota chapter of the AIA had been given no role. Gibert then submitted a personal entry in the second competition and survived an initial cut of five out of forty-one designs, but was unable to garner a majority or even a plurality of the commissioners' votes in any public ballot. But following a closed meeting of the commission, Seabury suddenly announced that Gilbert had been selected, much to the disgust of his more senior colleagues.

Gilbert carried out the job as energetically as he sought it. He demanded perfection in the turning of every column. Inside the dome, he placed an innovative supporting cone of steel and brick. He prescribed details as small as the design of toilet fixtures, wastebaskets, and doorknobs. The building was completed in 1907 at a cost of $4.5 million and was considered at the time to be one of the more dazzling statehouses in the country (Figure 1.2).

Gilbert went on to become a major figure in the profession and served as the national president of the AIA. Among many other structures he designed over his career were the United States Custom House and the Woolworth Building in New York and the buildings that house the Chamber of Commerce and the Supreme Court in Washington, D.C. Gilbert also designed the capitol of West Virginia and contributed to the completion of the Arkansas statehouse. He failed, however, in efforts to win statehouse commissions in Missouri, Montana, and Wisconsin. He died in 1934 in the sad position of a professional outcast, since the neoclassic orthodoxy popular at the turn of the century had gone out of style.[3]

AN OBJECT OF ART, EDUCATION, AND PRIDE

The ceremony in St. Paul in July 1898 and the events surrounding it are useful to introduce our subject because they say so much about it. The American state capitol, or statehouse, is not just a government building. To paraphrase Charles Graves, it is an object of art, education, and pride for each of the fifty states. Moreover, this is as true today as it was a century ago, when the cornerstone of the Minnesota State Capitol was laid.

Statehouses have been referred to as symbols, temples, and icons, all rightly so, for they are

Figure 1.2. The Minnesota State Capitol, St. Paul. The cornerstone is to the left of the front doorways. The main sculptor of the figures on the facade was Daniel Chester French.

deeply vested with cultural meaning. For political figures and ordinary citizens alike, this meaning is emotionally charged. For some, entering one's statehouse is like entering a civic church, which perhaps is why these buildings are visited by tens of thousands of citizens and schoolchildren, as would be a shrine. This heightened meaning is one reason for all the pageantry on such an occasion as cornerstone laying; similar rituals are performed at ceremonies for ground breaking, dedication, and rededication.

At the same time, statehouses are eminently *political* artifacts in every sense of the word. It is in the self-interest of government officials to whip up proauthority sentiment through parades of infantry and bands, as occurred in St. Paul. Whether or not they are conscious of it, legislators like the air of legitimation fostered by meeting in a civic church. Governors and other elected executives see their physical quarters in the statehouse as the literal fulfillment of their personal dream to ascend to high public office. Citizens who are proud of their state's unique locality and heritage in a vast and varied country seek tangible ways to affirm and validate their pride. The consequence is often building policies whose underlying aim is to create the "best" statehouse in the nation—or, at a minimum, a capitol equal to those of rival states.

Henry-Russell Hitchcock and William Seale contend that the state capitol is one of two unique American contributions to monumental architecture, the other being the skyscraper.[4] Although each statehouse is unique, almost all of them share certain key characteristics, such as prominent building site, parklike setting, monumental size, cruciform ground plan, dome and rotunda, and classic temple front. Its common set of architectural features makes the statehouse, along with the traditional county courthouse and older federal post office, one of the few distinctively governmental buildings to be found in what is essentially a private-sector architectural landscape in the United States.

Most statehouses were built a century or so ago, and thus they have an antiquated and ornamented appearance that sets them apart from utilitarian and self-consciously "modern" architecture. Their neoclassic and revivalist designs are generally European in origin, adapted in endless American stylistic variations. With its visual prominence, long horizontal mass, and upward-thrusting yet rounded dome, the statehouse is often the most notable structure on the skyline, especially in smaller capital cities. Even if not so dominating, it is the central physical symbol of state government and, in many ways, of the state itself. As a signature building with which everyone is familiar, the statehouse embodies elements of symbolic contradiction: the natural pride that citizens feel for their state, on the one hand, and the inevitable distrust with which individualistic Americans view government, on the other.

Another capitol building that is symbolically much on the mind of Americans is the United States Capitol in Washington, D.C. Because of television and other forms of mass media that transmit its image incessantly to every corner of the nation, it is one of the country's most powerful physical symbols. Its paradoxes of referential meaning also embrace mixtures of contradictory attitudes toward the United States Congress, the federal government, and the nation itself.

Partly because of its national exposure, the United States Capitol is capable of diminishing the perceived importance of the state capitol. Yet while the Capitol is obviously of enormous significance and is the largest such structure in the nation, its tendency to overshadow the statehouses should be resisted. From a governmental standpoint, the laws passed and administered in the fifty statehouses collectively authorize more generic police powers and public services that affect the American population than those originating in the Capitol. The presidents of the United States are, it is easy to forget, formally elected in the fifty statehouses (by members of the Electoral College). Furthermore, all but one of the amendments to the Constitution were ratified in them or their predecessor buildings, the Eighteenth Amendment being ratified by convention.

From an architectural standpoint, the state capitols constitute all but one of the country's examples of this unique building form. In fact, the United States Capitol was not the first capitol in the nation to be built, nor is it the oldest one in continuous use. Contrary to popular impression, its design did not dictate the shape of the statehouse form. Yet as Graves's reference to familiarity with the Capitol suggests, the multiphased construction of that building and the emergence of the form at the state level were closely intertwined.

The history of the Minnesota State Capitol brings out other important points as well, including how the construction of these edifices can stir up great political controversy. Struggles over cost, regional self-benefit, and competing ambitions took place during the creation of not just the Minnesota State Capitol, but every statehouse erected since colonial times. Battles erupted among rival political parties or factions seeking to control the state, various towns and cities desiring to be named the state capital, competing advocates of domestic or foreign building stone, and recipients of the graft that was routinely paid in association with large state construction contracts a century ago.

The statehouse in St. Paul illustrates many other common characteristics of this peculiarly American form of public architecture as well: frequent siting at a high elevation, referred to in many cities as "capitol hill"; location near the banks of a river, a practice that was almost inevitable before the construction of modern roads and railroads; replacement of a primitive statehouse that had become inadequate or had burned down by a "successor" building; lavish attention to ornamentation, art displays, and statuary, making the structure a combined civic temple, art museum, and war memorial; and adoption of the official name state capitol, a practice followed by most, but by no means all, of the states (for the official names see Table 1.1).

The example of the architect of the Minnesota State Capitol, Cass Gilbert, is also instructive. His exposure, along with that of his contemporaries, to the World's Columbian Exposition of 1893 and the American approach to neoclassicism represented by the firm of McKim, Mead and White

in New York was in large part responsible for the rather standard architectural vocabulary that came to be used in designing statehouses. Like most capitol architects, Gilbert was an ambitious entrepreneur in obtaining important commissions. He was also an establishment figure and a mainstream AIA professional rather than an avant-garde innovator. In addition, Gilbert was one of several American architects who worked on more than one statehouse in his lifetime, a tradition established in the early nineteenth century and continued into the twentieth. The relatively small group of men (and they were all men) who designed these buildings knew one another, fought one another, and copied one another, helping to create a common architectural model.

AN OBJECT OF SOCIAL INTERPRETATION

State capitols are the subject of hundreds of publications of various kinds, although the vast majority concern only single buildings and do not analyze them as a group. The most important scholarly treatment of statehouses as a whole is Henry-Russell Hitchcock and William Seale's *Temples of Democracy*.[5] This book was written from the standpoint of the architectural historian and is based on extensive archival research. Its treatment is definitive with respect to the history of the capitols, predecessor buildings, stylistic attributes, and design competitions that preceded construction. Even though the book is now over a quarter century old, it would be difficult to improve on its authors' discussion of these matters.

Temples of Democracy is additionally helpful to this inquiry from two specific standpoints. First, its title captures a fundamental truth about these buildings that was confirmed by my own analysis, and at the end of this book I return to this point. I also borrow their terminology in its subtitle. Second, in conducting my research, I was influenced by Hitchcock and Seale's concept of a key "clustering" or convergence of architectural symbols that took place during the development of this building form. They argue that the con-

Table 1.1
STATE CAPITALS AND CAPITOLS

	Capital City	Official Name of Statehouse	Prior Capitols in Capital (extant)
Alabama	Montgomery	State Capitol State House[a]	
Alaska	Juneau	State Capitol	
Arizona	Phoenix	State Capitol	
Arkansas	Little Rock	State Capitol	Old State House
California	Sacramento	State Capitol	
Colorado	Denver	State Capitol	
Connecticut	Hartford	State Capitol	Old State House
Delaware	Dover	Legislative Hall	State House
Florida	Tallahassee	The Capitol	The Old Capitol
Georgia	Atlanta	State Capitol	
Hawaii	Honolulu	State Capitol	'Iolani Palace
Idaho	Boise	State Capitol	
Illinois	Springfield	State Capitol	Old State Capitol
Indiana	Indianapolis	State House	
Iowa	Des Moines	State Capitol	
Kansas	Topeka	State Capitol State House[b]	
Kentucky	Frankfort	State Capitol	Old State Capitol Old Capitol Annex
Louisiana	Baton Rouge	State Capitol	Old State Capitol
Maine	Augusta	State House	
Maryland	Annapolis	State House	
Massachusetts	Boston	State House	Old State House
Michigan	Lansing	State Capitol	
Minnesota	St. Paul	State Capitol	
Mississippi	Jackson	New Capitol	Old Capitol
Missouri	Jefferson City	State Capitol	
Montana	Helena	State Capitol	
Nebraska	Lincoln	State Capitol	
Nevada	Carson City	Legislative Building	State Capitol[c]
New Hampshire	Concord	State House	
New Jersey	Trenton	State House	
New Mexico	Santa Fe	State Capitol	Palace of the Governors Bataan Memorial Building
New York	Albany	State Capitol	
North Carolina	Raleigh	State Legislative Building	State Capitol[c]
North Dakota	Bismarck	State Capitol	
Ohio	Columbus	State House	
Oklahoma	Oklahoma City	State Capitol	

Table 1.1
STATE CAPITALS AND CAPITOLS (*continued*)

	Capital City	Official Name of Statehouse	Prior Capitols in Capital (extant)
Oregon	Salem	State Capitol	
Pennsylvania	Harrisburg	State Capitol Building	
Rhode Island	Providence	State House	Old State House
South Carolina	Columbia	State House	
South Dakota	Pierre	State Capitol	
Tennessee	Nashville	State Capitol	
Texas	Austin	State Capitol	
Utah	Salt Lake City	State Capitol	Social Hall Council Hall
Vermont	Montpelier	State House	
Virginia	Richmond	State Capitol	
Washington	Olympia	Legislative Building	Old Capitol Building
West Virginia	Charleston	State Capitol	
Wisconsin	Madison	State Capitol	
Wyoming	Cheyenne	State Capitol	

[a] State Capitol is the name of Alabama's historic structure. State House is the official name given to a renovated state highway department building to which the legislature moved during the restoration of the capitol and where it has remained.

[b] State Capitol is the name currently used for the Kansas statehouse, but it appears that State House was its original name.

[c] In Nevada and North Carolina, the governor and some other officials maintain offices in the historic capitol, even though the legislature has moved to a newer legislative building.

vergence first occurred with the construction in 1810 to 1821 of the Pennsylvania State Capitol designed by A. Stephen Hills (a building no longer extant).[6] While I disagree with some details of Hitchcock and Seale's analysis, I found it useful in my own study to stress the architectural commonalities of these buildings, rather than their individualities.

My analysis of the statehouse from a social standpoint is based on several orienting ideas. First, my topical focus is the *political* analysis of architecture: the way in which statehouses reflect and affect aspects of authority, influence, hierarchy, and culture as they relate to public governing. To achieve this aim, the interests of the political scientist energize the investigation, but the concepts of many other disciplines are also needed to carry it out. These include sociology, psychology, anthropology, and material-culture

studies, not to mention architectural history, architectural theory, and behavioral studies of the built environment. Other political scientists have also undertaken interdisciplinary inquiry at the confluence of politics and architecture, including Murray Edelman, Cortus T. Koehler, J. A. Laponce, Harold D. Lasswell, David Milne, Lawrence J. Vale, and James S. Young.[7] Over the past several years, I also have published a number of studies in this field, including *The Social Meaning of Civic Space*.[8]

Second, I utilize as an instrument for my analysis the concept of *building type*. This is a more ambitious notion than Hitchcock and Seale's idea of clustered symbols. It seeks to achieve an aggregative level of analysis by which broad, conceptual points can be made about the buildings' collective meaning that transcend the individual structures. The term is often attributed to George

Kubler, who used it to construct a framework for conducting research on colonial architecture. Nikolaus Pevsner later employed the term to organize a famous historical review of European architecture, and, more recently, Karen Franck and Lynda Schneekloth have urged architects to enliven their thinking and work by means of the notion of building type.[9] In my own use of the concept, I draw more on sociological than architectural theory, linking the idea to Max Weber's concept of ideal type: an abstraction that captures the essence of a diverse phenomenon by isolating its central functional characteristics.[10]

Third, in carrying out the analysis, I consciously employ the *comparative method*. With a study universe of precisely fifty examples, I had a big enough data set in which to uncover patterns, yet one that was small enough to allow in-depth analysis. This helped in a number of ways. Explicit comparisons of individual cases brought to my attention pecularities and innovations that would be lost from view if each building were studied in isolation. The method also permitted me to reduce the overwhelming mass of detail to sets of general patterns, from which contrasting meanings could then be deduced. At the same time, I searched for fundamental, overarching tendencies that allowed broad generalization despite individual exceptions and departures.

Fourth, the research itself was centered on *personal observation and interviews* at the statehouses. I conducted fieldwork at forty-nine of the fifty statehouses, with the Alaska State Capitol left out since it is an adapted territorial office building. My research visits, which lasted from one to four days each, took place from 1991 to 1998. I made personal observations, took photographs, collected documents, and interviewed 307 knowledgeable individuals. The persons to whom I talked were elected and appointed state officials; legislators and legislative staff members; facilities managers and statehouse employees of all types; local architects, preservationists, and historians; state librarians and archivists; lobbyists and protesters; and members of the print and broadcast press.

My final tool is *three conceptual frames or lenses* by which I examined and interpreted these buildings. Together, they provide three distinguishable but compatible avenues for acquiring an understanding of what I call architecture's social meaning. I refer to these conceptual frames as the expressive lens, the behavioral lens, and the societal lens. Together, they reveal the ideas and values that were implicitly embedded in statehouse designs by their builders, the ways in which the capitols affect their users, and the impact of these buildings on the broader society. A summary of these lenses and their use in this book is found in Table 1.2.

The Expressive Lens

By means of the expressive lens, citizens infer ideas, values, and concepts of state governance that may have been held by the originators or rebuilders of capitols or been generally current in their own time. The underlying assumption is that the structures embody, whether consciously or unconsciously, broad conceptions of what was considered right and proper within a system of state governmental authority during their era of construction. That the buildings are made of durable materials—stone, iron, wood, and glass—allows them to function as carriers and perpetuators of social ideas over time. The long-lasting components serve as a kind of enduring text that we can judiciously attempt to "read." Accordingly, architecture, design, decoration, and unchanged furniture placement can be regarded as constituting a kind of "imprint" or set of residual markers of collective ideas.

Such inquiry is not without its pitfalls, it should quickly be pointed out. As Bill Kinser and Neil Kleinman have noted, buildings and other material objects are not discursive or logical as communicators.[11] An architectural text is not like a language text—it cannot be automatically "decoded," even if its "readers" had the right dictionary or codebook. Furthermore, no decisive act of writing or encoding the text ever occurred. A building is a definite but complex object and never the product of a single mind, not even that of the

Table 1.2
THE THREE LENSES AND THEIR USE

	Expressive	Behavioral	Societal
Types of social meaning sought	Ideals and values embedded in features of design	Design elements that shape user conduct	Symbolic impact of statehouse on the public
Issues faced in interpretation	Unstated, subjective, and culturally bound nature of meaning	Degree of causality, individualized and interactive effects	Ambiguity and subjectivity of symbolic meaning
Evidentiary basis of analysis	Cross-cultural and repeated use, contextual logic	Observation, informants, quasi-experiments	Conceptual reasoning and indirect indicators
Topics of analysis (by chapter)			
Building type (chapter 2)	Ideas projected by building site and grounds	Effects on access, circulation, and identity	Aspects of site and design that intimidate or attract
Creation (chapter 3)	Early spatial treatment of governors and legislative bodies	Effects of all of state government in one building	Historical aspects of symbolism at the statehouse
Construction (chapter 4)	Attempts to preserve and restore old statehouses	Human effects of capitol construction	Symbolic meanings of statehouse construction
Objects (chapter 5)	Themes revealed by displayed objects and decor		Apparent effects of symbolic display on the public
Space (chapter 6)	Spatial treatment of separation of powers in mature type	Behavioral effects of growth of government in one place	How the nature of the American state is depicted architecturally
Interiors (chapter 7)	Depiction of institutional cultures in design and features of rooms	Effects of room design on political conduct	Impressions given by room design on the public
Conduct (chapter 8)		Behavioral effects of rotunda and settings of influence	Effects of security measures and electronic media

chief architect. Then, too, accepted contemporaneous ideas that might be embedded in architecture are elusive, changing, subjectively held, and possibly a source of controversy. Finally, the interpretion of objects created in the past requires understanding one culture, that of the past, from the vantage point of another, that of the present—always a problem in material-culture study and related fields.

Nonetheless, with appropriate methodological precautions and a reflective, informed, and prudent research strategy, such inquiry is potentially revealing and informative, in ways not present in more conventional social research. Conceptual and methodological tools for the task can be derived, and generalizations are possible at an appropriate level. Amos Rapoport, the most distinguished present-day student of the interaction of architecture and culture, notes that the built environment's symbolic messages sent from other times and places carry multiple meanings, but are capable of some pan-cultural significance.

Examples are the superiority of height (as in the castle on the hill) and the importance of centrality (as in the middle object in a picture). But in deriving inferences from the environment, Rapoport cautions, we should examine many cases, make explicit comparisons, consciously seek patterns, and be prepared to infer indirectly as well as directly.[12]

One attraction of this line of study is that those who originated the messages were not necessarily aiming at future generations or were even conscious of creating a decipherable message. Hence such imprints may provide us with relatively deep understandings that go below surface descriptions or self-reports. Juan Pablo Bonta provocatively discusses the possibility of architectural "indexes" of cultural reality, a term that implies direct and even quantitative readings of the architectural past.[13] If, for example, the concept of superiority of height is applied to the interior spatial organization of the statehouse, the fact that the legislative chambers are typically situated on upper floors, while the governor's office is usually downstairs, takes on added meaning.

My own bias is that, to pursue this avenue effectively, the researcher must be careful to seek numerous and collaborative sources of information before formulating an interpretation. In addition, the research must draw from alternative sources and include a generalized understanding of the architectural, political, and historical context. Even then, it is important to make needed qualifications and not overreach.

In a pioneering essay written some years ago, the eminent political scientist Harold Lasswell argued that the height of buildings on a city's skyline could be viewed as an index of relative sectoral power. If, for example, corporate skyscrapers are the tallest buildings in the city, the business sector supposedly is dominant within the community's power structure. By contrast, if church steeples or the town hall is the most visible, organized religion or government presumably is paramount.[14] This kind of deduction would be a good example of interpretive overreaching, unless bolstered by much additional evidence.

In my book on civic space, I outlined the results of studying the spatial composition and accommodations of city council chambers and related public spaces in seventy-five city halls across the country. These buildings varied by era of construction from the post–Civil War years to the present day. By means of some twenty-nine variables, as well as contextual study, I uncovered three distinctly different presentations of authority in these ritual spaces: authoritarian, confrontational, and communal, each stemming from a different period of construction.[15]

Admittedly, such research assumes that something "real" exists ontologically to discover. My own view on this fundamental philosophical question is to accept the material objectivity of physical matter while regarding its social meaning as subjectively derived by human observers. When these individually constructed social "realities" fuse into a common, intersubjective whole, the meaning seems irrefutably "objective." This can perhaps happen with particular ease when the social constructions are tied to perceived material objects rather than verbal abstractions. "Discovering" these constructions in a full sense is impossible, although we can accept tentative understandings of them by looking for clues in the documentary record and by thoughtfully interviewing informed users. If we find in this inquiry that repetitive architectural patterns correspond logically to certain social ideas, we have not achieved certainty of understanding but perhaps a very plausible interpretation.

In this book, expressive insights are sought from the overall physical setting of the statehouse, the way institutions of government are treated spatially over time, the decorative displays in and historic-preservation projects undertaken in the capitol, and the design of specific rooms.

The Behavioral Lens

Turning now to the behavioral lens, this second kind of inquiry into architecture and politics asks not what buildings say about their originators or eras of construction, but how they may shape the attitudes and conduct of contemporary users and others affected by them. This frame is used to look for ways in which the built environment affects, not reflects, the social world. Putting the distinction another way, architecture is seen not as an imprint of earlier ideas, but as a pathway that steers or conditions current behavior.[16]

Winston Churchill was, in effect, employing the behavioral lens when in 1941 he gave his reasons for insisting that the bomb-damaged House of Commons be rebuilt exactly to its original design. The opposing sets of Government and Opposition benches discourage ideological factions, he believed, and the absence of desks keeps members from banging desk lids to get attention. Furthermore, the small size of the Commons chamber, in which only about two-thirds of members of Parliament can find a place to sit, keeps the House from seeming empty on routine days and fills it with "a sense of crowd and urgency" on momentous occasions. In a quote learned by every architecture student, Churchill said, "We shape our buildings, and afterwards our buildings shape us."[17]

A conceptual foundation for this line of inquiry was laid in the 1960s by environmental psychologist Roger G. Barker. He contended that human beings act within a "behavior setting" that forms a physical and social "nesting structure" of understood patterns of behavior.[18] In his work, Barker opened a new field of research, but left many issues unsettled. Even if one accepts the existence of such understood patterns (for example, that people speak in a low voice in a cathedral), the degree to which they succeed in influencing individuals is open to question. Early researchers tended to assume some level of controlling influence, a view later labeled as "deterministic" by those less impressed with the behavioral influence of the built environment. Revisionists suggested a more modest concept of causal linkage between the physical setting and human conduct, such as the affording of possibilities, the fostering of probabilities, or a potential mutual influencing along with other causal factors.[19]

Amos Rapoport, a champion of the concept of mutual interaction between people and their settings, describes the built environment as "mnemonic," by which he means it contains memory cues for eliciting appropriate emotions and behaviors. He regards its design as a form of nonverbal communication, albeit one that involves subjective interpretation and varied reactions by each individual.[20] Certainly, a building or space can have different effects on different classes of people—for example, first-time visitors to a statehouse compared with state employees who regularly work in the building and thus are habituated to it. Still another variable is the degree to which a given physical setting is occupied alone or in the company of others; one of the characteristics of the statehouse's public spaces is that over the cycle of the political year, they vary from being quite empty to very crowded, causing significant changes in the overall milieu.

A certain amount of experimental research has been done on the behavioral influence of the physical environment, and its results suggest a measurable impact in at least some situations. Speakers have been found to speak slower in more reverberant rooms. Lecture audiences perceive that time passes faster in halls decorated in red rather than blue. When speakers are separated from their audiences by more than 12 feet, they use a more formal style of speech.[21] With respect to government buildings, Koehler found that the presence of a physical barrier or raised platform separating officials and citizens in a city council chamber correlates with less verbal communication and public participation.[22]

My three lenses, of course, are only analytic categories, offering different perspectives on the same thing rather than incommensurate images. For example, the barriers noted by Koehler not only may discourage public participation in a behavioral manner, but, in an expressive manner, may reflect elitist attitudes in the first place. It is probably impossible to determine the independent variable, and the aphorism about the chicken and the egg offers good counsel in suggesting that we do not even try. The value of the separate frames is not to segregate types of social meaning, but to facilitate more orderly inquiry into this complex field.[23]

My own behavioral inquiry regarding statehouses differs from the standard approach in environmental psychology, which is to employ survey research or conduct experimental simulations.[24] Each of these methodologies presents problems. Surveys require that the researcher know which questions to ask in advance, plus faith that replies to brief, fixed-response questions offer insights beyond a superficial level. For their part, manipulative experiments involving physical models, role-play, or computer images could not begin to capture the subtleties of a political setting like the statehouse. If one attempted to use them with busy politicians the results would probably be disastrous.

For this book, I did not pretend to follow the canons of "rigorous" social science. Rather, I conducted in-depth, open-ended interviews with numerous players, employees, and users of the statehouse. I supplemented them with personal observation and sought corroboration where possible. My interviewees were treated as informants instead of respondents, asked not to generate objective data about causal variables, but to open a window into a subjectively experienced, complex, and unique world.

Admittedly, the resulting analysis yields an interpretation of possible environment–behavior relationships, not proven fact. In some instances, I found myself influenced by what I consider to be a particularly keen insight put forward by an interviewee that seemed pertinent to many, if not all, statehouses. In addition, certain key ideas in the literature provoked my thinking; an example is Grady Clay's "political venturi" notion of spontaneous, funneled social mixing along busy streets.[25] Another strategy was to take special note of changes experienced by interviewees when the physical setting was altered, as when offices or functions are moved from one place to another.

The behavioral perspective is used in this book to speculate on the consequences for behavior of the design and setting of the statehouse, the effects of placing all parts of state government in one building, the contemporaneous consequences of constructing the capitol, and space as a setting for political conduct.

The Societal Lens

The societal lens draws attention to how buildings present themselves to the external society. All buildings are "public" in the broad sense of being visible to those who physically come upon them. Large edifices are obvious to the eye and may dominate the landscape. Distinctive building types, such as the church and the bank, are capable of becoming symbols of social subcultures and economic interests. Distinctive government buildings, like the county courthouse and state capitol, may symbolize a geographic locality, legal jurisdiction, government body, political regime, or system of authority, whether negatively or positively.

It is the nature of symbols that their meaning is ambiguous. Their message to the inner self of each person is uniquely constructed, even though we are socialized to interpret common symbols in common ways. Hence what the statehouse "means" as a societal symbol is not an objective matter to be discovered empirically, but a subjective one to be interpreted within our various communities of thought.

A community of thinking prevalent among certain theorists of and commentators on architecture is that large and majestic government buildings should be understood as instruments of deliberate intimidation of the populace. Otherwise, they would not be grand and imposing and built of permanent materials.

This conviction is presented in various forms. One is to contend that the designed world as a whole represents attempts by powerful elites to perpetuate their position. Postmodernists argue that all architecture must be deconstructed in order to lay bare its underlying values and claims to power. Poststructuralists and others maintain that the mere presence of an imposing and permanent building asserts a presumed continuing legitimacy whose implicit acceptance becomes a masked form of control and repression.

This point of view can also incorporate a neo-Marxist perspective, according to which the modern state appropriates space in order to reproduce the capitalist system of class dominance. Other anti-Establishment theories assert that in constructing large buildings, the state is able to control the inner life of the individual by shaping the presumed character of the outside world. Jeremy Bentham's Panopticon prison design, which enables wardens to observe prisoners secretly, is regarded as the future architectural model for governmental repression. Landscape architecture, for its part, is considered to be a means by which power statements are disguised by making them look like nature.[26]

Some theorists who write about government buildings from this perspective put an even finer point on the argument. Political theorist David Milne argues that public buildings enshrine each civilization's code of law and order and thus perform a conservative, stabilizing function for the society. This is done by means of an architecture designed to make regimes appear mighty and everlasting. According to political scientist Murray Edelman, the monumentality of public buildings reminds citizens that when using them they are entering the precincts of power and must act as supplicants who will be susceptible to arbitrary rebuffs and favors. Architectural theorists Michael Parker Pearson and Colin Richards claim that monumentality in buildings portrays established power as presumably eternal and integral to an imperishable social order. Applying this approach to specific governmental structures, historian Ron Robin contends that the design of United States embassy buildings and overseas military cemeteries constitutes deliberate attempts to assert government authority over the masses and accomplish strategic international objectives.[27]

Thus these authors, when looking through what I call the societal lens, perceive a dark picture. Controlled space in general and government architecture in particular are seen as manipulative, coercive, and intimidating. Furthermore, this underlying reality is both intentional and hidden, suggesting the presence of guile, if not conspiracy. The functional consequence is the enhancement and maintenance of state power, elite influence, class domination, regime stability, and resistance to competing social forces. The

effects of architecture on society are, in short, great indeed.

This matter may be viewed in other ways, however. To begin with, as noted in the discussion of the behavioral lens, the notion of a determinist impact by the physical environment has long been held suspect; perhaps government buildings as a whole are less compelling in influencing human beings than is sometimes thought. While people may be impressed on *entering* a monumental structure, their capacity to act or think independently may well reappear after they cross its threshold. While a building's observer may be initially overawed by exposure to an intimidating facade, with time this conditioning could recede as issues of leadership and policy press to the fore. Another whole scenario would be the ironic turn of events whereby the building becomes so identified with hated authority that the imposing presence itself nurtures anti-regime sentiment.

The societal effects of government buildings also can be seen in positive ways. Even when large buildings attract public attention and some degree of deference, it may not be because of a successful campaign of architectural intimidation, but because the structures satisfy certain group needs. Speculating on the possible functions performed by buildings that serve as corporate headquarters, Per Olof Berg and Kristian Kreiner suggest the following: (1) the totem, or uniting symbol for all employees; (2) the strategic profile, or embodiment of the organization's approach or "soul"; (3) packaging, or the extension of its product or service; (4) the symbol of status, potency, and good taste, as with the offices of key leaders; and (5) a marker of time, ideas, and existence, as with the retention of old buildings or construction of new ones.[28]

With respect to Berg and Kreiner's last point, James P. Armstrong and four co-authors studied a famous Washington, D.C., landmark: the State, War and Navy Building, designed by Alfred B. Mullett. This huge Second Empire edifice, completed in 1888, is presently known as the Dwight D. Eisenhower Executive Office Building. Among the several social functions that are performed by this imposing structure is the encapsulation of history. Many historic deeds were done in this building by famous people, such as attempts by Assistant Secretary of the Navy Theodore Roosevelt to precipitate war against Spain and moves by Assistant Secretary of the Navy Franklin Roosevelt to prepare for America's entry into World War I. In short, the spaces of this old building are capable of bringing history alive to later generations.[29]

In a book on buildings and power, Thomas A. Markus analyzes, among other building types, monasteries, courthouses, and concert halls. He notes how these structures represent an exercise of power, by having for example, consumed large quantities of scarce resources to be built in the first place. Moreover, the head occupants of them—the abbot, judge, and orchestra conductor—are installed inside the buildings in prominent, central places that reinforce their high status. Yet, Markus goes on, in addition to supporting power asymmetries, the buildings perform a bonding function. The monks, lawyers, and musicians who use the structures are given by them tangible symbols of their collective occupations and identities. This affects their sense of self and thus their impact on society. Hence the buildings not only empower elites, but enrich communities of nonelites.[30]

This book uses the societal perspective to examine, among other topics, the overall impressions made by various aspects of the design and setting of statehouses, the origin of their symbolism and their association with history, the treatment of the public in room design and security measures, and the consequences of television for projecting the statehouse image to society. Only then does it draw a conclusion in the debate over whether the American statehouse is inherently intimidating to citizens or is capable of projecting more positive emotions.

2 | *The Statehouse as Building Type*

The fifty statehouses of the United States have many unique features. The rotunda of the Hawaii State Capitol is a metaphoric volcano. In Tennessee, the architect and chairman of the capitol building commission are buried in the building's walls. The Idaho State Capitol is heated by underground geothermal springs. There are a great many more such interesting oddities.

To capitol tour guides, such details are not mere trivia. They are part and parcel of each building's treasured character and history. Yet a description of these quirks, so important to appreciating each statehouse on its own, does not afford an understanding of the statehouse as a building type. Indeed, encyclopedic detail can crowd out such an understanding.

The statehouse as a generic form of government architecture emerged and came to fruition in the United States, ultimately being adopted throughout the country. Even though modified in more recent statehouses, the form persists as the quintessential symbol of state government. State capitols, when they became cramped or outdated, were not torn down and replaced, as usually happens with public buildings. On the contrary, they were the objects of huge expenditures for historic preservation and restoration.

The German sociologist Max Weber is identified with the concept "ideal type."[1] This analytic construct seeks to portray the essence of a class of varied but similar phenomena. It goes beyond the mass of detail and variation to the critical, underlying characteristics of members of that class. By stripping away unessential detail and isolating key properties, the ideal type helps us think more deeply about vital functions and relationships. The term "ideal" refers not to hypothetical perfection, but to a distilled essence that takes on its own meaning.

The ideal type of the American statehouse possesses six interrelated elements: (1) a promi-nent site, (2) parklike grounds, (3) cruciform massing, (4) a central dome, (5) a temple front, and (6) a grand central space.

A PROMINENT, OPEN SITE

The state capitols are, of course, located in the capital cities of the American states (see Table 1.1). The words "capitol" and "capital" stem etymologically from the Latin word *caput*, which means "head." Hence the statehouse is the *head*quarters building in a *head*quarters city—the center of the center of a state's governance, so to speak.

The locations of state capitals is a large subject that would in itself deserve a book.[2] Their selection tended historically to be made in four ways: (1) the acceptance of an existing headquarters location, such as the colonial centers Annapolis, Maryland; Boston, Massachusetts; and Hartford, Connecticut, and territorial capitals Cheyenne, Wyoming; Phoenix, Arizona; and Salt Lake City, Utah; (2) a conscious attempt to place the capital in a geographically central location, as illustrated by Indianapolis, Indiana; Jackson, Mississippi; and Tallahassee, Florida; (3) the outcome of an often bitter intercity struggle for the prize, exemplified by Charleston, West Virginia; Helena, Montana; and Pierre, South Dakota; and (4) a decision to construct a capital city de novo in a largely unpopulated place, such as Columbia, South Carolina, and Jefferson City, Missouri.

With respect to the location of the capitol building within the capital city, a mix of practical, principled, and political reasons were operative as well. Frequently, the site of an earlier transitory or predecessor capitol was a factor. In more than one state, pressures by local land speculators seeking handsome profits were brought to bear. But regardless of how and why the siting choices were made, those making the selection almost always followed—whether consciously or unconsciously—the criterion of visual prominence.

This salience is achieved in three ways. First, many statehouses are noticeably situated on high ground. Thus the enduring principle of superiority of height seems to apply to some extent. Eighteen of the fifty statehouses are sited on a prominent rise, often the highest in the area.[3]

One of the earliest examples of an elevated capitol site is Beacon Hill in Boston, created by leveling off the top of an eminence earlier known as Trimountain. It was on this location overlooking Boston Harbor that Charles Bulfinch, later the third architect of the United States Capitol, built two great monuments: a tall shaft commemorating American independence, and, later, the original front portion of the Massachusetts State House (Figure 2.1).

Other hills on which capitols were built include Brown's Bluff in Denver,[4] Goat Hill in Montgomery, Smith Hill in Providence, Shockoe Hill in Richmond, Arsenal Hill in Salt Lake City, Campbell Hill in Nashville, and Wabasha Hill in St. Paul. This identification of important public places with hills is an ancient practice, evidenced by Mount Olympus in classical Greece and Capitoline Hill in ancient Rome. (The latter apparently is the original source of the American use of the term "capitol.") The United States Capitol, too, is located on elevated ground, a feature once known as Jenkins Hill.

The second way in which prominence is achieved is centrality of urban location, another common physical indicator of importance. The Maryland State House, the oldest in the country, still stands in Annapolis in the centrally located State Circle, which is a short distance from the smaller Church Circle, the site of St. Anne's Church. The South Carolina State House is at the center of the city square laid out by Columbia's original planners, at the corner of streets appropriately named Assembly and Senate.

Figure 2.1. The Massachusetts State House on Beacon Hill facing Boston Common. The original front part of the building, completed in 1798 and later restored, was designed by Charles Bulfinch.

Similarly, the capitols of Illinois and Michigan are placed at axial intersections of the grid-organized midwestern cities of Springfield and Lansing. In Salt Lake City, the capitol overlooks the critical urban centerpiece of Temple Square, and in Atlanta, it stands near the old zero mileage point of the railroad. Reminiscent of imperial Rome, where all roads radiated from a designated stone in the center of the metropole, or present-day Spain, where the origin is the *kilometro zero* golden disk in Madrid, Bulfinch's dome on the Massachusetts State House is the zero mileage point for the calculation of highway distances to Boston. A marker on the grounds of the Virginia State Capitol performs a similar function for distances to Richmond. Several statehouses are sited on old communication routes important to the settlement of the West. The Ohio and Indiana State Houses are adjacent to what was once the National Road. The Idaho State Capitol faces a street that follows the route of the Oregon Trail; the Nevada Legislative Building bears a similar

relationship to the Overland Trail, as does the New Mexico State Capitol to the Santa Fe Trail.

Proximity to water is the third siting commonality. This is explained by the importance of rivers and other bodies of water as the primary means of transportation when travel over land routes was difficult. Until railroads became common following the Civil War, the only practical location for a capital city was either along the coast or on a navigable river. No fewer than thirty-three statehouses are next to or near water. Of these, twenty-seven are "riverine" in the sense that the nearby water is a moving stream, and, within that group, nine originally overlooked the river from its banks or a bluff.[5] Examples of the last are in Albany, which is on the Hudson River; Baton Rouge, the Mississippi; Charleston, the Kanawha; Harrisburg, the Susquehanna; Jefferson City, the Missouri; Richmond, the James; and Trenton, the Delaware (Figure 2.2).

A visually prominent site is, therefore, the first major attribute of the statehouse building type.[6]

Figure 2.2. The Missouri State Capitol, Jefferson City. Overlooking the Missouri River, it was completed in 1917. Jefferson City became the capital in 1826, supplanting St. Charles.

The second element concerns the grounds surrounding the structure. All but the oldest statehouses are set back from surrounding roads or streets by a considerable distance and thus are ringed by open space, setting them off visually and contributing further to their prominence.

Architectural theorists have dealt in various ways with the concept of siting a major building on open land. James Holston distinguishes this "void" location from the "solid" concentration of buildings that typifies urban settings. Michel Foucault argues that "heterotopias," his term for "different places" like gardens and cemeteries, create enclaves of refuge or timelessness in the urban fabric. Denis Cosgrove regards the English rural estate as an encapsulation of the hierarchical Victorian social order. To Bill Hillier and Julienne Hanson, the placement of a public building in sparse surroundings permits ideological manipulation of the outdoor landscape in order to control thinking indoors. Lawrence Vale and other commentators on capital cities argue that the grand architectural vistas at Versailles, in Vienna, and at the Vatican seek to extend the image of a potentate's power beyond the immediate palace.[7]

Certainly, the surrounding grounds of the American state capitol help accentuate its presence. The building is visible from afar and as a totality. Its "void" setting, like that of the rural courthouse on its open square, makes it seem special and different from more solid concentrations of structures. When approaching the formal entrance to the statehouse, especially on foot, the experience is often one of crossing a greensward transected by sidewalks and driveways and dotted with trees, gardens, and statuary. War memorials, monuments to state heroes and heroines, and replicas of the Liberty Bell are in evidence. They may be supplemented by fountains, floral clocks, and even small lakes or arboretum trails. Other state buildings may be nearby, but are separated from the capitol by grassy areas in the manner of a college campus. In smaller capital cities, the grounds are a kind of small-scale central park, integral to the downtown. Although the scene may include geometric

gardens or processional lines of sight, relatively unstructured landscapes are more common (Figure 2.3).

A point to be emphasized is that the grounds are open, not surrounded by a barricade. The American statehouse is the farthest thing from a walled-off fortress. This makes it very different from most palaces, presidential mansions, and houses of parliament in the world, even in democratic countries. A few statehouse grounds are enclosed by ornamental cast-iron fences, but they keep no one out. In the early nineteenth century, many statehouses were surrounded by board fences, but they were constructed to exclude livestock, not citizens.

The absence of a secure perimeter enclosure is often astonishing to foreign visitors. In many countries, such as Japan, the parliament grounds are not only securely fenced, but patrolled by armed guards. The only visible security personnel near the statehouse tend to be low-key and nonthreatening, such as the "squirrel guards" in Austin (Figure 2.4).

The statehouse grounds may not be a barricaded fortress or an outdoor extension of indoor power, but two kinds of intrusive architectural presence are possible. One is the placement of high-rise office buildings near the capitol. Aside from its dome, the statehouse is a relatively low building, and hence nearby office towers can easily obscure or overshadow it. In some cities, attempts have been made to protect the capitol's viewshed with zoned height limitations, but once the damage is done—as in Columbus, Nashville, and Sacramento—there is no way to turn back.

The other architectural intrusion is an overbuilt capitol plaza or mall, designed in a style entirely different from that of the statehouse. The worst examples are in Albany, Lansing, and Indianapolis, where huge government office complexes have been built immediately adjacent to the capitol building. Albany's latter-day addition, called the Governor Nelson A. Rockefeller Empire State Plaza, consists of a mammoth platform base from which rise ten major structures, including a forty-four-story office tower. This "city of marble," planted in the middle of Victo-

Figure 2.3. The South Dakota State Capitol, Pierre, as seen from Hilger's Gulch Park. Beyond the building is the Missouri River, at a point some 800 miles upstream from the Missouri State Capitol.

Figure 2.4. Car guards, also known as "squirrel guards," make sure that tourists do not park in official spots on the grounds of the Texas State Capitol, Austin. They are genial but effective.

rian Albany but looking like Brasilia, abuts the nineteenth-century capitol. Built between 1964 and 1976, it displaced 3,300 houses in 40 city blocks, along with 3 churches and 2 schools (Figure 2.5). The Michigan State Capitol is adjacent to a smaller platform complex derisively called Fort Romney after its gubernatorial progenitor. In Indianapolis the nineteenth-century capitol is joined to Government Place, a 1,000-foot-long closed street flanked by huge bureaucratic buildings that are topped with nonfunctional watchtowers. The massiveness of these unified structures dwarfs the statehouse and conveys an impression of monumental power (Figure 2.6).

A DOMED, LOW CROSS

What, then, is this building like that rises from a prominence and is girded by a park? The first characteristic to mention, and the third element of the statehouse building type, is that the "footprint" of the classic American statehouse is a cross. Its two primary axes intersect at 90 degrees. The arms of the cross constitute two, three, or four wings that project from a center point. Typically, the building is longer than it is wide, creating a major lateral axis crossed by one or more minor axes (see Figure 2.6). The Wisconsin State Capitol is unusual in that it consists of four equivalent wings, oriented to the four points of the compass. Because of this symmetry, the capitol has no obvious front (Figure 2.7).[8]

With its cross shape, the statehouse as a structure is strung out in opposing directions rather than constituting a compact mass. Hence it possesses discernible subparts that can be disaggregated by the eye and mind. This segmented form seems appropriate to the American form of government, based as it is on the doctrine of separation of powers. Indeed, the separate wings of the building are often occupied by the constitutionally differentiated branches of government.

As was traditional in classical architecture, the facade of the statehouse is characterized by bi-

Figure 2.5. The Governor Nelson A. Rockefeller Empire State Plaza, Albany. Designed by Wallace K. Harrison and built adjoining the State Capitol in 1964 to 1976, it displaced more than 3,000 homes.

Figure 2.6. The Indiana State House, Indianapolis. Designed by Edwin May and built in 1878–1888, it is almost lost against the backdrop of the Indiana Government Center, a vast state office complex (upper right).

lateral symmetry: in each major elevation, the left side mirrors the right, as illustrated by the Beaux-Arts Mississippi New Capitol (Figure 2.8). The Senate wing (left side in photograph) is an exact counterpart of the House wing (right side), in perfect accord with the principle of bicameral equality. The visual result of bilateral symmetry generally is an image of regularity, balance, and completeness. The argument can be made that this orderly presentation not only can be aesthetically satisfying, but also implies characteristics of dignity, dependability, and significance on the part of the institutions housed within the building.

The main entrance of the typical statehouse is at the center of one of its long sides, bisecting the symmetrical facade. This contrasts with the Roman temple or Gothic cathedral, which is entered at one of its projecting ends rather than in the middle of a side. The interior plan of the cathedral is such that, upon entering the front, one moves through a succession of spaces (narthex, nave, and chancel) in order to reach the sacred east end. The most "sacred" space of the capitol, however, is the rotunda, which is located in the center of the building. Because of the centrality of both rotunda and main entrance, access to the heart of the capitol is not ritualistically processional, but quickly attained. Despite its dignity and sobriety, then, the statehouse is symbolically quite open to the external world.

Proportionally, the principal massing of the statehouse is relatively low. Put differently, the building is long for its height. A roofline 40 to 70 feet high and a length of 300 to 500 feet are ranges that would include most statehouses. These proportions yield, in the side view, an aspect ratio of 6:1 or 7:1. The structure typically has only three or four floors, permitting vertical movement between stories by stairway rather than elevator, a matter of some behavioral importance.

Figure 2.7. The Wisconsin State Capitol, Madison. Designed by George B. Post and completed in 1917, the building is unique among statehouses in that it has four equal wings oriented to the points of the compass.

Figure 2.8. The Mississippi New Capitol, Jackson, constructed in 1901 to 1903. This Beaux-Arts edifice, designed by Theodore C. Link, illustrates the classical principle of bilateral symmetry.

The vertical reach of the statehouse does not end at the roofline, however. The most dramatic feature of its design is a dome rising above the principal mass. Projecting 150 to 400 feet above the ground, the dome often more than doubles the building's overall height (Figure 2.9).

The dome is positioned directly over the primary axis crossing, with its own centerline rising in a perfect vertical from that point of intersection. Its height gives a vertical thrust to the building that complements the horizontality of the massing. Furthermore, the curves of the dome contrast strongly with the square angles of the cruciform shape of the building. In terms of religious symbolism, the verticality of the dome can be thought of as representing an *axis mundi,* or radius of the world, that connects an earthly existence below with the celestial realm above.[9]

Thus a compounded "intersectedness" may be said to exist at the center of the classic statehouse. On the horizontal plane, the axes of the cruciform plan intersect, at 90 degrees. On the vertical plane, this point is itself intersected by the dome's *axis mundi* reaching skyward, also at 90 degrees. Symbolically, this primary point of origin can be said to constitute a centrum where the mundane concerns of political conflict below meet the lofty ideals of public life above.

The dome, like the cross, is an ancient physical form. It was invented before the time of the Romans, who used it creatively. By means of such permanent materials as ashlar, brick, and cement, Roman engineers developed gravity-defying examples of the arch, the vault, and the dome. The most famous dome from antiquity covers the Pantheon in Rome. Its circular, low, oculus-pierced roof stands as an architectural marvel to this day. Thomas Jefferson was enamored of the low Roman dome and used it at Monticello; he also wanted such a low dome built on the new national capitol in Washington, but an essentially hemispheric dome was constructed instead. It was designed by Charles Bulfinch, comparable to the dome he had placed on the Massachusetts

Figure 2.9. The Kansas State Capitol, Topeka, built between 1866 and 1906. The tip of the dome lantern is 304 feet from the ground, and the dome itself contains a large empty space.

State House nearly a quarter century earlier (see Figure 2.1). In the mid-nineteenth century, Thomas U. Walter replaced the rounded dome of the Capitol with a taller, more pointed, and more elaborate structure, inspired by the domes of such churches as St. Peter's Basilica in Rome, St. Paul's Cathedral in London, and the Invalides in Paris.

When large-scale capitols in the neoclassical architectural tradition began to be built in the state capitals after the Civil War, this more elaborate and elongated dome design became popular for the statehouse as well. Its elements are a colonnaded drum, on which the dome rests; a rounded portion or tholos, which is ribbed or scored to accentuate the sense of height; and a lantern at the top, on which a statue is sometimes placed.

In view of its prominence, as well as its unexpectedly rounded form, the dome automatically attracts the eye. Its vertical thrust, when juxtaposed against the horizontal mass of the building on which it rests, combines tension with repose and seems to mark an important place.

One can analyze the form using three levels of meaning proposed for architecture by Amos Rapoport.[10] The "low," or instrumental, level of meaning is the dome's attention-getting ability from afar. In some capitols, this feature is augmented by gilding the tholos. The "medium," or status-marking, level is the dome's identification of the building as a government capitol. In the United States, the association is remarkably universal. As for the "high" level, which for Rapoport is cosmological, one thought that comes to mind is the dome's anthropomorphic resemblence to a giant head of authority seen on the distant horizon, covered perhaps by an antiquated helmet (Figure 2.10). E. Baldwin Smith, the leading scholar on domes, indeed points out that one of the ancient cosmological meanings of the dome is that of celestial helmet.[11] Moreover, as we know, the Latin root of "capitol" is "head."

Figure 2.10. Dome of the Washington Legislative Building, Olympia, as seen from the east. A symbolic meaning of dome is a celestial helmet, and with an exercise of the imagination it looks like one.

Figure 2.11. North portico of the West Virginia State Capitol, Charleston. Built in 1924 to 1932, its pediment, entablature, columns, steps, and podium arms constitute a classic temple front.

A CIVIC TEMPLE

The principal doorway of the American state-house is at the center of the longitudinal side considered to be the front. This entrance is not a mere functional opening, but an architectural composition of grand design—a facade ensemble known as the temple front, the fifth element of the statehouse building type.

This composition is taken from Greek and Roman antiquity, passed on by the Renaissance and repeated in neoclassical revivalist styles of the nineteenth century. As the architectural historian William L. MacDonald notes, its image is almost universally recognized around the world and is perhaps the strongest visual design ever produced in Western architecture.[12]

The temple front is, in simple language, a splendid front porch, or portico. The portico projects from the mass of the building and shelters a raised rectangular podium, or landing, in front of the doorway. The upright structure of the portico consists of several columns (often, but not necessarily, six) that support an entablature, or horizontal lintel. Above the entablature rises the triangular pediment, or gable. Steps lead several feet from the ground up to the portico, between two side blocks known as podium arms (Figure 2.11).

The most striking feature of this stylized porch is its columns. The column as an architectual form descends from the tree trunk and became—in the hands of Egyptian, Greek, Roman, and Renaissance builders—a beautiful and dignified device for post-and-lintel construction. As reported in the first century B.C. by Vitruvius, in *De architectura*, the ancients codified the decorative detailing of the column into several classical orders —Doric, Ionic, Corinthian, and Tuscan—creating the most influencial architectural typology of all time. The column's erectness serenely defies gravity in its solitary, rounded perfection, making it a powerful symbol of authority. The Greeks wrapped their temples on all four sides with rows of beautiful columns, the ruins of which can still be seen on the Acropolis in Athens and at countless other sites. A small number of Greek Revival statehouses exist in America, and in these, too, the spare beauty of Greek architecture is evident.

The Romans borrowed Greek ideas to build their temples, but at the same time elaborated on them. A surviving Roman temple in Nîmes, France, known as the Maison Carrée, attracted the attention of Thomas Jefferson, who visited it when he was minister to France. When, at Jefferson's insistence, the capital of Virginia was moved from Williamsburg to Richmond to make it less vulnerable to British assault, Jefferson also decreed that the new capitol building be modeled after the Maison Carrée. The Nîmes temple is in the "prostyle" form, possessing a temple front at only one end. The original core of the Virginia State Capitol was built in this form, absent front stairs and entrance (Figure 2.12). When in 1906 legislative wings were added to the core, steps and a doorway were built in front, converting the

capitol symbolically from a temple to be admired to a building to be entered. In the nineteenth century, the temple front became a staple of American architecture and is found on countless banks, churches, college buildings, and halls of government. Two-thirds of the statehouses have a full version of the ensemble incorporated into their facades, and in a few more only the triangular pediment is missing.

MacDonald regards the psychological impact of the temple front as both assertive and accepting. Its superhuman height, projecting nature, columned verticality, and pointed peak assert authority. The podium serves as a natural viewing platform of the lesser world below, and the podium arms—likened by MacDonald to the forelegs of a recumbent sphinx or lion—suggest poised energy. Yet, his analysis continues, the temple front is also a roofed overhang and thereby offers shelter. Its visibility and clarity bring the building and the observer into a focused, connected relationship. The dramatized entranceway

Figure 2.12. The Virginia State Capitol, Richmond. The design of the center core building was modeled by Thomas Jefferson after the Maison Carrée, a Roman temple in Nîmes, France.

Figure 2.13. South facade door of the West Virginia State Capitol, the last statehouse on which Cass Gilbert worked. Its ornate entrances signal the importance of the spaces within.

suggests the accessibility of the interior, and the scooplike shape of the stairs and its arms receives as well as projects.[13]

To gain access to the interior of this civic temple, one passes through the portals accentuated by the temple front. Appropriate for a temple, the doors are large and ornately designed. In Beaux-Arts statehouses, they are often constructed of cast bronze and weigh a ton or more, with Cass Gilbert's entrance to the West Virginia State Capitol offering a good illustration (Figure 2.13).

Upon passing through the front portal, and after traversing antechambers, the rotunda is entered. The word "rotunda" means "round room." These spaces are sometimes perfectly circular, and other times only roughly so, due to the presence within a square space of four corner piers that bear the weight of the dome.

The rotunda is large, sometimes huge. It may be 50, 60, or more feet across and 120, 180, or even 260 feet high. This height is achieved by having the rotunda cut through all the floors of the building and reach up into the drum and tholos of the dome. The ceiling of the rotunda is at times the underside of the exterior dome. More commonly, to avoid placing this upper surface too high for observers below to see clearly, only the underside of a false inner ceiling is visible, positioned some distance below the outer dome with dead space between. Balconies encircle the rotunda at various levels, allowing the grand space below to be viewed from various perspectives. Principal corridors connect the rotunda with radiating wings at each floor level (Figure 2.14).

This large round space, situated at the cruciform intersection and directly beneath the dome, is an essentially empty room. No throne occupies it, as in a castle, or altar graces it, as in a church. Nonetheless, the importance of the space is clearly stated by means of ornate decoration: bas-relief pendentives, painted lunettes, stained-glass windows, scagliola pilasters, historical murals, carved exhortations, likenesses of distinguished figures, Civil War banners, and even Roman firepots. Grand stairs, complete with marble balusters and elaborate newel posts, lead to the upper stories.

In the center of the floor, the state seal may be rendered in bronze, glass, or terrazzo, sometimes roped off to avoid defilement. Below the floor lies the crypt, but, unlike the cathedral equivalent, it is used for meetings or storage, not the burial of saints.

The rotunda ceiling is painted and adorned with particular intricacy and brilliance. According to ancient tradition, such ceilings represent the heavenly vault (Figure 2.15).[14] In some statehouses, an oculus, as in the Roman Pantheon, pierces the ceiling, above which a circular painting may be mounted, visible through the heavenly aperture. Another format is to suspend a huge chandelier in the upper volume of the rotunda by means of a heavy chain that is paid out of the oculus. This arrangement is in keeping with another ancient idea associated with sacred spaces: the egg of creation floating in the void of the world (Figure 2.16).[15]

The rotunda has no permanently assigned function. Rather, it is a place where inaugurations take place, holiday concerts are held, and deceased heroes lie in state. Otherwise, the space is chiefly a central point of public circulation, connected to all other parts of the building. Public tours begin in the rotunda, which is a convenient place to meet, get from one corridor to another, or people-watch from the balconies. Symbolically, the room may be the sacred heart of a civic temple, yet on a day-to-day basis, it is a quite democratic place of common use.

DEPARTURES AND CHANGES

This description of the statehouse building type —incorporating the elements of prominent site, parklike grounds, cruciform ground plan, pointed dome, temple front, and central rotunda—applies to the majority of the fifty state capitols. Thirty statehouses (or their preserved predecessor buildings, as in Alabama, Arizona, and Florida) embody the essence of all six elements. Thirteen more statehouses are missing only one or two.[16] All features of the type also apply, incidentally, to the United States Capitol in Washington, D.C.

Figure 2.14. Rotunda of the Wisconsin State Capitol, as seen from the second-floor level of the East Gallery and looking toward the West Gallery, which contains the lower house, or Assembly, chamber.

Figure 2.15. Rotunda ceiling of the Mississippi New Capitol. This concave surface is typically the subject of intricate decoration. In Renaissance churches, it represents the heavenly vault.

As an ideal type, this model does not capture the individuality of each building. Yet departures from the model are relatively uncommon. No statehouse is not prominently sited in one way or another. In not a single state capitol are the grounds closed off, and all have some degree of parklike quality, even though the administrative plazas in Indiana, Michigan, and New York supplement the grass with much concrete.

With respect to cruciform massing, significant departures from this norm are limited to Alaska's reused office building, Delaware's Georgian hall, Hawaii's rectangular composition, New Hampshire's organic design, New Mexico's circular plan, New York's Second Empire block, North Dakota's asymmetrical row, and Vermont's asymmetrical grouping. Even with these buildings, the departure is not complete; in all the statehouses save those of Alaska, New Hampshire, and Vermont, the two houses of the legislature are internally opposed, even if not in opposing wings.

Eleven existing or predecessor statehouses have no dome: those of Alaska, Delaware, Hawaii, Louisiana, Nevada, New Mexico, New York, North Dakota, Oklahoma, Tennessee, and Virginia. Domes were planned for New York and Oklahoma, but were never built. The capitols of Ohio and Oregon have domes, but they are flat, not rounded. The Nebraska State Capitol, often cited as the first statehouse to break the traditional mold, has a gilded, round dome atop its famous tower. While the Nevada Legislative Building is topped by a feature that is closer to a cupola than a dome, its new legislative building incoporates a low dome painted silver.

Eleven statehouses or predecessor capitols are without temple fronts in any recognizable form: those of Alaska, Connecticut, Delaware, Hawaii, Lousiana, Minnesota, Nebraska, New Mexico, North Dakota, Oregon, and Texas. As for a rotunda-like central space, only the capitols of

Figure 2.16. The "Angels of Mercy" chandelier suspended in the rotunda of the Washington Legislative Building. Made of cast bronze, it weighs 5 tons and is hung by a 101-foot chain.

Alaska, Delaware, Nevada, New York, and Vermont are absent this feature.

Most statehouses have changed in major ways over time. The most radical change has been to move the legislature out of the statehouse and into a new building, keeping the old capitol for other purposes, such as the governor's office or a museum. This has occurred in Alabama, Arizona, Florida, Nevada, and North Carolina. The more common modification has been to enlarge the statehouse by constructing additions or extensions. This has happened in California, Maryland, Massachusetts, Montana, New Hampshire, New Jersey, Ohio, South Dakota, and Vermont. In Connecticut, Louisiana, Tennessee, and Texas, additional space either has been created underground or is reached by underground passage, without disturbing the historical building or its grounds.

A larger point related to statehouse change is that, despite the fact that these old structures are chronically outgrown by an expanding state government, they are not throw-away objects that are cavalierly dumped in favor of bigger and better buildings. On only two occasions in American history has a permanently constructed and still usable capitol been razed, in New York in 1883 and Idaho in 1919.[17] This testifies to the enduring value attached to these icons.

SOCIAL MEANINGS OF THE BUILDING TYPE

Aspects of the statehouse building type, viewed through the expressive lens, seem to make implicit statements about the nature of state governance. The open character of the statehouse's parklike setting points to the relatively open nature of American state government. The absence of a high fence around the building, punctuated by entrances secured by locked gates and armed guards, suggests a willingness on the part of authorities to be visited by the public and to receive scrutiny from the outside world. Unlike the barricaded palace or ministry found in many capital cities of the world, the grounds of the statehouse manifest no evident fear of popular rioting or

coups d'état. Although concerns for physical security certainly exist in American state government, they are manifested by hidden precautions rather than blatantly visible means, such as the closed streets and cement bollards found in front of the Capitol and White House in Washington, D.C.

Other physical features of the area surrounding the statehouse register the changing context of state government. The threat posed to viewsheds of the capitol by high-rise office buildings is a product of the urban and economic growth that, over the lifetime of the statehouse, greatly expanded the functions of state government. By the same token, the construction of government office complexes near the statehouse indicates how these added functions increased the number of state employees and state agencies.

Turning to social meanings uncovered by the behavioral lens, several of the features of the statehouse contribute to the ability of the public to reach and identify it. When the capital city is located in the geographic center of a state, distances to it are minimized. In the vast interior of the country, the siting of a capitol on a navigable river made access to the building feasible before the advent of railroads and highways. In the old West, the placement of the capitol on the routes of early trails was critical to making contact with state authorities. The building's hilltop location and characteristic dome helped to make it stand out clearly on the landscape. This is still true, even in the crowded urban fabric of contemporary cities.

Another set of behavioral consequences pertains to public circulation into and within the building. The temple front unmistakably marks the front door. The rotunda's nearness to this doorway and its central location in the floor plan allow for ease of circulation through all parts of the structure. Axial corridors that lead from the rotunda into and along each wing permit access to the deepest parts of the building. The low massing of the three or four floors allows vertical circulation to be accomplished by stairway rather than elevator, creating the possibility that movement from floor to floor can have a public rather than merely a private character.

The ease of circulation notwithstanding, the cruciform shape of the statehouse permits its separate wings to disaggregate the interior space. Constitutionally autonomous institutions housed in the building, such as separate branches of government or houses of the legislature, can have their "own" wing or floors in that wing. The bilateral symmetry of the facade design invites institutions housed in opposite wings to conceive of themselves as equals.

A final behavioral consequence is that certain places created by the elements of the building type are particularly conducive to ceremonial activity. The parklike grounds are perfect for outdoor political rallies, not to mention informal relaxation in good weather. The steps of the temple front are ideal for staged political theater, with the podium and arms acting as a stage, the columns as scenery, and the entablature and pediment as proscenium arch. Within the building, the rotunda is a space that lends itself to displays and rituals of all kinds. Its round shape and large size create 360 degrees of extended audience visibility, plus a natural sound amplification that can permeate the building.

Finally, the societal lens finds that the statehouse neither totally intimidates nor completely attracts. In a word, its presentation seems ambivalent or even contradictory.

From one standpoint, the statehouse articulates the final and inescapable authority of government, and does so in a manner that to many citizens must seem overwhelming. It is a big building, conspicuously located, laid out with ordered symmetry, festooned with columns and grand porches, entered through heavy doors, and topped by a high dome shaped like a giant head of authority. Within, the building's highlight is a large sacred space positioned at the physical center of state government. The rotunda is lavishly decorated with historical murals, heroic statues, exhortative inscriptions, a brilliant celestial vault, and a hanging egg of creation.

From another perspective, however, the statehouse is relatively low, divided into wings to accommodate a pluralist government, graced by a porch that is sheltering as well as grand, and surrounded by open, unfenced parkland. Within, the building does not subject the visitor to a procession of elegant spaces. Rather, the citizen quickly enters a large room that, despite its rich decoration, contains neither throne nor altar, but functions primarily as a place for ordinary people to walk and meet.

Thus the building type both affirms the suspicions of those who view government architecture as an instrument of domination and the thinking of the less cynical who believe that public buildings can, as well, have more benign meanings for citizens and even unite or inspire. This mix of possibilities suggests that the task of interpreting this complex and subtle physical landmark of state government will not be a simple one. The next step in exploring the subject will be to learn how the American statehouse came into being.

3 | The Creation of the American Statehouse

The process by which the statehouse building type came into being can be conceived as having taken place in two steps. The first was the *creation* or conceptual development of the type, which is the subject of this chapter. The second was the *construction* of the actual capitols we now know, the topic of the next chapter.

HEADQUARTERS OF COLONIAL GOVERNMENT

Although we usually equate our colonial past with English settlements along the Atlantic seaboard, the oldest former colonial headquarters in America is the Palace of the Governors in Santa Fe, New Mexico. This adobe structure, perhaps the oldest public building in the United States, dates in its original form to about 1610 and was used to serve colonial governors for both Spain and Mexico. After the Mexican War of 1846 to 1848, American territorial authorities occupied the structure. A fund depository was located in one of its front corners and legislative halls in the other. Placed at the center front of the building were the governor's several rooms (Figure 3.1).[1]

The first building to be called a capitol in America was the structure known by that name in Williamsburg, Virginia. It was constructed between 1701 and 1705 to house the legislative and judicial organs of the colonial government of Virginia after the capital of the colony moved inland from Jamestown in 1699. Perhaps at the personal insistence of Governor Francis Nicholson, the act directing the move called the government building a "Capitoll," said by some scholars to be the first recorded use of the term in this manner. As noted earlier, the word comes from the Capitoline (or Tarpeian) Hill in ancient Rome, on which were built two temples: one to the god Jupiter Optimus Maximus, and the other to Juno Moneta. While the temples were primarily for religious purposes, the Roman government performed some civil functions in them, such as minting coins in the basement of the temple of Juno Moneta, thereby also coining the word "money." The Roman Senate, contrary to an impression sometimes given, did not meet on the Capitoline Hill except for performing religious ceremonies or taking of oaths. Nonetheless, it may have occurred to Nicholson that the word "capitol" would be an appropriate name for the new Williamsburg building, which was intended not as a palace but to house governing bodies, with the governor provided a separate mansion some blocks away.[2]

The capitol in Williamsburg burned in 1747. The only object saved was the Speaker's chair from the House of Burgesses, now on display in the Virginia State Capitol in Richmond. A second capitol, built on the same site but in a different design, also burned, in 1832. When Williamsburg was reconstructed at the initiative of John D. Rockefeller, Jr., in the 1920s and 1930s, the first capitol and not its successor was re-created.

The building has an H-shaped plan with two wings connected by an arcaded crossbar. The House of Burgesses, or elected assembly of landowners, met in a chamber in the east wing. The west wing housed the General Court and the Council chamber. The governor, representing the Crown, presided over both Court and Council.[3]

The relationship between these wings is revealing. The east wing, associated with the colonial burgesses, is less fancy than the west wing, the home of royal power. A second-floor conference room above the connecting arcade was available for meetings on neutral ground.

Figure 3.1. Palace of the Governors, Santa Fe, New Mexico. Perhaps the oldest public building in the United States, it was used, in various forms, by governments for some three centuries.

Within the wings, the chamber of the king's Council was on the second floor of the building, while the House of Burgesses was on the first, conforming elevation-wise to the distinction between the "upper" and "lower" houses of a legislature.

Thomas Jefferson, like Nicholson before him, liked the term "capitol." This preference was an outgrowth of his wish, along with that of several other Founders, to evoke the spirit of the Roman republic as inspiration for the new country. He thus insisted on the name capitol not only for his Maison Carrée copy in Richmond, but also for the legislative building being planned for the District of Columbia. When Pierre L'Enfant presented his designs for the new federal city, the structure intended for Jenkins Hill was labeled "Congress House," to complement the separate "President's House" down Pennsylvania Avenue. When Secretary of State Jefferson reviewed the plans, he marked out "Congress House" and substituted "Capitol."[4]

In the New England colonies, the more domestic name house was used instead of capitol, as in the Old State House in Boston, constructed in 1712 to 1713. Although burned more than once, used for commercial purposes, and almost razed, this venerable structure recently has been restored (Figure 3.2). It, like the capitol in Williamsburg, is revealing with respect to the use of its interior space. Originally, the first floor provided a commercial area known as a merchants' walk. Allowing commerce at this level followed a practice associated with early English town halls, where an open, arcaded lower story often served as the public market. In Boston, the lower floor was also used as a post office and a place for securing public records.

The second floor of the Massachusetts Old State House was divided among the decision-making components of colonial government. A chamber for the royal governor and his Council was located on the east side of the building, facing the harbor. A back room was reserved for the courts of Suffolk County. Between the two was a chamber for the province's General Assembly, made up of representatives from each town.[5] Hence this small building, the seat of Massachusetts government until Charles Bulfinch's statehouse was opened in 1798, provided an early precedent for placing all governmental functions under one roof.

A number of other architectural details and changes in the building are politically telling. The Crown emblems of lion and unicorn, prominently displayed on the upper corners of the east or harbor side of the building, were removed after the American Revolution, but were replaced in the 1880s in the name of historical accuracy. A shallow balcony located in the middle of the east facade, accessible from the governor's chamber, was used to announce royal proclamations to the public on the street below. The tables were turned, however, in 1776 when the Declaration of Independence was read from this balcony to an en-thusiastic crowd of newly proclaimed republican citizens. A decade earlier, a seating gallery for the general public had been installed in the Assembly chamber, creating what is perhaps the earliest American example of a legislative visitors' gallery.

Antecedents of what we call federalism had early architectural manifestations in colonial New England. The colony of Rhode Island and Providence Plantations, just to the south of Boston, was settled by separate dissident groups, including those opposed to the Massachusetts Bay theocracy. Rhode Island was made up of five counties, each of which cherished its separate set of groups and individual autonomy. In light of this disunity, the colony's General Assembly did not meet in one central location, but rotated its sessions among five buildings, each located in a county. Two of them still exist: Colony House in Newport, built from 1739 to 1743, and the Old State House in Providence, constructed in 1760 to 1762.

Figure 3.2. The Massachusetts Old State House, Boston. Dating from 1713, this oldest of Boston's public buildings served successively as headquarters for colonial, state, and municipal government.

The lower floor of these structures contained community gathering rooms for the public, comparable to the first-floor commercial area in Boston. As in Massachusetts, the second floor was devoted to the business of government, with one chamber provided for the Council, composed of the governor and his magistrates, and another for elected deputies.

The grounds of the Old State House feature a tree-lined front walkway known as The Parade. Visitors of importance approached the building by ascending this formal path up the hill (Figure 3.3). When the Marquis de Lafayette, hero of the Revolution, visited America in 1824 and went to Providence, his procession up The Parade was greeted by rows of young girls dressed in white who sprinkled flower petals in his path.[6]

One colonial edifice became the cradle of the nation: the Old State House in Philadelphia, now known as Independence Hall. Its construction commenced in 1732, with the defining central

tower built from 1750 to 1753. The building's purpose was to house the government of Pennsylvania, which it did until 1799, with the state supreme court remaining until 1816.[7]

Since Philadelphia was centrally located along the eastern seaboard and the largest city in the colonies, it became a natural gathering point for those seeking to forge a new nation. The First Continental Congress, called in 1774 to secure colonial unity in the face of Parliament's detested tax policies, met in Carpenters' Hall. The Second Continental Congress, which convened the following year, met in the Assembly Room of the Old State House. Over the next dozen years, this 30- by 40-foot space, located on the east side of the first floor, witnessed an incredible series of historical events: agonizing debates over war with the mother country, the signing of the Declaration of Independence, the naming of George Washington as commander of the Continental Army, the direction of the war itself (except

Figure 3.3. The Rhode Island Old State House, Providence. It was completed in 1762 and used for a variety of governmental functions until 1975. Its front walkway was known as The Parade.

when, at one point, the building was occupied by the enemy), the formation of a national government by means of the Articles of Confederation, and, finally, in the summer of 1787, the drafting of the Constitution of the United States.

It can be argued that no other single confined space has ever been as important to American history. While the Old State House was being utilized for these momentous purposes, the Pennsylvania Assembly obligingly met upstairs. But soon the room's glory faded. After a few years, both the national and state governments had left Philadelphia, and the Assembly Room was used successively as courtroom, museum, art gallery, and art studio, occupied by Charles Willson Peale and his son Rembrandt. The room's paneling was stripped away and its furniture sold, with only an inkstand and the famous "rising sun" Speaker's chair saved. Only after Lafayette's visit to Philadephia in 1824 was the loss caused by this deterioration comprehended; in due course, the room was redecorated, given the Liberty Bell to guard for a time, declared a national shrine, and eventually restored and re-restored for all future generations to contemplate.[8]

HEADQUARTERS FOR THE NEW REPUBLICS

After the Revolutionary War, the colonies became independent republics, the first of their kind on earth. As soon as wartime conditions permitted, the young governments began to act: constitutions were drawn up, leaders were elected, and assemblies began to enact laws to lay the basis for a new society. These new governments, faced with tremendous challenges of initial organization and postwar change, required adequate physical quarters in which to operate.

In 1771, the construction of a new headquarters for the province of Maryland had been initiated in the port town of Annapolis, and by the time war broke out, much of the basic structure was in place. After the Revolution, it seemed natural to complete the building intended for colonial use and turn it over to the new republic. The Maryland State House was first occupied

in 1779 and eventually completed in 1797, making it the oldest functioning capitol in America (Figure 3.4).[9]

Annapolis had been laid out in 1695 by Governor Francis Nicholson, who a few years later planned Williamsburg and coined the present definition of the term "capitol." Annapolis was one of the earliest examples of baroque town planning in the New World, and on a knoll at its heart Nicholson platted land for public use. This became the location of the new government building, and after its post-Revolutionary use was determined, the site was named State Circle.[10]

The Maryland State House was radical for its time. The architect, probably Joseph Horatio Anderson, rejected the usual Georgian rooftop steeple or cupola in favor of an octagonal dome built of wood. Beneath the dome was a public lobby, a kind of predecessor to today's rotunda. In a few years, the dome's timbers began to rot, and in 1788 a second octagonal wooden dome was built, this time of enduring cypress. At the same time, the dome's height was increased to 200 feet, a substantial construction feat for its time.[11]

Steps were incorporated into the dome, so visitors could climb to an exterior viewing platform. In September 1790, none other than Thomas Jefferson and James Madison, in the company of Thomas Lee Shippen, climbed into the dome and spent three hours looking over the Annapolis harbor. This experience seems to have made an impression on Jefferson and may have led to his promoting the idea of a dome for the new national Capitol.[12]

Like Independence Hall, the Maryland State House has witnessed many important events in American history, including the ratification of the Treaty of Paris, which ended the Revolutionary War, and George Washington's relinquishment of military command, which occurred on December 23, 1783. On the morning of that day, this lionized figure, having said goodbye to his officers a few days earlier at Fraunces Tavern in New York City, presented himself at the statehouse in full dress uniform. In the Old Senate Chamber,

Figure 3.4. The Maryland State House, Annapolis. First occupied in 1779, it is the oldest functioning capitol in America. A rear addition, built in 1902 to 1904, serves today's needs.

he read his resignation to those delegates present (Figure 3.5) and immediately thereafter departed for Virginia to spend Christmas with his wife. That simply, the American Cincinnatus rejected any opportunity for the lifetime dictatorship he might easily have assumed. In another six years, Washington would came out of retirement to become the new nation's constitutional head of state.[13]

The next capitol to be built, for the new state of South Carolina, also received a visit from George Washington. Its capital, Columbia, was planned de novo, just as Annapolis and Williamsburg had been laid out by Nicholson. In 1786, the South Carolina General Assembly ordered the construction of a statehouse that would provide rooms for itself, courts of justice, and certain public officers. Space in the building for the governor was not mentioned, although a separate residence was anticipated for him. Completed in 1790, the building had two floors, with the upper more commodious one, reached by portico with side steps, housing the legislative chambers and committee rooms. Offices for the treasurer, secretary, and surveyor general were placed on the lower level, partly below ground and entered beneath the portico.[14]

President Washington paid a visit to Columbia in 1791 and was received at the capitol for a state dinner and grand ball. Legend has it that because of this visit, Washington was instrumental in having its architect chosen to design the new President's House in Washington, D.C. This would have been James Hoban, a Charleston professional who could conceivably have designed the statehouse, but probably did not—even though the connection makes a good story. Washington did help Hoban became the original White House architect, however, and Hoban later supervised early construction of the United States Capitol.

Figure 3.5. Old Senate Chamber of the Maryland State House. In this room, the Continental Congress concluded the Revolutionary War and accepted George Washington's resignation of command of the Continental Army.

The South Carolina State House was burned in 1865 during Sherman's March to the Sea.[15]

As we have seen, in colonial Virginia and republican South Carolina, as well as the District of Columbia, architectural attention to the chief executive centered on a palace of residence, not a business office. The governor's physical presence in the legislative capitol was not regarded as particularly necessary. But as elected governors took office and their powers expanded, a new pattern evolved.

In the Maryland State House, which was originally intended for colonial use, the governor had space above the Senate chamber, where Washington resigned his commission, but it was reached by a steep and unpretentious back stair. More respectable gubernatorial treatment is found in the State House of Delaware. This Georgian structure, facing Dover's common known as The Green, was constructed from 1788 to 1792 and restored in 1972 to 1976. In 1792, Delaware adopted a new constitution that granted the gov-

ernor enhanced powers, allowing him to operate with less oversight from a legislatively controlled privy council. This enlarged status is reflected in the official's placement in the new building: in a corner front office on the first floor with independent access to an outside door (Figure 3.6). Although not a central-front location, as in the Palace of the Governors in Santa Fe, the arrangement was a big improvement over what was offered in Maryland.

Spatial enhancement for the legislative branch is also found in the Delaware State House. Unlike the capitols of Pennsylvania and Maryland, where assemblies were downstairs within earshot of the street, and unlike those in New England, where they occupied part of the upstairs "government" floor, the structure in Delaware provided each of the two houses with a simple but elegant upstairs chamber for its sole use. These rooms were of equal dimensions, located in the front of the building, and built with elevated public galleries reached by a back stair. A set of handsome

Figure 3.6. The Delaware Old State House, Dover. The Delaware legislature met upstairs at the front of the building. The governor's office was downstairs in the right corner.

curved stairs gave access from the first floor to the upper level, conveying the importance of the bodies housed there.[16]

The next new republican headquarters to be built was the Connecticut Old State House, erected between 1792 and 1796 and recently restored (Figure 3.7). The construction of the capitol, at one time the largest building in Hartford and facing down the hill to the Connecticut River, was regarded as an affirmation of government's newly positive role in the postcolonial era. Some contend that this building, with its pedimented portico and tall steeple, was Charles Bulfinch's first public commission.

Following the Delaware pattern, the two houses of the Connecticut legislature occupied individual chambers of equal size on the second floor, reached by double stairs in a main hall. Facing the front of the building, the chamber of the House of Representatives is on the right and that of the Council (later Senate) on the left. With respect to floor plan, councillors sat as a cor-

porate body around one side of a semicircular dais. House members originally occupied opposing benches in the English manner, but in 1836 they were turned to face the speaker. Placement of the governor also replicated the accommodations in Delaware by giving him a large office on the first floor. The Old State House contained the supreme court chamber as well.[17]

TEMPLES IN THE WILDERNESS

Following the building of statehouses by the new republics along the Atlantic seaboard, it was inevitable that with expansion westward statehouses would be erected in the interior of the country. New states began to enter the union in the 1790s, and admissions became more frequent after the turn of the century. In addition, Virginia, Pennsylvania, and the Carolinas had, for various reasons, moved their capitals away from the coast, requiring the construction of new capitols.

Figure 3.7. The Connecticut Old State House, Hartford. It was used by state government from 1796 to 1879, with the legislature housed upstairs and the governor and supreme court, downstairs.

One of the striking things about many of the early western statehouses is that instead of being low-cost, minimalist, utilitarian buildings of a frontier character, they were exceedingly elegant, especially for their time. While relatively small in scale and simple in decoration, they exhibited refined design characteristics, careful workmanship, and the best materials. Moreover, their architects took to heart the urgings of Jefferson and other Founders to emulate the architecture of antiquity as a way of symbolizing the new republican order.

Hence several temples sprang up in the wilderness in the early nineteenth century. They not only contrasted with their frontier settings in terms of refinement, but also presented the anomaly of Greco-Roman forms deep in the interior of a new land. By means of the quality and style of these statehouses, western politicians could present an image of political and economic importance for their region as well as a demand for cultural respect from the eastern elite.

The earliest and most important precedent of a wilderness temple has already been discussed, the Virginia State Capitol in Richmond (see Figure 2.12). This was Jefferson's personal example of a proper public building for the new America. Although Charles-Louis Clerisseau designed its details, Jefferson himself dictated the configuration, measurements, spatial organization, and site. He was in fact quite emotional about the project, and became furious when, after returning from France, found that construction was not proceeding exactly along the lines he wanted. He insisted on several changes, but because of various compromises and lack of "proper ornaments," Jefferson was never fully satisfied with the results.[18]

Others of the time held Jefferson's creation in awe, however. Benjamin Henry Latrobe, later the second architect of the United States Capitol, was so taken with the building that he executed four handsome watercolors of it, showing the displaced Maison Carrée standing in splendid isolation above the James River. William Loughton Smith, a South Carolina Federalist, visited the site and wrote, "The different views of Richmond, with its immense Capitol, towering above the Town on a lofty eminence, with its antique appearance, arrested my attention. . . . The loftiness of this building, and its eminent situation render it a very striking object, and it is the first thing which strikes the traveler."[19]

In 1799, the government of Pennsylvania began to depart from the Old State House in Philadelphia. Its move to the western outpost of Harrisburg required the construction of a new capitol. A large, handsome site on the banks of the Susquehanna River was chosen. Under the direction of architect A. Stephen Hills, a capitol was built from 1810 to 1821 that departed markedly from the Georgian flavor of Independence Hall and the New England statehouses. Its low dome and colonnaded portico, which projected outward in rounded form, were inspired by the architectural legacy of classical antiquity. Below the dome, Hills placed a central circular open space, the first true statehouse rotunda in America.

With its dome, rotunda, portico, and riverine site on open land, the only element of the statehouse building type entirely missing from the capitol in Harrisburg was a cruciform ground plan. Although Hills positioned the commonwealth's two legislative chambers on opposing sides of the rotunda, the original structure had no externally visible cross axis. One was not created until a rear office wing was added in 1868. Even so, this capitol, which burned in 1897, constituted a notable advance in the emergence of the statehouse building type. Between 1837 and 1860, a near copy was built under the same architect's direction on an even more western riverbank, the Missouri, for the government of the state of that name. It, too, has not survived.[20]

The first new western state to join the union was Kentucky, carved out of Virginia in 1792. This frontier land west of the Alleghenies had been opened up by explorers like Daniel Boone, who laid out the Wilderness Road. The tiny river settlement of Frankfort (derived from "Frank's Ford") was chosen for the capital of the new commonwealth. The infant state government initially convened in some private residences, later moving to a simple stone building on Public Square.

It burned in 1813 and was replaced by a brick structure with portico and steeple, but it, too, burned, in 1824.

Gideon Shryock, a native of Lexington then twenty-five years old who had studied for a year in Philadelphia with architect William Strickland, responded to the call for proposals for a new Kentucky statehouse. Shryock's design was based on the Greek temple of Minerva Polias, resulting in the creation of such a temple on Public Square in 1827 to 1830. Its highlight is a hexastyle (six-columned) front portico in simple Ionic form (Figure 3.8). The interior was crafted simply but elegantly, the centerpiece being a keystone-supported circular stone stairway in the rotunda. The legislative chambers were located on the second floor, with the Senate in the front of the capitol and the House in the rear.[21]

Other new republics in the western wilderness followed this example. For neighboring Tennessee, the next state to join the union, a Greek Revival temple was constructed from 1845 to 1859. Its architect was Shryock's teacher, William Strickland. Ohio then was admitted to the union, and it acquired a Greek temple as well. Three designs in Greek Revival style were submitted for the statehouse in Columbus, and New York architect Alexander Jackson Davis was hired to coalesce them. The capitol's cornerstone was laid in 1839, but it was not fully completed until 1861.[22]

In the next state to the west, Indiana, Davis helped design yet another Greek temple in the planned city of Indianapolis. A domed, Parthenon-like edifice in amphistyle form, with a temple front at both ends, was built in 1832 to 1835. Two hundred feet long, it incorporated Ionic, Doric, and Corinthian orders in its many columns and pilasters. "Nothing tends more to refine the taste, and to divest it of all taint of vulgarity," an observer wrote in reference to the new building, than "those exquisite forms of beauty transmitted to us in the remains of ancient art." Unfortunately, the temple had to be replaced in a few decades, after its House chamber collapsed in 1867.[23]

ALL ELEMENTS CONVERGE

In addition to bringing perceived cultural refinement to the frontier, these temples in the wilderness were an avenue for the development of the statehouse building type as the nineteenth century unfolded. The prominent site, parklike grounds, central dome, portico, and rotunda were all coming into being. The last element to be added was the cruciform ground plan. Looking ahead, the final step was taken with respect to the national Capitol by 1825, and its appearance at the state level occurred in 1840.

An interesting transitional case on the way to the full emergence of the type is the Old State House in Little Rock. It was constructed between 1833 and 1842, during which time, in 1836, the territory of Arkansas became a state. Gideon Shryock advised its design, and the core of the building is a Greek temple somewhat like Shryock's statehouse in Frankfort, Kentucky, but without the domed lantern. Nearly identical porticos terminated each end of the core structure in the amphistyle manner, with the facade on the Arkansas River side considered to be the front.

This end-to-end symmetry facilitated a switch of the building's directional orientation in 1885. After the dominant mode of transportation in Little Rock changed from riverboat to carriage and train, the riverside portico was removed and the building was extended in that direction, while new doors and windows were cut on the street side (Figure 3.9). When the switch occurred, the Senate chamber was moved from the old front end to the new front end, with the House of Representatives moved to the expanded back.[24]

To supplement the main building, Shryock had had two identical smaller structures built, placed symmetrically beside the central one and attached to it by covered walkways. This was not an unusual arrangement for the time—Independence Hall in Philadelphia has connected flanking buildings, for example. But it appears that in Little Rock there was, for the first time, an allocation of outbuildings to particular functions of government. Early occupancy patterns are not known for sure, but it is likely that the eastern

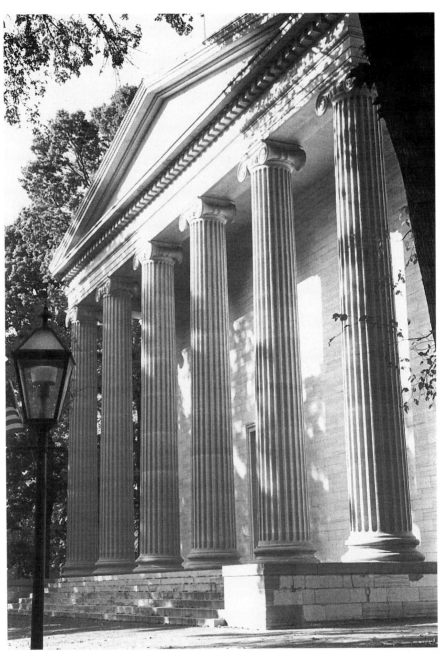

Figure 3.8. The Kentucky Old State Capitol, Frankfort. Designed by twenty-five-year-old Gideon Shryock and completed in 1830, this work is said to have introduced the Greek Revival style to the American West.

Figure 3.9. The Arkansas Old State House, Little Rock. Although the building was constructed between 1833 and 1842, the street side of the buiding, created in 1885, previously faced toward the Arkansas River.

auxiliary building contained courtrooms and judges' chambers, while the western building housed state officials, including the governor. Meanwhile, the central core was the home of the Arkansas legislature.

Some years before the directional switch in Little Rock, the covered walkways linking the three structures were rebuilt into largely enclosed connectors to provide additional office space. This created a rough equivalent of the cruciform floor plan. Its long axis consisted of an east–west set of opposing judicial and executive wings; its short axis, a north–south set of opposing legislative chambers. The axes crossed at the center of a middle hall; although it was not a true rotunda, curved stairways and a round skylight were incorporated into the hall in 1885.

The North Carolina State Capitol in Raleigh, constructed between 1832 and 1840 and hence a contemporary of the Arkansas Old State House, fully embodies the statehouse building type, even if at a modest scale. It was initially designed by

Alexander Jackson Davis and Ithiel Town, with David Paton later replacing them. The building possesses a clear cruciform shape; unlike the connected auxiliary structures found in Little Rock, its wings project directly from a central core, at all the cardinal points of the compass. The longest dimension of the resultant cross, 160 feet, is the north–south axis, with the old Senate chamber situated on the north side and the former House chamber on the south. The east–west axis, 140 feet in length, terminates with a temple front at each end. The east facade is considered the front of the building, even though the west side is identical (Figure 3.10).[25]

In addition to its cruciform ground plan and temple front, the capitol in Raleigh exhibits the other elements of the statehouse building type. It is located in the middle of a landscaped block in the center of the city. It is crowned by a low dome centered directly above a rotunda, positioned at the intersection of the two axes. As for interior organization, the first floor is divided

Figure 3.10. The North Carolina State Capitol, Raleigh. Completed in 1840 and still in use, it represents the earliest convergence of all the elements of the capitol building type at the state level.

by crossed corridors into four quadrants, each initially devoted to a separate function of government: (1) southwest quadrant, governor; (2) southeast, state treasurer; (3) northwest, auditor and secretary of state; and (4) northeast, comptroller and supreme court. These uses have long since changed, but the governor still occupies some space on the floor, with ample supplementary offices in a nearby state building.

At one time, the North Carolina legislature met on the capitol's second floor, with the state library and state geologist's office on the third. In 1963, the North Carolina legislature moved to its own quarters, the State Legislative Building, abandoning its old chambers for restoration and exhibition use. Nonetheless, the capitol remains a beloved anchor to North Carolina political life, continuing to attract both the powerful and the ordinary. Legends pertaining to hidden tunnels, secret rooms, and an upstairs bar known as the Third House show no sign of losing their appeal.

Another statehouse of the early nineteenth century is the Old Capitol of Mississippi, authorized in 1833 and completed in 1840, and hence a contemporary of the early statehouses in Arkansas and North Carolina. In 1832, Mississippi adopted a new constitution and selected a site for a permanent capital, a point on the Pearl River at the geographic center of the state that was christened Jackson in honor of Old Hickory.

Designed by English architect William Nichols, Mississippi's first statehouse, still standing, has some Greek Revival detailing, yet like its counterpart in North Carolina, the low dome and temple front are more Roman than Greek (Figure 3.11). In 1840, soon after the capitol was opened, an aged Andrew Jackson paid a brief visit to his namesake town in honor of the twenty-fifth anniversary of the Battle of New Orleans. He was greeted by an adulatory crowd from the portico balcony. Inside the building, physical features can be found that preserve the spirit of Jacksonian democracy. One egalitarian gesture is the absence of doors that could close courtrooms to public entry. Another doorway oddity is the entryway to the governor's first-floor suite; it is barely distinguishable from all the other doors along the corridor, said to be a deliberate reflection of the weak powers given the chief executive in the constitution of 1832 (Figure 3.12).[26]

The Illinois Old State Capitol in Springfield was designed by John Francis Rague, using Greek Revival copybooks of the time. Built from 1837 to 1840, it reflects all the elements of the statehouse type, except the rotunda (Figure 3.13). Perhaps more than those of any other present or past state capitol, its halls evoke the spirit of famous historical figures. Stephen A. Douglas was boss of the state Democratic machine that ruled the building with an iron hand for many years. Ulysses S. Grant's first role in the Civil War was as a clerk in the adjutant general's office on the second floor, and later he received his first command in the building.

The old capitol's mightiest ghost, however, is that of Abraham Lincoln. Shortly after he moved to Springfield, Lincoln and other local legislators helped manipulate a self-serving move of the capital from Vandalia to Springfield. As an aggressive railroad attorney whose offices were across the street from the statehouse, Lincoln researched cases in the building's library and argued them in its courtoom. As a four-term member of the Illinois House, he studied election returns in the secretary of state's office, swapped stories in the clerk's office, and drew pay warrants in the auditor's office. In Representative Hall (Figure 3.14), Lincoln launched his campaign for the United States Senate against his archrival Douglas, delivered the famous "House Divided" speech, and lost his Senate bid (until 1913, United States senators were elected by state legislatures). In the governor's reception room across the hall, Lincoln planned his campaign for president and received job seekers following his

Figure 3.11. The Mississippi Old Capitol, Jackson, now the Mississippi State Historical Museum. This early statehouse bears physical signs of the principles of Jacksonian democracy, such as courtrooms without doors.

Figure 3.12. First-floor corridor of the Mississippi Old Capitol. The five circles above the end door on the right are the only indication that it was the entrance to the governor's office.

Figure 3.13. The Illinois Old State Capitol, Springfield. In state use from 1839 to 1876, the building is tied to the careers of Stephen A. Douglas, Ulysses S. Grant, and Abraham Lincoln.

Figure 3.14. Representative Hall, as restored, Illinois Old State Capitol. The end of the front rostrum desk closest to the camera is where Lincoln likely delivered his "House Divided" speech in 1858.

victory in 1860. After his assassination five years later, Lincoln's body lay in state in Representative Hall.[27]

Intriguing historical parallels to this lore about the Illinois Old State Capitol are found at the Alabama State Capitol in Montgomery. This building, whose initial portion was constructed in 1850 and 1851, embraced from the start all the features of the statehouse type, including a rotunda. Several additions were made to the capitol, but the temple front facing Dexter Avenue to the west is original (Figure 3.15). Although the Alabama legislature now meets in the State House, this building is still the state capitol.[28]

Just as the principal leaders of the Civil War's Union cause, Lincoln and Grant, began their careers in the Illinois Old State Capitol, so the Confederate cause and its prime leader were launched into history in the Alabama State Capitol. On February 4, 1861, in the second-floor Senate chamber, the Confederate States of America was organized. Two weeks later, on the

capitol's portico steps, Jefferson Davis of Mississippi was inaugurated as president of the new government. A quarter century later, in 1886, Davis returned as an old man to lay the cornerstone of a Confederate monument on the capitol grounds. The monument took twelve years to build, and the day before it was unveiled the aged Davis died. As was that of his wartime rival Lincoln, Davis's body lay in state in the capitol building where his presidency began.

The historical ironies do not end there. Only a single block down Dexter Avenue from the building's temple front, another great and not unrelated cause was launched: the civil rights movement. After Rosa Parks was arrested in late 1955 for having refused to surrender her seat on a Montgomery city bus, a boycott of the local buses was organized with the cooperation of a young Martin Luther King, Jr., in the basement of the Dexter Avenue Baptist Church, located just 200 yards down the street from the capitol (Figure 3.16). A decade later, by which time King

Figure 3.15. The Alabama State Capitol, Montgomery. Its front portion was built in 1850 and 1851, with many extensions added later. The Confederate States of America was created in this statehouse in 1861.

Figure 3.16. Looking west from the portico balcony of the Alabama State Capitol. The Dexter Avenue Baptist Church, a birthplace of the civil rights movement, is visible on the left.

had become the national leader of the civil rights movement, his famous march from Selma to Montgomery took place. On March 25, 1965, the march ended at the same capitol steps where Jefferson Davis had been inaugurated as president of the Confederacy a century earlier.

EMERGENT SOCIAL MEANINGS

As the conceptual development of the statehouse building type proceeded, its social meanings emerged. With respect to meanings to which attention is drawn by the expressive lens, several ideas are embodied in the way space within the early buildings was organized.

Under colonialism, governors were clearly central. In the Palace of the Governors in Santa Fe, the governor's suite is at the front center of the building. In the capitol in Williamsburg, the upstairs rooms in which Crown authority was exercised are more elaborately decorated than the downstairs House of Burgesses. In the Old State

House in Boston, the royal governor and Council occupied the preferred harbor end of the building, complete with a balcony overlooking the street.

Following the Revolution, governors became objects of deep republican suspicion, which was registered spatially. In the Maryland State House, the governor originally occupied an obscure upstairs office reached by a back stair. The statehouse in South Carolina provides no office space at all for the governor. In the Virginia State Capitol, the governor was relegated to a small corner upstairs office on the third floor, still occupied by that official. The Old Capitol of Mississippi located the governor behind a barely enhanced door on the first floor.

With the adoption of second-generation state constitutions that gave state governors more power, their spatial treatment was improved. In the Delaware Old State House, the chief executive occupied a corner-front office on the first floor, equipped with an independent doorway to the street. The governor's suite was situated in a similar position in the Connecticut Old State House, and in the North Carolina State Capitol, the chief executive's office took up the southwest quadrant of the first floor, while in the Alabama State Capitol it occupied a front corner on the first floor.

As for spatial treatment of the legislature, in early colonial times assemblies representing the colonists met in secondary space. In Santa Fe, it was a small side corner; in Williamsburg, a less ornate wing; and in Boston, a middle room sandwiched between Crown and court. Following the Revolution, things changed. Beginning with the Delaware and Connecticut Old State Houses, a set of specially designed legislative chambers was installed on the second floor. This pattern was continued in the original statehouses of Kentucky, Arkansas, and Mississippi and in the first capitols of North Carolina, Alabama, Tennessee, and Ohio.

With respect to the separate chambers of the legislature, the colonial tradition was to give the smaller body more distinguished space, on the grounds that its origin was a privy council or governor's council. Favoritism to the Senate often continued in the republican era, sometimes by placing its chamber in the front of the statehouse and that of the more popular body in the rear. This can be seen in the original layout of the Virginia State Capitol, the Kentucky Old State Capitol, and the Arkansas Old State House. Yet the more common emergent pattern was to give the two chambers strictly equivalent space in terms of prestige, if not volumetric size. Usually this was done by placing each house on one side of the central dome and rotunda, along the longitudinal axis of the building. The concept of bicameral equity is visible in the old statehouses of Delaware, Connecticut, and Mississippi and the capitol of Pennsylvania designed by A. Stephen Hills.

Turning to emergent meanings generated by the behavioral lens, the situation whereby each of the five counties of Rhode Island had its own government house meant that functions of the colony and later the state were geographically dispersed. Meetings of the General Assembly of this nascent federal polity rotated among towns. The practice must have created difficulties of access to meetings by assemblymen and citizens. By contrast, the emergent statehouse concept became the conceptual opposite of such dispersal. Not only was there a single capitol in each state, but all headquarter components of government were housed under one roof. This concept was present as early as 1610, the date of construction of the Palace of the Governors, which housed the military, fiscal, and legislative functions of government, as well as the governor and his family. The Old State House in Boston was also an important precedent, since three adjacent rooms on the second floor were used for the executive, legislative, and judicial functions of government.

The consolidation of all headquarter components of state government in the statehouse prevailed for more than a century, creating for the time being the opportunity for intimate behavioral interaction across branches and departments. Another unitary feature of the building was the street-level merchant's walk, which followed the English town hall custom of integrating commerce with government in one building. This idea was not to survive in the statehouse per se, although it is seen in recent city halls and federal structures, such as the Ronald Reagan Building in Washington, D.C.

Emergent social meanings are also seen from the perspective of the societal lens. The earliest statehouses were capable of articulating authority to the public, as evidenced by the lion and unicorn emblems in Boston, the processional Parade in Providence, and State Circle in Annapolis. But Jefferson had more in mind than evoking the leftovers of colonial symbolism in the new republic. He and other Founders were committed to expressing the authority of the infant state and national governments in a fresh symbolism taken from Greco-Roman antiquity. More than any other statehouse, his arresting capitol on the James River—copied from a Roman temple, sketched by Benjamin Latrobe, and admired by William Smith—set the directions, at the state level, of this symbolic architectural campaign. It was called a capitol, sited on a substitute Capitoline Hill, and given a majestic temple front whose size and image were striking for the time. Other temples sprang up in the frontier wildernesses of Pennsylvania, Kentucky, Tennessee, Indiana, and Ohio.

The early statehouses eventually became repositories of history. Distinguished figures of the past—including Washington, Jefferson, Lafayette, Jackson, Lincoln, Grant, and King—walked their halls. The buildings have been settings for momentous events, such as the signing of the Declaration of Independence, the drafting of the Constitution, the delivery of the House Divided speech, the birth of the Confederacy, and the launching of the civil rights movement. Their continued existence enshrines the past.

4 | The Construction of the American Statehouse

By 1840, the building type of the American statehouse had been created. Its basic conceptual elements were in place, even though the building was modest in scale compared with what would come. The statehouses we know today were, for the most part, erected during the last third of the nineteenth century and first third of the twentieth. These buildings were enormous construction projects for their time from the standpoint of capital costs, skilled labor, and available technology. From a political standpoint, bringing them into being was often accompanied by intense conflict and controversy, resulting in mixed legacies of pride and bitterness.

FIFTY BUILDINGS IN BRIEF

We have already encountered exceptions to the generalization that the contemporary statehouse is a post–Civil War phenomenon. These include the capitols of Maryland, Massachusetts, Virginia, Alabama, and North Carolina, all of which contributed to the emergence of the building type and are still in use. The buildings in Annapolis, Boston, and Richmond have been extended, and those in Montgomery and Raleigh have been supplemented by the creation of separate legislative buildings. The Alabama legislature meets in a former highway department headquarters, and North Carolina legislators convene in a 1960s-era structure designed by Edward Durell Stone.

Other statehouses with early origins that are still in use in some way are those of New Jersey, New Hampshire, and Maine. The earliest segment of the New Jersey State House, a small fragment buried deep within the greatly extended structure, dates from 1792. The New Hampshire State House, significantly transformed twice, was originally built in 1816 to 1819. The front core of the Maine State House was Charles Bulfinch's last contribution to American capitol architecture, produced between 1829 and 1832 just after he finished work on the United States Capitol (Figure 4.1).

In addition, the Greek Revival statehouses of Ohio and Tennessee were built in the decades before the Civil War and may be thought of as latter-day temples in the wilderness. Subsequently, an annex was added in the rear of the capitol in Columbus, and that in Nashville was enlarged underground. The Vermont State House, initially built in the 1850s in the Classical Revival style, was later extended in the back by two unusual asymmetrical additions. The South Carolina State Capitol, also Classical Revival, was begun in 1851, but not completed until the twentieth century. The construction of the California State Capitol was launched just before the Civil War and completed a few years after the war ended. In retrospect, the American Renaissance style pioneered in Sacramento became in effect the "standard" capitol architecture, which was to take root in the nation's capital and spread throughout the country over the next several decades (Figure 4.2).

These thirteen exceptions aside, the heyday of state capitol construction in America was the six decades following the Civil War (Table 4.1). Of the remaining thirty-seven statehouses, twenty-seven were built in what might be thought of as two successive waves of construction. The timing of these waves, from 1866 to 1886 for the first wave and from 1895 to 1924 for the second, is measured by the year of commencement of construction.

During the first wave, eleven statehouse projects were begun. These resulted in the current capitols of Colorado, Connecticut, Georgia, Illinois, Indiana, Iowa, Kansas, Michigan, New York, Texas, and Wyoming (see Figures 2.6 and 2.9).

Figure 4.1. The Maine State House, Augusta. Its front portion, but not the dome, was designed by Charles Bulfinch and built between 1829 and 1832, just after he completed the early United States Capitol.

Figure 4.2. The California State Capitol, Sacramento. Its front portion, constructed from 1860 to 1869, was the first statehouse to be built in what came to be known as the American Renaissance style.

Table 4.1
CONSTRUCTION DATES

	Original Structure	Additions and Extensions	Major Renovation	Restoration or Preservation
Alabama	1850–1851	1885, 1905–1907 1911–1912, 1989–1992		1976–1992
Alaska	1929–1931		1967	1980
Arizona	1899–1901	1918–1919, 1938–1939 1957–1960, 1973–1974		1976–1981
Arkansas	1899–1917			
California	1860–1869	1949–1954		1975–1981
Colorado	1886–1908			
Connecticut	1873–1879			Ongoing
Delaware	1932–1933	1970		
Florida	1973–1977			
Georgia	1884–1889		1929, 1956	
Hawaii	1965–1969		1991–1996	
Idaho	1905–1912	1919–1920	1992–1993	
Illinois	1868–1888		1932	1968–1988
Indiana	1878–1888		1917–1920, 1945–1948, 1958, 1966	1975–1988
Iowa	1871–1886			Ongoing
Kansas	1866–1906			
Kentucky	1905–1910			
Louisiana	1931–1932		1980s	
Maine	1829–1832	1890–1891, 1909–1910		
Maryland	1771–1797	1858, 1886, 1902–1904		
Massachusetts	1795–1798	1831, 1853–1856 1889–1895, 1914–1917 1958–1960, 1990		
Michigan	1873–1878			1980s, 1990s
Minnesota	1896–1907			
Mississippi	1901–1903			1979–1982
Missouri	1913–1917			
Montana	1899–1902	1909–1912	1963–1965	
Nebraska	1922–1932			
Nevada	1970	1977	1990s	1977–1991
New Hampshire	1816–1819	1864–1866, 1909–1910	1969	
New Jersey	1792	1845, 1860s, 1870s 1880s, 1890s, 1900s 1910s, 1920s, 1990s		Ongoing
New Mexico	1964–1966		1992	
New York	1867–1899			1979 on
North Carolina	1963	1982		
North Dakota	1932–1934	1977–1981		

Table 4.1
CONSTRUCTION DATES (*continued*)

	Original Structure	Additions and Extensions	Major Renovation	Restoration or Preservation
Ohio	1839–1861	1899–1901		1988–1997
Oklahoma	1914–1917		1921	Ongoing
Oregon	1936–1938	1975–1977		
Pennsylvania	1902–1906	1982–1987		1982 on
Rhode Island	1895–1904			
South Carolina	1851–1907			1995–1997
South Dakota	1907–1910	1932	1941	1975–1989
Tennessee	1845–1859		1950s	1980s
Texas	1882–1888	1991–1995		1991–1995
Utah	1912–1915			
Vermont	1857–1859	1884–1886, 1898–1900	1987	
Virginia	1785–1800	1904–1906	1962–1964	
Washington	1919–1932		1949, 1976	1987
West Virginia	1924–1932			
Wisconsin	1906–1917			Ongoing
Wyoming	1886–1888	1890, 1915–1917		1974–1980

The societal context of several of these first-wave projects was the aftermath of the Civil War. The statehouses of Connecticut, Illinois, Iowa, Kansas, Michigan, and New York were begun in the late 1860s and early 1870s, as if to memorialize the Union cause and express confidence in peacetime economic growth. This was not the case in Georgia and Texas, of course, and their capitols were not begun until the 1880s, when Reconstruction was well over. Indeed, for many years after the war, the depleted southern economy prevented extensive public investments of any kind, as manifest in the long delay in completion of the South Carolina State House.

The very opposite was true in the victorious North. The state governments had both funds and pretensions. Several new statehouses were astonishingly large and ornate for their time—for example, the huge Illinois State Capitol, built in Italianate style over the two decades of 1868 to 1888 (Figure 4.3). Its contemporaries include an elaborate Victorian Gothic edifice in Hartford, a multidomed Beaux-Arts capitol in Des Moines, and an ambitious Second Empire replacement statehouse in Indianapolis (see Figure 2.6).

The construction of capitols in the West during these years was a particularly emphatic gesture of optimism. The land was thinly settled, and the construction of a statehouse constituted an assertion of faith in westward migration. Land speculators hoping to make a profit from the West's development donated land for capitol construction, with the hope that it would raise the value of adjoining property. Moreover, capitol construction could also fit into the entreprenurial plans of corporations. The Wyoming State Capitol, started eighteen years after chief engineer Grenville Dodge of the Union Pacific Railroad laid out the capital town of the new territory, was sited so that it faced down Cheyenne's main axis toward the Union Pacific depot. Its construction was an enormous feat for the frontier and stood as a claim that the Wyoming Territory deserved statehood despite its suffragette radicalism (Figure 4.4).

Figure 4.3. The Illinois State Capitol, Springfield. This huge Italianate edifice, constructed after the Civil War, replaced the smaller capitol, in which Abraham Lincoln had served.

Figure 4.4. The Wyoming State Capitol, Cheyenne. Its central core was built to be the territorial capitol. The suffragette statue is a reminder that Wyoming pioneered in granting women the vote.

Relevant contextual forces operating during the second wave of statehouse construction were urban growth, rapid industrialization, continued westward migration, and the Progressive commitment to an enlarged role for government. The construction of sixteen capitols was launched during this period: those of Arizona, Arkansas, Idaho, Kentucky, Minnesota, Mississippi, Missouri, Montana, Oklahoma, Pennsylvania, Rhode Island, South Dakota, Utah, Washington, West Virginia, and Wisconsin (see Figures 1.2, 2.2, 2.3, 2.7, 2.8, and 2.11).

From a style standpoint, most of these buildings may be classified as American Renaissance, in which a number of European stylistic influences are eclectically melded into a new version of themes echoing from antiquity and the Renaissance. First used in Sacramento at the state level, the American Renaissance image became standard for the statehouse building type in the early twentieth century and is the most easily recognizable popular model for what a state capitol "should look like."

A good example of American Renaissance style is found in the Pennsylvania State Capitol Building, which replaced the capitol built by A. Stephen Hills (Figure 4.5). Dedicated with fanfare by President Theodore Roosevelt in 1906, the building is replete with facade detailing and architectural sculpture. Inside, the rotunda is grandly conceived as an improvement on the lobby of Charles Garnier's Opéra in Paris. The ceremonial spaces are decorated with fine murals and artwork of all kinds, suggesting a kind of state government palace suitable for the dawning twentieth century.

Not all second-wave statehouses are the same, however. Some were influenced by the resurgence of classicism following the architectural success of the White City, built for the World's Columbian Exposition, held in Chicago in 1893. Its temporary buildings were seen as dazzling examples of avant-garde architecture executed in the Beaux-Arts style, a self-conscious kind of neoclassicism taught at the Ecole des Beaux-Arts in Paris. Examples are the Mississippi New Capitol, completed in 1903 (see Figure 2.8), and

the Rhode Island State House, finished the following year. The latter capitol, strikingly white like the exposition buildings, was designed by Charles Follen McKim of the famous New York architectural firm McKim, Mead and White (Figure 4.6).

The statehouses built later than these two great waves of construction may be divided into two categories. The first is a set of varied and occasionally creative structures dating from the 1920s and 1930s. The most important is the Nebraska State Capitol, an elaborate Art Deco edifice built between 1922 and 1932 (Figure 4.7). Another Art Deco creation is the Oregon State Capitol, a "modern" version of Greek Revival (Figure 4.8). Others of this period are the Louisiana State Capitol, inspired in part by the Nebraska capitol; the North Dakota State Capitol, whose modernist exterior hides an Art Deco interior; the Delaware Legislative Hall, the only Georgian statehouse in the country; and, finally, the Alaska State Capitol, a territorial office building designed by the federal government that was converted into the capitol after statehood was conferred in 1959.

Completing the fifty American statehouses is a group of five relatively contemporary edifices. One is the North Carolina State Legislative Building by Edward Durell Stone (Figure 4.9). The Hawaii State Capitol, completed ten years after statehood, is a columned block somewhat like Stone's building but dominated by an open atrium that serves as metaphor for a volcano (Figure 4.10). The Florida Capitol, also designed by Stone, consists of a complex of five connected structures with a high-rise tower in the center (Figure 4.11). Its detractors claim that from afar, the group's two low domes with middle upright tower embarrassingly suggest the male genitalia. The New Mexico State Capitol, which bears the nickname The Roundhouse, is in the form of a circular Zia sun symbol, pervasive in the state's iconology. The nation's most recent statehouse is the Nevada Legislative Building, whose 1970s core was expanded and reconstructed in the 1990s. Its detailing is modestly postmodern and includes a low silver dome (Figure 4.12).

Figure 4.5. The Pennsylvania State Capitol Building, Harrisburg. Dedicated by President Theodore Roosevelt in 1906 amid charges of corruption, this statehouse is known for its mural art.

Figure 4.6. The Rhode Island State House, Providence. Charles Follen McKim's strikingly white Beaux-Arts structure was probably inspired by the White City at the World's Columbian Exposition, held in Chicago in 1893.

THE POLITICS OF LOCATION AND FUNDING

We turn now from a panoramic survey of the final products of statehouse construction to a more focused examination of the construction process itself. As might be expected, the size, importance, and publicness of capitol building projects generated political controversy from the start. At the time of their construction, these buildings typically cost more than $1 million, and sometimes $5 million, $10 million, or more. In the late nineteenth and early twentieth centuries, such sums were perceived as enormous outlays. Carrying out the projects usually took many years, even several decades. Building a capitol was often the most ambitious public-works project ever attempted by a state government, dwarfing all others in scale.

Key decisions about whether to build a new capitol, where to build it, and how to finance it were major issues of public debate. State legislatures could wrangle for years before coming to the point of authorizing construction. A commission, usually made up of elected officials and others intended to represent various constituencies, would often be formed to develop and oversee the project. The commission's deliberations frequently erupted into well-publicized squabbles, with political opponents and a sensationalist press amplifying all disagreements and criticisms. With rare exceptions, these were highly politicized public works, from beginning to end.

Political controversy over building a capitol was often intertwined with conflict over which town or city should serve as the state capital. Various communities would vie strenuously for this honor and provide incentives to obtain it. Tuscaloosa was the capital of Alabama for twenty years before Montgomery won out against it, in part because of a gift of land and money for a statehouse. In Vermont, several towns competed.

Figure 4.7. The Nebraska State Capitol, Lincoln. This eclectic, towering, cathedral-like statehouse was designed by Bertram Grosvenor Goodhue, who did not live to see it completed in 1932.

Figure 4.8. The Oregon State Capitol, Salem. Constructed in the 1930s with New Deal help, this Art Deco capitol has a flat dome that bespeaks its Greek Revival stylistic origins.

Figure 4.9. The North Carolina State Legislative Building, Raleigh. Designed by Edward Durell Stone in the 1960s, it is square with curtain walls on all four sides.

Figure 4.10. Hawaii State Capitol, Honolulu. Its principal design metaphor is the island volcano, represented by the sloped cone behind the columns, crater opening in the roof, and surrounding pools of water.

Figure 4.11. The Florida Capitol, Tallahassee. Designed by Edward Durell Stone in the 1970s, the office tower flanked by two domed chamber buildings is often compared to the male genitalia.

Figure 4.12. The Nevada Legislative Building, Carson City. Built in the 1970s and reconstructed in the 1990s, it houses the legislature, while the governor occupies the historic State Capitol nearby.

This happened on no less than three occasions: in 1805, when a temporary capitol was first contemplated; in 1836, when a permanent structure was being planned for Montpelier; and in 1857, after a fire had destroyed much of the statehouse. At all three times, Montpelier's cause was greatly aided because its townspeople privately raised funds to subsidize their beloved community project.[1]

Portland was the temporary capital of Maine for seven years after the state's admission to the union, and its leaders were furious when in 1827 the tiny inland town of Augusta was named the permanent capital and Charles Bulfinch built a statehouse there. In later years, a group of Portland businessmen erected a large merchants' exchange in their city, hoping that it would entice the state government to move downstate. Then Portland built a new domed city hall, with an eye to its serving as the capitol. None of these inducements worked, yet members of the Portland legislative delegation pressed their case on two more occasions when the capitol in Augusta was in need of enlargement.[2]

Such struggles were repeated in many states during the nineteenth century. Work on the Ohio State House was delayed for six years in the 1840s while legislators argued over whether to keep the government in Columbus. In New York, after discussion of building a new capitol surfaced during the Civil War, many cities made bids for relocation of the capital from Albany. New York City offered several prime sites, including one in Central Park. West Virginia, after its separation from Virginia during the Civil War, confronted the contentious issue of whether Charleston or Wheeling would become its capital city. The struggle between the two localities was so continual and unresolved that temporary capitols were built in both cities, and all state records and furniture were shipped up and down the Kanawha and Ohio Rivers three times: in 1870, 1875, and 1885.[3]

The construction of permanent statehouses in Oklahoma and South Dakota had to await the outcome of bitter fights for the seat of govern-

ment. According to a story still circulating, Oklahoma City "stole" the capital from the town of Guthrie by secret transfer of the state seal in a laundry basket. In South Dakota, two rival railroads, the Chicago Northwestern and the Milwaukee, fought intently to have towns they served named as the capital. Eventually, Chicago Northwestern, which favored Pierre, won the struggle, and in 1890 a temporary wooden capitol was erected there at private expense on railroad land to secure the prize.[4]

Developments other than the establishment of the capital city precipitated the construction of new statehouses. One was to rebuild following a fire. The use of wood-burning stoves to heat wooden predecessor buildings and gas fixtures to light them caused many statehouses to burn down in the nineteenth century. Those built later of stone also burned on occasion because of the chimney effect of rotundas. These fires were traumatic events to residents of the state capital and would be remembered for years. Invariably, rumors would fly that political opponents had had a hand in setting the blazes. Major statehouse conflagrations occurred in Vermont in 1857, Texas in 1881, Minnesota in 1887, Pennsylvania in 1897, Wisconsin in 1904, Missouri and New York in 1911, West Virginia in 1921 and 1927, North Dakota in 1930, and Oregon in 1935. Nor are such fires entirely a thing of the past; in 1983, a young person was killed in a localized fire in the Texas State Capitol, leading to a major reassessment of the building's safety. On New Year's Day 1992, a fire broke out in the Idaho State Capitol and was within minutes of taking the entire building when the flames were contained.

In addition to fires and struggles over the capital city, the construction of a new statehouse could spring from a politician's personal agenda. Huey Long, the legendary populist boss of Louisiana, made a new statehouse a principal plank in the platform of his campaign for governor in 1928. The idea was strongly opposed by Long's legislative enemies, who, among other things, suspected his motives. Not above artful shenanigans, Long allegedly had a hole drilled in the roof of the old statehouse above an opponent's desk so that water from Baton Rouge's frequent rains would remind everyone of the need for a new building.

After the construction of a new capitol was authorized, Long's only instructions to the architects were that it must have a tall tower and be built quickly. Indeed, it was completed in just fourteen months and became the highest structure in the South at the time. Although Long never served in an official capacity in the new capitol, he controlled Louisiana politics from it with an iron hand until he was fatally shot in one of its corridors in 1935. Long's body was buried in the building's front grounds, forever associating it with his legacy.[5]

Financing these capital projects, huge and costly for their time, inevitably stirred the political cauldron. Voters had to be convinced to support bond issues and, in some instances, approve special tax levies. When financial panics or depressions hit and state revenues sagged, projects had to be delayed. Sometimes only lump-sum windfalls into state coffers made it possible to go ahead. In 1879, Texas sold for 50 cents each 3 million acres of state land to a Chicago syndicate to finance its new capitol. This enormous piece of property embraced most of ten panhandle counties and eventually formed the basis for the largest cattle ranch in the world, the XIT—which means "10 in Texas."[6]

Other special financing sources for capitol construction include a war-damage settlement won by Kentucky from the Department of War for $1 million in 1901. In 1911, the widow of Edward H. Harriman, president of the Union Pacific Railroad, paid an inheritance tax of $798,546 to Utah, a sum that allowed the capitol to be built. At least seven western states received federal land grants in the late nineteenth and early twentieth centuries from which they acquired income to invest in state buildings.

With financing difficult and profits to be made if a new statehouse was built, unsavory development schemes sometimes unfolded. In the 1830s, a Wisconsin land speculator named James Duane Doty purchased property in Madison on the isthmus between what are now Lakes Mendota and Monona, hoping to cash in on the land values that would be escalated by building a territorial capitol on the site. By cutting legislators in on the deal, he generated the political support needed to place the territorial capitol on this land. Doty eventually became territorial governor and brought about the construction of the first capitol, nicknamed Doty's Washbowl because of its hemispheric dome. The state's current capitol stands on the same site.[7]

Similar activities took place in a number of western states. In Colorado, homesteader and developer Henry Cordes Brown donated 10 acres, for which he had paid $1.25 each, for a territorial capitol. He was planning to develop a well-to-do residential neighborhood on the surrounding land, and the capitol's presence would enhance its value. Funds were not appropriated to construct a building at the location for nearly a decade, however. Brown, embittered, sued to reclaim his land; twice the case went all the way to the United States Supreme Court, with Brown losing both times. Eventually, the Colorado State Capitol was built on this property, but Brown refused to attend the dedication ceremony.[8]

In Phoenix, developer Moses H. Sherman sold 10 acres of land for the sum of $1 to the Arizona territorial government for its capitol, with the understanding that a streetcar line be built to connect his outlying property to the center of town. The ploy succeeded, and the city spread westward, as expected, to Sherman's land. In a parallel incident, Oklahoma City landowners William Fremont Harn and J. J. Culbertson donated parcels of adjoining land for a state government site, far to the north of the settled area. As in Phoenix, streetcar connections to the donated lands were required as a part of the deal. When a legal dispute arose over the exact site on which to locate the statehouse, a judge ruled that it straddle the two parcels equally. Harn's donation included mineral rights, but Culbertson's did not, a distinction that had enormous financial implications when oil was discovered beneath the capitol.[9]

THE ARCHITECTS AND THEIR DESIGNS

After decisions were made about whether, when, and where to build a capitol and how to finance it, states had to select architects and approve their plans.

In the early nineteenth century, a number of professional and amateur architects—Thomas Jefferson, Charles Bulfinch, A. Stephen Hills, Gideon Shryock, William Strickland, Alexander Jackson Davis, William Nichols, and John Francis Rague—fashioned, for the first republican states in modern history, a new kind of government headquarters and, in so doing, created the statehouse building type.

Later, particularly during the two great waves of statehouse construction, the nature of architectural creativity in designing capitols changed. Instead of forming new building types, architects in effect set out to refine the existing one. In order to satisfy demands for more room and prestige, their task became making the capitol ever more spacious and elaborate. The major design elements that had converged by 1840 were not challenged until Bertram Grosvenor Goodhue made his plans for the Nebraska State Capitol in the early 1920s.

Why this eighty years of relative architectural conservatism? It would seem to run counter to the tendency of creative minds to reject the past and innovate in order to win lucrative commissions. In part, the answer lies with the general tendency of governments, as architectural clients, to favor conventional styles and thereby avoid controversy. In the case of statehouses, this natural risk aversion was tempered by a desire among states to outshine one another by building a bigger and better capitol—an even finer example of the standard building type. Thus rivalries over the "best" state capitol blossomed; it was not unknown to witness public arguments among states, well covered in the media, about which one had the highest dome and whether its height should be measured from the steps or the sidewalk.

Two other specific factors are also important, however, for explaining the continuity of statehouse design, especially during the two major waves of construction. One relates to the men who were the architects of these buildings; the other is the influence of the national Capitol.

Eighteen architects were the dominant figures in designing the first- and second-wave capitols (Table 4.2):

Frank Mills Andrews	Kentucky
Charles Emlen Bell	Montana, South Dakota
Cass Gilbert	Arkansas, Minnesota, West Virginia
John M. Huston	Pennsylvania
John Hacket Kent	Montana
Richard K. A. Kletting	Utah
Solomon A. Layton	Oklahoma
Theodore C. Link	Mississippi
George R. Mann	Arkansas
Edwin May	Indiana
Charles F. McKim	Alabama, Rhode Island
Elijah E. Myers	Colorado, Michigan, Texas
Alfred H. Piquenard	Illinois, Iowa
George B. Post	Wisconsin
Egerton Swartwout	Missouri
John E. Tourtellotte	Idaho
Richard Michell Upjohn	Connecticut
Walter Robb Wilder	Washington

Although, of course, these individuals varied greatly from a personal standpoint, as architects they had much in common. They were not isolated artists of unique genius, but members of an established inner circle. Unlike the Louis Sullivans and Frank Lloyd Wrights of the world, these architects adhered to the conventional canon. They knew one another, competed with one another, sometimes collaborated with one another, in some cases hated one another, and always watched one another.

As Establishment architects, these men belonged to the American Institute of Architects and were active in its local chapters. They read the same professional journals, in which the latest capitol competitions were described and discussed.

Table 4.2
ARCHITECTS AND DESIGN INFORMATION

	Initial Principal Architect(s)	Design and Period
Alabama	Special committee and builders	Classical Revival Core from formative period
Alaska	Office of Supervising Architect of Treasury	Converted federal territorial building
Arizona	James Reily Gordon	Classical Revival Core from second wave
Arkansas	George R. Mann Cass Gilbert	American Renaissance Intact from second wave
California	Miner Frederick Butler Reuben Clark	American Renaissance Core from 1860s
Colorado	Elijah E. Myers	Beaux-Arts Intact from first wave
Connecticut	Richard Michell Upjohn	Victorian Gothic Intact from first wave
Delaware	E. William Martin	Georgian Revival Core from 1930s
Florida	Edward Durell Stone	International Style Tower group from 1970s
Georgia	Willoughby J. Edbrooke Franklin P. Burnham	Beaux-Arts Intact from first wave
Hawaii	John Carl Warnecke	International Style Intact from 1960s
Idaho	John E. Tourtellotte	American Renaissance Intact from second wave
Illinois	John Crombie Cochrane Alfred H. Piquenard	Italianate Intact from first wave
Indiana	Edwin May	Second Empire Intact from first wave
Iowa	Alfred H. Piquenard John Crombie Cochrane	Beaux-Arts Intact from first wave
Kansas	Edward Townsend Mix John G. Haskell	Classical Revival Intact from first wave
Kentucky	Frank Mills Andrews	American Renaissance Intact from second wave
Louisiana	Leon C. Weiss	Eclectic Art Deco Intact from 1930s
Maine	Charles Bulfinch	Greek Revival Core from formative period
Maryland	Joseph Horatio Anderson	Georgian Core from formative period
Massachusetts	Charles Bulfinch	Classical Revival Core from formative period
Michigan	Elijah E. Myers	American Renaissance Intact from first wave
Minnesota	Cass Gilbert	American Renaissance Intact from second wave

Table 4.2
ARCHITECTS AND DESIGN INFORMATION (*continued*)

	Initial Principal Architect(s)	Design and Period
Mississippi	Theodore C. Link	Beaux-Arts Intact from second wave
Missouri	Egerton Swartwout	American Renaissance Intact from second wave
Montana	Charles Emlen Bell John Hacket Kent	Classical Revival Intact from second wave
Nebraska	Bertram Grosvenor Goodhue	Art Deco synthesis Intact from 1920s and 1930s
Nevada	Dolven Simpson Associates	Postmodern Rebuilt in 1990s
New Hampshire	Stewart James Park	Neoclassic Core from formative period
New Jersey	Lewis Broome and others	Beaux-Arts Core expanded many times
New Mexico	W. C. Kruger	Circular Zia design Intact from 1960s
New York	Thomas W. Fuller Leopold Eidlitz H. H. Richardson Isaac G. Perry	Second Empire Intact from first wave
North Carolina	Edward Durell Stone	International Style Intact from 1960s
North Dakota	John A. Holabird John W. Root	International Style exterior, Art Deco interior Intact from 1930s
Ohio	Henry Walter William R. West	Greek Revival Intact from mid-nineteenth century
Oklahoma	Solomon A. Layton	American Renaissance No dome Intact from second wave
Oregon	Francis Keally	Art Deco Intact from 1930s
Pennsylvania	Joseph M. Huston	American Renaissance Core from second wave
Rhode Island	Charles F. McKim	Beaux-Arts Intact from second wave
South Carolina	John R. Niernsee Frank P. Milburn Charles Coker Wilson	Classical Revival Begun in mid-nineteenth century, completed in early twentieth
South Dakota	Charles Emlen Bell	Classical Revival Core from second wave
Tennessee	William F. Strickland	Greek Revival Intact from mid-nineteenth century
Texas	Elijah E. Myers	American Renaissance Intact from first wave
Utah	Richard K. A. Kletting	American Renaissance Intact from second wave

Table 4.2
ARCHITECTS AND DESIGN INFORMATION *(continued)*

	Initial Principal Architect(s)	Design and Period
Vermont	Ammi B. Young Thomas W. Silloway	Classical Revival Core from nineteenth century
Virginia	Thomas Jefferson Charles-Louis Clerisseau	Neoclassic Intact from formative period
Washington	Ernest Flagg Walter Robb Wilder	American Renaissance Intact from second wave
West Virginia	Cass Gilbert	American Renaissance Intact from second wave
Wisconsin	George B. Post	American Renaissance Intact from second wave
Wyoming	David W. Gibbs	American Renaissance Core from first wave

Like their colleagues, they were socialized into common admiration for the various European revivalist styles then popular. Gilbert sketched buildings in Europe as a young man, McKim attended the Ecole des Beaux-Arts in Paris, and those who did not visit or study abroad were affected by Parisian currents of thinking that crossed to the New York art world. Link and Piquenard were Europeans, while Layton and Upjohn were British, the last the son of a famous church architect.

The World's Columbian Exposition was another source of common inspiration. The temporary buildings of the White City seemed radically light and modish in comparison with the heavier styles popular immediately after the Civil War, such as Second Empire and Romanesque and Gothic Revival. Andrews was an architect in Chicago at the time and worked on several buildings for the exposition, as did Post, who was from New York. McKim, now in partnership with William Mead and Stanford White, contributed even more to the exposition's architecture. Later, the three established the firm McKim, Mead and White, which became the leading exponent of this form of neoclassicism for several decades, winning such prestigious commissions as the Boston Public Library and the office wings of the White House.

Another source of design consensus resulted from the personal ties among members of the group. There was ample opportunity, beyond normal professional communication, for their ideas to coalesce. Both McKim and Post advanced in their careers with the help of the influencial New York architect Richard Morris Hunt. Andrews studied for a year under Post, while Mann and Wilder worked at the New York offices of McKim, Mead and White.

The crossing of paths went on outside New York as well. When Myers was a young architect in Springfield, Illinois, his home was located a few blocks from the architectural office of Piquenard, and each morning on his way to work he passed the windows through which the linen sheet drawings of the new Illinois State Capitol could be seen.[10] After winning the design competition for the Michigan State Capitol, Myers moved to Detroit, and Kent was on his staff there. Later, in Council Bluffs, Iowa, Kent entered into partnership with Bell, and together they designed the Montana State Capitol.

Still another way in which concepts stabilized was the multiplicity of opportunities given these architects to set forth their ideas, affording them more exposure than would otherwise have been the case. Several designed more than one capitol. The champion statehouse architect was Myers, designer of the capitols of Michigan, Texas, and Colorado, in that order. In addition, he planned the territorial capitol of Idaho, which is no longer standing. Close behind was Gilbert, who designed the Minnesota State Capitol at the beginning of his career and the West Virginia State Capitol at the end. In addition, he was brought in late to advise the completion of the Arkansas State Capitol.[11]

Others in the group had multiple statehouse commissions as well. Although technically in partnership with John Crombie Cochrane, Piquenard was in reality the key architect of two statehouses: those of Illinois and Iowa. Bell codesigned the core of the Montana State Capitol and, later, was the sole architect of the South Dakota State Capitol. Andrews designed the statehouse of Kentucky and added the wings to that of Montana. McKim was the primary architect of the Rhode Island State House and the expansion consultant for the Alabama State Capitol. Thus these six men—Myers, Gilbert, Piquenard, Bell, Andrews, and McKim—had a hand in the design of thirteen capitols, approximately half the total output of the two primary waves of statehouse construction.

Several of these architects entered statehouse competitions that they did not win. While this obviously kept them from creating the buildings under consideration, their ideas were given a presence in the ongoing professional discourse. Mann was initially selected to build the Montana State Capitol, but he withdrew when funding was reduced, only to take the same plans to Arkansas. Bell submitted losing proposals for the capitols of Idaho and Utah and for the expansion wings of that of Montana. Kent, following the breakup of his partnership with Bell, also lost in bids for these three jobs. Gilbert, too, submitted a proposal for the wings, and unsuccessfully sought commissions for the statehouses of Missouri and Wisconsin. Myers submitted proposals for the Connecticut project to no avail, drew plans for Colorado but was dismissed during construction, and entered the Indiana competition only to charge that the winner, May, had stolen his plans.

The second special factor behind the similarity of statehouse designs was the example of the United States Capitol. This great building, con-

siderably larger (but not taller) than any state capitol, was built in a series of stages over many years. George Washington laid the cornerstone in 1793, and the old Senate wing was occupied in 1800. These dates make the Capitol's origins precede those of most contemporary statehouses, but not all; the Maryland State House was first occupied in 1779, and Bulfinch's original core in the Massachusetts State House was completed in 1798.

The original legislative wings of the new national Capitol were largely complete by 1811, when work was suspended because of the imminence of war with Great Britain. In 1814, the British invaded Washington, D.C., and burned the interior of the building. Its reconstruction, together with construction of the central core, including its original dome, was completed by 1825, under the direction of Bulfinch. With a prominent, open site, plus a dome, rotunda, temple front, and modest cruciform ground plan, the Capitol exhibited all six elements of the statehouse building type.

If we compare this state of progress with what was contemporaneously occurring in the states, many early statehouses had been erected, but, notably, none yet had all the features of the statehouse building type. This convergence did not take place until the North Carolina State Capitol was finished in 1840. Thus while the basic idea of a republican capitol first appeared at the state level in America, its full flowering first emerged at the national level.

This duality suggests that the architectural ideas embedded in the capitol archetype were flowing both up and down the federal relationship. In effect, national and state governments were learning from each other about how to build their headquarters. This combined nexus of development is not surprising, considering that several of the same figures were in key positions at both levels of authority. They included Jefferson, who carried the term "capitol" from Richmond to Washington and was a lead proponent for adopting the architectural symbolism of the Roman Republic to legitimate authority at both levels of American government; Benjamin Henry

Latrobe, who supervised construction of the Capitol following James Hoban, as well as painted watercolors of Jefferson's temple in Richmond and tutored William Strickland; and Charles Bulfinch, who designed the statehouses of Massachusetts and Maine, but in between served as third architect of the Capitol and, in that position, brought the 1825 version of the building to fruition.

The United States Capitol reached the essentials of its present-day appearance between 1851 and 1916, with the dome completed in 1863 and much of the remaining major construction finished the following year. Its designer was the fourth architect of the Capitol: Thomas U. Walter. Walter's work was well known around the country, and because of the significance and publicity attached to his designs for the Capitol, they had considerable potential for influencing the design of state capitols after the Civil War.

A retrospective analysis suggests that such influence was definitely exercised, yet not right away. The California State Capitol, designed by Miner Frederick Butler and Reuben Clark in American Renaissance style, resembles Walter's Capitol in many respects (see Figure 4.2). It was, however, built from 1860 to 1869, so if a cross-continent transfer of ideas from Washington, D.C., to Sacramento had taken place it would have had to be efficient. The more likely scenario would seem to be a reaction delayed over several decades. Of the eleven first-wave statehouses, only the Texas State Capitol, designed by Myers in the 1880s, bears signs of a relationship, but only in the pointed, tiered, and fluted dome. Other statehouses of that group are strikingly different, such as Connecticut's Victorian Gothic edifice (Figure 4.13) and New York's enormous Second Empire structure (Figure 4.14).

It is among the second-wave statehouses, whose construction began in 1895, that several close resemblances are evident. While each of these buildings is distinctive, the homogenizing influence of the Capitol seems present in ten of the sixteen: the capitols of Arkansas, Idaho, Ken-

Figure 4.13. The Connecticut State Capitol, Hartford. Built in the 1870s, this elaborate Victorian Gothic edifice was designed by Richard Michell Upjohn, son of a famous church architect.

Figure 4.14. The New York State Capitol, Albany. In this Second Empire statehouse, completed in 1899 after taking thirty-two years to build, several famous Americans served as governor, including Theodore Roosevelt, Franklin D. Roosevelt, and Al Smith.

tucky, Mississippi, Missouri, Oklahoma, Utah, Washington, West Virginia, and Wisconsin.

Statehouse architects eventually broke with the standard model. By the 1920s, American Renaissance styling was passé, and the architectural symbols of antiquity were out. Yet elements of the traditional statehouse did not totally disappear. If one looks closely at Bertram Goodhue's radical creation in Nebraska, a dome is found at the top of the tower and a rotunda at the base (see Figure 4.7). As for Francis Keally's Greek Moderne statehouse in Oregon, it incorporates a flat dome, rotunda, and cruciform ground plan (see Figure 4.8). Even at the most avant-garde statehouse of all, W. C. Kruger's Zia sun symbol Roundhouse in New Mexico, exterior projections at four perpendicular axial points correspond to interior corridors that intersect at a central rotunda (Figure 4.15). Hence signs of an early design orthodoxy live on.

BIG AND BOISTEROUS PUBLIC WORKS

Statehouses were no ordinary buildings to construct. They are massive. They are made of stone, a material that is not easy to transport and use. Erecting their domes, which reach hundreds of feet into the air and cover great volumes of space, is technically demanding. As symbols of each state's constitutional status and unique history, statehouses were built for the ages, with all that implies for quality of materials, skill of workmanship, solidity, and permanence. As very visible and costly public-works projects, building capitols was a very worldly matter always capable of fueling political controversy.

It often took many years or even decades to build the statehouses (see Table 4.1). Statehouses constructed in the first wave took an average of fifteen years to build and those in the second

Figure 4.15. The New Mexico State Capitol, Santa Fe. Built in the 1960s and renovated in the 1990s, W. C. Kruger's innovative circular structure was inspired by the Zia Pueblo sun symbol.

wave, seven. But the total duration of projects sometimes extended to twenty, thirty, or even more years.

One reason for what now seems to be an excessive lapse of construction time is the state of building technology in the nineteenth century. Since in early public buildings, masonry walls bore all loads directly, they had to be thick and massive. Quarrying and cutting the requisite granite, limestone, sandstone, or marble required enormous manpower, even after steam-powered saws became available. Convicts were often used for this purpose, shown in old photographs in their prisoner stripes under the watch of guard dogs. In South Carolina, slaves hand-dressed the stone, with their careful markings visible to this day. To transport the stone to the building site, special railroad lines were built, sometimes several miles long. At the site, the stone pieces would be laid out on the ground, cut and matched by skilled masons often brought from Italy, and raised to wall height by stiff-leg derricks powered by horse, steam, and eventually electricity. Even as late as 1905, for the erection of the Kentucky State Capitol, only one power machine was used, a steam-driven concrete mixer; the crane and steel bender were operated by hand.[12]

Domes required special care and took extra time. Those constructed entirely of stone, such as that on the Rhode Island State House, demanded great stonecutting skill. The use of interior iron trusses or masonry cones, more common methods of construction, called for sophisticated techniques of ironmongering and bricklaying. To bear the great weight of the dome, giant supporting piers had to be built from deep footings or even from bedrock up through the center of the building. In addition to presenting a pleasing form outside and an inspiring celestial ceiling within, the dome had to be built to withstand the effects of temperature and wind, provide a roof that did not leak, and, in the electronic age, accommodate an internal forest of antennae.

The large spaces required for the legislative chambers also were not easy to construct. Large floor areas with high ceilings were called for, unimpeded by supporting center columns. Elaborate interiors with visitors' galleries and vaulted ceilings complicated matters further. Before the age of structural steel and reinforced concrete, these requirements were sometimes not satisfied. The collapse of the House chamber in the Indiana State House in 1867 instigated its replacement. In another example of failure, in 1870 the second-story Virginia Supreme Court chamber, packed for a trial, crashed down into the House of Delegates chamber, killing sixty-two persons. In 1887, stones began to fall on the desks of Assembly members in New York, requiring the evacuation of the body and the construction of an enormous repair scaffold in the center of the chamber. In 1883, the south wing of the second capitol of Wisconsin suddenly collapsed during construction, killing six workmen and seriously injuring eighteen. The accident was witnessed by fourteen-year-old Frank Lloyd Wright, making a deep impression on the future architect.[13]

Another reason for long construction times was an interruption in the flow of funds. When financial panics or depressions hit, appropriations would dry up and voter referenda on bonds or levies to raise more funds would be rejected at the polls. Construction of the half-completed Illinois State Capitol was delayed for seven years because funds were exhausted and the voters balked at more. Similar problems occurred in Ohio, New York, and Colorado, all of whose statehouses took decades to complete. In Montana, when the capitol commission tried unsuccessfully to float a bond issue in 1898, the day was saved only when a wealthy Helena prospector named Thomas Cruse purchased the entire issue, allowing construction to commence the following year. In Washington, a foundation was dug in 1894 for a capitol designed by the New York architect Ernest Flagg. The effects of the panic of 1893 and the new governor's disinterest in the project resulted in the unfinished walls serving as a sandbox in summer and skating rink in winter for the next quarter century. When work on the project was resumed in 1919, it was with an entirely new architect and a wholly new plan.[14]

For various reasons, the time required to construct the South Carolina State House took on mythic proportions—more than a half century. After three years of work beginning in 1851, a crack developed in the largely erected walls. They were torn down, and the whole project was begun all over again. After five more years of work, during which new walls were put up, construction was halted again because of the Civil War. During Sherman's artillery bombardment of Columbia in 1865, shells hit the unfinished walls (at points now marked by iron stars), but did not knock them down. They continued to stand unfinished, covered by a temporary roof, for the remainder of the nineteenth century as the state's economy languished. Finally in 1900, Frank Milburn was appointed to finish the building, but this consumed seven more years.[15]

In another project almost as drawn out, construction of the Kansas State Capitol took forty years. Work began in 1866 on the Senate wing, but after a year the foundations were found to be crumbling. They were reconstructed with new rock, and the wing was available for occupancy in 1869. But for the next dozen years, it stood in splendid isolation on the Kansas prairie, surrounded by corn and cattle. In 1881, work on the House wing began on a site 150 feet distant. When it was completed, a temporary covered walkway was built to connect the two structures; its wind-tunnel properties gave it the nickname "cave of the winds." Construction of the central core of the building, with its high dome, began three years later. Again, an alarming crack developed on a facade arch, but construction resumed after repairs were completed.

The interior detailing of the Kansas State Capitol was delayed further by open warfare between Republican and Populist factions of the legislature. Bathrooms installed for officials were deemed too lavish. Objections were raised to murals depicting Grecian women with uncovered breasts and paintings of pigs with tails curled in the wrong direction. It was not until six years into the twentieth century that the building was finally finished.[16]

Controversies over the stone to use could also delay construction. This was a sore problem for Cass Gilbert, designer of the capitol of Minnesota, where local political interests pressed for St. Cloud granite over cheaper stone from out of state. Elijah Myers faced similar problems in Colorado, where plans called for white sandstone. The Denver press took the position that only more costly granite would be sufficiently strong, creating a public furore over the issue. Work could begin only when a granite quarry near Gunnison offered free stone.

A similar incident happened during the construction of the Texas State Capitol, also designed by Myers. After the architect proposed using Bedford limestone from Indiana, a battle royal ensued. Newspapers in Austin amplified public opinion that a Texas statehouse *must* be made of Texas rock. The situation was resolved when the owner of a granite mountain 50 miles from Austin offered pink granite free of charge, provided that the state dig the quarry on his property, build a railway to Austin, and supply 1,000 convicts as labor.[17]

Suspicious deals and investigations of wrongdoing were also causes of delay. For two years, the half-finished Arkansas State Capitol was left exposed to rain and vandals as rival politicians traded charges over bribery and unsafe construction. Among the spectacles witnessed in Little Rock were two capitol commissions claiming jurisdiction over the project, the governor personally directing the use of a battering ram to enter the boarded-up structure, and weight tests on floors from which pro-contractor legislators scrambled for safety when the load gave one-fifth of an inch.[18]

Charges of graft and corruption arose in connection with other statehouse projects, too. In Illinois, John Cochrane, Alfred Piquenard's partner, was alleged to have paid members of the statehouse commission a bribe of $2,700 to secure the job.[19] In Montana, public disclosure of bribery allegations resulted in the probable suicide of a closely involved architect, John C.

Paulsen.[20] In Pennsylvania, the administration that came into power after the statehouse was completed in 1906 discovered extensive overcharging for purchases, especially furniture. An investigation concluded that of the $12.5 million spent on the building, more than $5 million had been used for fraudulent overpayments to suppliers. A number of state officials and contractors were convicted, and architect Joseph Huston was briefly imprisoned.[21]

A LEGACY AND ITS SOCIAL MEANINGS

The American statehouse has been a presence on the architectural and political landscape for more than a century and a half. Many capitols were constructed during the horse-and-buggy era and are still in use in the information age. What has happened to this legacy over the decades?

For the most part, the buildings are in good physical condition. In several cases, demands for additional office space led to the erection of temporary "plywood cities" in corridors and rotundas. They are now gone, made unnecessary by the building of additions or extensions to the statehouse itself as well as constructing underground floors or annexes. In several states, separate office buildings for legislative use have also been rented or built. Also alleviating the space shortage was a tendency for the departure of many executive and judicial functions to buildings of their own, often clustered in a campuslike complex around the statehouse.

In other ways, too, the statehouse legacy has received good care. State governments, to save money, often defer maintenance on their office buildings, but seldom on their capitols. As symbols, they are simply too important to neglect. This contrasts with the repair record of older corporate or retail buildings of a city, whose condition is often allowed to decay along with the city center in general. Even the capital-city neighborhoods around the statehouses continue to thrive for the most part.

In addition to routine maintenance, extensive renovations have been carried out in several capitols over the years (see Table 4.1). They have been associated with such purposes as asbestos removal (Hawaii), roof replacement (New Hampshire), chamber refitting (Indiana and New Mexico), and damage repair (Idaho, Oregon, South Dakota, and Washington).

The legacy of the statehouse has been further enhanced since the advent of the preservation movement. Efforts to preserve or restore the statehouses began in the 1960s, and they are now widespread (see Table 4.1). Millions of tax dollars have been spent to restore individual rooms and rotundas, as in the capitols of Michigan, Ohio, Pennsylvania, and Wisconsin. Another strategy has been to gut and rebuild large interior portions of the buildings as a whole, as in the statehouses of Alabama, California, and Texas. This preservation activity has been so extensive and significant that it may be regarded as the final stage of the process of constructing the American statehouse.

As with earlier stages of statehouse construction, preservation has not been accomplished without controversy. Questions of unnecessary cost have been raised in many states, with California being a good example. To build legislative and public support for projects, preservation advocates have at times conducted sophisticated public-relations campaigns. They have featured the formation of "friends of the capitol" groups, the distribution of professionally produced videotapes, and the artful placement of appealing demonstration projects, such as a patch of redone wall along a busy corridor.

As an example of one controversial incident, Edward Durell Stone wished to remove the Old Capitol in Tallahassee, built in 1845, to clear the site for his new Florida Capitol. In reaction, Secretary of State Bruce Smathers refused, in the glare of much publicity, to depart from his office in the Old Capitol. This genteel sit-in generated a tide of support across the state for keeping most of the old structure. It was then converted into a museum, a step that also has been taken in Arizona, California, Maryland, and Nevada. As is shown in Figure 3.5, the resultant exhibition spaces are sometimes equipped with mannequins or explained by docents dressed in period cos-

tume. A rival point of view, manifest in Texas and Wisconsin, has been to adapt the restored spaces to present-day functions, such as visitor centers or meeting rooms.

The act of preservation that seems to attract the most controversy is the regilding of domes. Several statehouse domes have always been covered with gold paint or leaf, while others were gilded later to make them more visible against the increasingly dense urban fabric. In either case, renewed treatment of the surface is periodically required. But since gold symbolizes wealth and the capitol dome symbolizes state government, the act of regilding invariably sparks public discontent over "waste" in government.

In West Virginia, the issue traumatized the body politic for some decades. The gold paint insisted on by Cass Gilbert kept lifting off, and its recurring replacement using taxpayer dollars always stirred up discontent. Finally, a lasting solution of applying gold leaf was tried, but the ensuing antipolitician outcry made it impossible to proceed. Although eventually the job was done, the bitterness of its aftermath can still be sensed. When the same issue arose in Georgia, a different strategy and outcome resulted. Opposition to regilding was deflected in advance by enlisting the state Jaycee organization to raise private funds for the task. To publicize the fundraising, a wagon train drawn by mules crisscrossed the state from the small town of Dahlonega, the site of a gold rush in 1828 that still arouses sentiment in Georgia's collective memory.

To sum up, the construction of the American statehouse was a physical act of massive proportions for its time, requiring great resources, keen skills, and years of effort. It was also a social act that bore important meanings.

The expressive lens draws attention to the significance of the latest and ongoing stage of constructing the American statehouse: the many historic-preservation projects undertaken in them. Great sums and much political capital have been spent on the restoration of statehouses, and many large programs are under way. Some of them have involved gutting whole buildings and reconstructing interiors to duplicate original or early spaces as closely as possible.

This suggests that these old buildings are highly valued by a powerful segment of officialdom. That millions of dollars can be garnered for this purpose indicates as well a latent degree of political support. That no usable capitol has been razed for well over a century speaks to how these buildings have worked their way into the affections of Americans in all fifty states. This seems quite remarkable in a throwaway society that is not particularly enamored of government to start with.

From the perspective of the behavioral lens, the construction of the statehouse inevitably affected many people's lives. The scale, duration, complexity, and ramifications of the project ensured its impact. Citizens of towns where the capitols were built prospered. The reputations of politicians who successfully advocated capitol construction projects were boosted. Architects who won capitol commissions went on to fame and fortune. Land speculators profited by "donating" properties as sites. Suppliers who offered bribes and officials who took them went to either the bank or the jail. European stonecutters who came to America to carve granite never went home. Convicts and slaves who dressed the stone at gunpoint would not forget their fear.[22] Artisans who created sculpture and murals would bask in their glory. Day laborers who actually erected the buildings could thereafter have something to tell their grandchildren.

Through the societal lens, statehouse construction is seen not as an expression of intrinsic value or a personal episode of defining experience, but as a founding ritual of republican governance—a kind of material equivalent to the enactment of statehood legislation or the ratification of a state constitution. This is because of the lengthy, public, trying, and yet predictable nature of the process by which this physical symbol, so intimately associated with state authority and identity, is created.

As in performing any ritual, several distinctive steps are solemnly taken: passing of authorization and appropriation acts, achieved after much wrangling and delay; appointing commissioners, with choices that balance numerous constituencies; selecting of a site, a step with both symbolic and profiteering implications; holding an architectural competition and picking an architect, a trigger to much professional and public debate; choosing a general contractor and type of stone, decisions of commitment and controversy; public ground breaking and excavating of a great hole, targets attracting wide publicity; laying railroad track to haul in stone and distributing pieces across the ground, undeniable signs of the project's magnitude; erecting piers, ironwork, walls, dome, and lantern, a specter of gradual upward progress that is closely watched across the state; and, finally, dedicating the building, the final step in a great collective ceremony experienced by the whole state.

Hence, in each state's history, the construction of the statehouse becomes recorded as a memorable event. Libraries and archives are full of testimony to this fact. It is so in all regions of the country, but with varying overtones of meaning. In the East, it symbolized transition from colony to republic; in the North and Midwest, it celebrated Union victory following the Civil War; in the South, it signaled that Reconstruction was over; in the West, it marked the end of the frontier and the dawn of the industrial age. In each era and each region, remarkably, basically the same type of building was constructed, which, combined with the model offered by the federal Capitol, points to one nation.

5 | *Objects and Decor at the Statehouse*

Having related how the American statehouse was created and built, we move to a more detailed level of description and interpretation.

The statehouse is, of course, a working headquarters of government. In addition, it is a display case for that government. The building is prominent, well known, and in the public domain. As the center of state government, it speaks for that government and for the state as a whole. Those who designed it and control it on a daily basis are perfectly aware of this function. They know that items displayed in, around, and on the building send powerful messages to the citizenry and to visitors that both assert power and reflect culture.

PROJECTIONS OF LEGAL AUTHORITY

Objects and items of decor displayed in the statehouse are specifically intended to project legal authority. The most ubiquitous such symbol used by governments around the world is the official flag. State and national flags fly at many points in and around the statehouse. Outdoors, flagpoles are often placed on the dome or near it, at key points on the roof, or on the grounds immediately in front of the main entrance. In keeping with convention, state flags fly below, behind, or to the right of the American flag as it is being faced. The Nevada legislature has its own flag, which is displayed in front of the Legislative Building in a position subordinate to the state banner, but only on days when the legislators are in session.

In Iowa, too, the flags that are flown depend on who is in the building. The American flag is hoisted above the dome of the appropriate chamber when the House or Senate meets. The national banner flies at the center of the statehouse

roof only when the governor is present. Whereas in a more regal setting this act might be considered a gesture of honor to attending officials, in democratic Iowa legend has it that originally the practice allowed Iowans arriving at the railroad station down the hill to know whether their elected representatives were available for a personal visit.

In certain southern states, controversy has arisen over flying the Confederate battle flag at the state capitol, below the national and state flags. In Alabama, after years of protest by civil rights organizations, the controversial Stars and Bars was removed in 1993. In South Carolina, where the Confederate flag was first flown in 1962 to symbolize resistance to the civil rights movement, acrimonious dispute over the removal of the symbol continued for several decades. In 2000, after drawing media attention across the nation, it was moved to the statehouse grounds nearby. Even in this high-tech information age, the symbolic significance of a flag remains real.

Flags are displayed at many points inside the statehouse as well. In the rotunda and other public spaces, military banners are exhibited in sealed glass cases. In the offices of all important officials, especially the governor, standards for the national and state flags are usually positioned to the right and left of the officeholder's desk, respectively. The same is true in legislative chambers, where they stand on each side of the rostrum. In some chambers, small flags are also mounted on each legislator's desk, creating a sea of patriotic color.

Second only to the flag as a condensation symbol of authority is the state seal. In times past, the secretary of state in each statehouse carefully kept, under lock and key, the "great seal." Originally, this was the die, mounted in a hand press, that imprinted the state seal on official documents. Today the seal is essentially an officially sanc-

Figure 5.1. General Assembly in session in the New Jersey State House, Trenton. A three-dimensional version of the state seal is mounted above the baldachin arch of the rostrum. The glassed loggia facing the floor on the right is used for private conversations by members.

tioned graphic design reproduced by means of modern printing techniques, thus allowing it to appear in state documents and publications of all kinds.

Statehouse interiors often display enlargements of the state seal in various places, rendered in different media. In Ohio, the seal is molded in plaster in the rotunda ceiling. It is embedded in stained glass above the entrances to the legislative chambers in California and carved in wood behind the rostrum in the House chamber in Florida. In the chamber of the New Jersey General Assembly, built in 1891 and decorated in late Victorian style, a three-dimensional version of the state seal is mounted above the baldachin arch of the rostrum. Sporting bright heraldic colors and featuring life-size figures of Liberty and Ceres, the seal immediately draws the attention of newcomers to the room (Figure 5.1).

An especially popular place for the depiction of the state seal is at the center of the rotunda floor, at the highly symbolic intersection of the building's horizontal and vertical axes. Examples are found in Arizona (old capitol), Montana, Oregon, Rhode Island, Texas, and Washington. Oregon's emblem, executed in bronze bas-relief, is roped off to avoid desecration by the human foot (Figure 5.2). The seal of New Mexico, based on the Zia sun symbol, is reproduced in travertine at the center of the rotunda floor.

A third category of displayed authority symbol is founding documents of a constitutional or similar nature. A replica of the constitution of Wisconsin is on view in the capitol rotunda in Madison. The original copy of Iowa's constitution is displayed under glass in the secretary of state's office in Des Moines. Encased in stone in the rotunda of the Utah State Capitol is the constitution for the State of Deseret, the basis of an application for statehood made in 1849, but never approved by Congress. The constitution of Puerto Rico, whose capitol in San Juan fulfills quite well the mainland's statehouse building type, is enshrined in a round marble urn at the center of the rotunda.

A set of several founding documents is on display in the Rhode Island State House. They are mounted in glass plates that swing from a fireproof safe located on a second-floor corridor. Exhibited are the royal charter of the Rhode Island and Providence Plantations, which served as the state constitution until 1843; the official copy of the Declaration of Independence given to Rhode Island by the Continental Congress; and the proclamation of King George III that in 1772 created the Gaspee Commission, a body that investigated the burning of a British revenue schooner by anti-Crown arsonists.

An authority symbol found in some legislative chambers is the mace. This ancient symbol of power is descended from the Roman fasces or lictor's ax and later the medieval battle mace.

Found in the lower rather than the upper house, as it is in Congress, the mace is often carried into the chamber in ceremonial opening processions and placed in a position of honor by the rostrum.[1]

At least five lower houses have maces, which differ widely in appearance. Pennsylvania's is a heavy staff topped with a gold ball and an eagle. The one in Arkansas is a long pole, while that in Maryland is a short rod. Virginia's mace is gold plated, 45 inches long, and crowned with a royal diadem in the manner of the mace of the British House of Commons. The mace in South Carolina dates from 1756 and is the only colonial mace that was not melted down as a nationalist gesture after the Revolutionary War. When sessions open in Columbia, the mace is taken from a locked vault in the chamber wall and placed on a special rack at the front of the rostrum. On those occasions when the South Carolina Speaker goes to the Senate chamber to ratify acts of both

Figure 5.2. State seal of Oregon, placed at the midpoint of the rotunda floor in the Oregon State Capitol. The rope barrier, which always protects it from being walked on, is festooned for the holiday season.

bodies, the mace goes along. In front of the rostrum, the object is placed on a special rack just below the Senate's own symbol of authority: a sword of state.

PROJECTIONS OF COERCIVE POWER

Artifacts that indirectly convey the coercive power of the state, associated with war and the sacrifice it entails, are also displayed in the statehouse. War, the ultimate prerogative of governments, is also one of the most terrible of human experiences, capable of producing deeply moving symbolism. Much symbolism of war is brought to the statehouse, transforming it in some degree into a patriotic shrine. Perhaps at an unconscious level, the blood of war is used to consecrate state power.

Many types of reference to war are found in almost all statehouses. One is regimental banners

and other flags that have flown in battle. In the rotunda and other ceremonial spaces are large display cabinets containing old wartime flags. The cases are hermetically sealed to protect the crumbling sacred cloth. In several states, attempts have been made to treat the flags chemically to preserve them, but veterans' groups are inclined to protest this effort as a sacrilege.

Particular reverence is shown for flags carried in the Civil War. This is in keeping with the idea that many statehouses seem to memorialize that conflict. In the capitols of Connecticut, Georgia, Massachusetts, New Hampshire, and New York, an entire ceremonial space, such as a lobby, is designated as the hall of flags and is used to display hundreds of carefully preserved banners. In Illinois, an enormous columned hall near the capitol serves this purpose (Figure 5.3).

The historically accumulated meaning of these banners is brought out vividly in the particularly numinous Massachusetts hall of flags, in which,

Figure 5.3. Display of banners carried by Illinois regiments in the Civil War, the Spanish-American War, and World War I. The room is a ceremonial vestibule of the Centennial Building in Springfield.

along with the flags themselves, is an arresting mural called *The Return of the Colors to the Custody of the Commonwealth.* Painted by Edward Simmons in 1902, it depicts the moment on December 22, 1865, when banners given by the governor to regiments heading forth to preserve the Union were returned to the statehouse after the Civil War was won. Forefathers Day, an annual event in Massachusetts, takes place on the anniversary of this ceremony.

References to war in the statehouse are not limited to battle flags. Guns, cannon, and other weapons are on display. Mounted outside the Maryland State House is a cannon brought from England by early settlers in 1634. On the portico of the Vermont State House, resting in a nineteenth-century gun carriage, is the brass barrel of a Revolutionary War cannon that was captured from Hessian troops at the Battle of Bennington in 1777. On the grounds in front of the capitol in Montpelier are two enormous Krupp naval guns taken from the Spanish war-

ship *Castilla* following the naval victory at Manila Bay in 1898. Their 17-foot muzzles point down the lawn, aimed, as it happens, in the general direction of the birthplace across the street of the battle's great hero, Admiral George Dewey (Figure 5.4).

Standing before the Idaho State Capitol is an iron seacoast gun cast in 1857 and deployed by the Confederate navy during the Civil War. It was shipped to Idaho in 1910 after Senator William Borah lobbied the navy for its release. Even loaded weaponry is not unknown in capitols. In the lobby of the Rhode Island State House is displayed a bronze cannon that was hit by Confederate shells during Pickett's charge at Gettysburg. The shelling caused a ball loaded in the cannon's barrel to be seized in place, capturing behind it a sizable charge of gunpowder that remained undiscovered for almost a century.

Many other artifacts associated with war are exhibited in state capitols. In the lobby of the Connecticut State Capitol stands a tree trunk

Figure 5.4. Naval gun in front of the Vermont State House, Montpelier. It was seized after Admiral George Dewey, who was raised across the street, defeated the Spanish fleet in Manila Bay in 1898.

with cannon balls embedded in it from the Battle of Chickamauga in 1863. In the rotunda of the Iowa State Capitol, an 18-foot model of the battleship USS *Iowa* rests in a glass display case, on permanent loan from the navy. Mounted on a corridor wall in Des Moines is a wide-angle, framed photograph of the officers and men of the Rainbow Division, taken upon their return from France in 1919. In the South Carolina State House, just inside the ground-floor entrance, stands the figurehead intended for the battleship USS *South Carolina,* scrapped in 1924 (Figure 5.5).

Outdoor war memorials are found on virtually all statehouse grounds. Those referring to the Civil War are particularly prominent, with subtle differences discernible between what is displayed in northern and in southern states. In the North, the memorials celebrate victory by means of "soldiers and sailors" monuments and, occasionally, victory arches. The latter are seen facing the statehouse grounds in Connecticut and New Hampshire.

In the South, by contrast, conventional statues of the standing soldier are accompanied by sculpted tributes to the Confederacy as a sentimentalized abstraction. A good example is the monument on the grounds of the Alabama State Capitol, whose cornerstone was laid by Jefferson Davis in 1886 (Figure 5.6). Another theme of romantic idealization of the lost cause is wartime sacrifices endured by southern women, found in monuments on the grounds of the statehouses of Mississippi and South Carolina.

Memorials are also erected to the fallen of all other wars, with their formats quite varied. In New Mexico, a crude but poignant outdoor memorial commemorates members of the state National Guard who perished during the Bataan Death March in 1942. In Rhode Island, four locked, book-shaped boxes executed in bronze serve as a reliquary for the names of all state residents who fought for their nation between 1941 and 1945. In South Dakota, an eternal flame burns in honor of the sacrifices made in all wars, and an All Veterans Memorial in the form of a small rectangular shrine stands in North Dakota.

Memorials to those who died in the Vietnam War are found on the grounds of most statehouses, with designs ranging from abstractions rendered in marble or metal to realistic representations of soldiers (Figure 5.7).

A more recent type of memorial to appear on statehouse lawns is the peace officer memorial, dedicated to fallen law-enforcement officers from government jurisdictions throughout the state. They have been placed on the grounds of the capitols of California, Florida, and North Dakota. Planted in the grass in Montgomery is a small marble block too low to be much noticed, dedicated to Alabama state troopers who have died in the line of duty.

PROJECTIONS OF TASTE AND PRESTIGE

Statehouses other than the less formal ones in the West exude an elitist air. Artistic works of museum quality are displayed, exterior facades are adorned with classical sculpture, ceremonial interiors are appointed with valuable furniture and carpets, and public rooms and stairways are illuminated by stained-glass windows and crystal chandeliers. The effect is to give the visitor the impression that those who occupy the building are persons of consequence. The house of democracy is presented as not vulgar or commonplace, but tasteful and refined.

The most readily visible art of the statehouse is the architectural sculpture found on the facade, especially of revivalist and neoclassical capitols. Cass Gilbert, who regarded statehouse art as an expression of state pride and a means of educating the populace, sought to obtain the services of the most prominent sculptor in America for the Minnesota State Capitol: Augustus Saint-Gaudens. The noted artist was, however, otherwise engaged and expensive, so Gilbert hired Daniel Chester French, later famous for his seated Lincoln in the Lincoln Memorial. French produced six allegorical figures for the portico entablature and, in association with Edward C. Potter, created a gilded-copper sculptural group for the base of the dome in the form of a quadriga.

Figure 5.5. Carved bow ornament or figurehead intended for the battleship USS *South Carolina*, on display in the South Carolina State House, Columbia. It was moved to the capitol after the use of figureheads was abolished.

Figure 5.6. Confederate monument on the grounds of the Alabama State Capitol. Jefferson Davis laid the cornerstone for the monument in 1886 and died the day before it was unveiled.

Figure 5.7. Vietnam War monument outside the War Memorial Building and Auditorium in Nashville, near the Tennessee State Capitol. Memorials to those who fell in the Vietnam War are found on the grounds of most statehouses.

Called *Progress of the State*, it consists of four horses harnessed abreast in the manner of ancient Roman practice (Figure 5.8; see Figure 1.2).[2]

Many other statehouses also have facade or roof sculpture, with interesting variations. The California State Capitol, built in the 1860s in American Renaissance style, was given sculptural embellishment by Pietro Mezzara, the state's first major sculptor. He created a statuary group in the triangular tympanum above the portico whose centerpiece is the Roman goddess Minerva, representing California. She is flanked by other classical figures symbolizing Education, Industry, Justice, and Mining. Mezzara created some thirty additional figures, urns, and emblems for the parapet balustrade, but they were removed in 1906 and lost. Remaining, however, are two equestrian statues at the acroteria, or ends of the pediment. These riders are not serene white males, but a Native American duo of warrior and woman under attack by large animals (see Figure 4.2).

Standing above the drum of the dome on the Victorian Gothic facade of the Connecticut State Capitol, constructed in the 1870s, are ten allegorical figures, fashioned by J. Q. A. Ward from 1877 to 1879 (see Figure 4.13). In the lower facade, twenty-four statuary pedestals are in place above the doorways, six on each side of the building. They are filled by historical figures, yet vacancies were left by Ward for future additions from the state's later history. Only a few years ago was added a representation of Ella Grasso, a popular governor who had prematurely succumbed to cancer.

The Wisconsin State Capitol, completed in 1917, presents numerous opportunities for ornamental sculpture because of its unique four equal wings, emanating from the central dome at the cardinal points of the compass. Each wing has a temple front, so artist Karl Bitter designed four tympana instead of one. They consist of deep bas-relief groups whose themes allude to the use of the wings: *The Unveiling of the Resources*

Figure 5.8. Gilded-copper sculptural group on the roof of the Minnesota State Capitol. Minnesota is depicted driving toward prosperity on a quadriga, or chariot drawn by four horses.

of the State (Assembly), *Liberty Supported by the Law* (supreme court; see Figure 2.7), *The Virtues and Traits of Character* (Senate), and *Learning of the World* (transportation hearing room). At the intersections of wings and dome, Bitter placed four statuary groups of allegorical figures. In accord with the gender stereotypes of the time, Faith and Prosperity-Abundance are depicted as female, while Knowledge and Strength are male.

The Nebraska State Capitol, constructed in the 1920s and early 1930s, is replete with Art Deco sculptural decoration. The sculpture and accompanying inscriptions were designed by Lee Lawrie of New York, once a student of Saint-Gaudens, and carved by Alessandro Beretta, an Italian artist who gave nine years of his life to the building. The themes, symbols, and texts of the carving were the work of Hartley Burr Alexander, a professor of philosophy at the University of Nebraska. The four exterior elevations of this great edifice are different, with the south facade

bearing heads representing Moses, Akhnaton, Solon, Solomon, Julius Caesar, and Justinian, together with scenes memorializing the Declaration of Independence, Magna Carta, and United States Constitution (Figure 5.9).

A final form of ornamental sculpture is the statue surmounting the lantern of several domes, such as the figure of Freedom that crowns the United States Capitol. Fifteen statehouses have such statues. Those on the capitols of Idaho, Mississippi, and New Hampshire are in the form of eagles (see Figure 2.8). The remaining are human allegorical figures: Agriculture in Vermont, Ceres (the goddess of agriculture) in Missouri, Commonwealth in Pennsylvania, Freedom in Georgia, Goddess of Liberty in Texas, Independent Man in Rhode Island (see Figure 4.6), Liberty in Montana, Oregon Pioneer in Oregon (see Figure 4.8), The Sower in Nebraska, Winged Victory in Arizona, Wisconsin in Wisconsin (see Figure 2.7), and Wisdom in Maine (see Figure 4.1).

Figure 5.9. South facade of the Nebraska State Capitol. Its exterior bas-relief detailing was planned by Hartley Burr Alexander, designed by Lee Lawrie, and carved by Alessandro Beretta.

While famous sculptors like Daniel Chester French and Lee Lawrie executed Wisconsin and The Sower, Vermont's Agriculture has quite different origins. The original Agriculture was carved from ponderosa pine in 1858. By 1938, it had rotted, been removed, and thrown in the town dump. The sergeant-at-arms at the time, an octogenarian named Dwight Dwinell, pulled the hulk from the rubbish and removed it to his workshop at the rear of the statehouse. There, with the help of two assistants, Dwinell produced a replacement that still surmounts the dome (Figure 5.10).[3]

Second to architectural sculpture in its prominence in statehouse decor is mural art. Wall and ceiling paintings were prolific in ancient times and a high art in Renaissance and baroque churches, but not an important medium in America until the late nineteenth century. The spate of capitol building around the turn of the century created new opportunities for mural artists and played an important part in bringing this art form to America, even though the actual painting did not always take place in the United States.

Cass Gilbert, eager to bring art to statehouses, succeeded in having eleven major murals installed in the Minnesota State Capitol, all of which were painted on canvas in studios elsewhere and then shipped to St. Paul to be permanently mounted. Most of the works are lunettes, or half-round paintings, placed high on the walls of the rotunda and the Senate and supreme court chambers and along the principal corridors. The artists —Edward Simmons, Edwin Blashfield, John La Farge, and Elmer Garnsey—used allegorical and metaphorical scenes to depict the pioneer's dream of Manifest Destiny, the American Indian as noble savage, the agricultural prosperity of the state, and great moments in the creation of lawful civilization. In his mural for the Senate, *Minnesota the Granary of the World,* the Paris-trained Blashfield placed small portraits of architect Gilbert and capitol commission chairman Channing Seabury at the left edge of the painting, in the medieval tradition of acknowledging patrons.[4]

The Pennsylvania State Capitol Building contains perhaps more murals than any other public building in the United States. Its most famous muralist was Edwin Austin Abbey, who committed the final years of his career to a vast program of painting for the building. His many works, which he executed in his English studio at a fee of $50 per square foot, include four lunette and four medallion paintings for the rotunda and, for the House chamber, the giant *Apotheosis of Pennsylvania,* which depicts actual historical personages rather than allegorical figures. Another mural, *Penn's Treaty with the Indians,* re-creates a major event in the history of the commonwealth.

Abbey died in 1911 before his work was finished, but a young Philadelphia muralist, Violet Oakley, was meanwhile receiving rave reviews for her narrative murals dealing with William Penn and religious liberty in the capitol's executive reception room. After Abbey's death, Oakley was hired to take over his unfinished assignments. She went on to produce a series of brilliant literalist works for the Senate (Figure 5.11) and a number of stylized calligraphic panels for the supreme court. Oakley contributed some forty-three murals to the capitol over a quarter century, and her work, as a female painter, was at the time unprecedented in scale and quality.[5]

The Wisconsin State Capitol is also well endowed with mural art. Kenyon Cox created glass mosaics for the rotunda that sparkle to this day. In the Senate, Cox painted an allegorical triptych called *The Marriage of the Atlantic and Pacific,* which celebrates the opening of the Panama Canal. Edwin Blashfield decorated the Assembly chamber with a mammoth mural representing the state's past, present, and future, but his masterpiece is a circular painting in the oculus of the rotunda ceiling. Called *Resources of Wisconsin,* it is 34 feet in diameter, is deeply concave, and shows a heavenly Wisconsin enthroned on the clouds and surrounded by figures offering bounty.

Most other statehouses also have mural art, some of which depicts subjects quite different from those portrayed in traditional allegorical or referential painting. In Montana, Charles

Figure 5.10. Gilded dome of the Vermont State House. The statue on the dome, which represents Agriculture, was carved by an untrained sergeant-at-arms after the original had rotted and been discarded.

Figure 5.11. Mural portraying the Constitutional Convention in the Senate chamber of the Pennsylvania State Capitol Building. It was painted by Violet Oakley, a pioneer female muralist in the early twentieth century.

Marion Russell's *Lewis and Clark Meet the Flat-heads at Ross' Hole,* painted in 1912, portrays a moment in the Lewis and Clark expedition (Figure 5.12). Although technically not a mural, since its canvas stands a few inches off the wall, the work measures 12 by 25 feet and is mounted at the end of the House chamber. The painting dominates the room and has become an object of immense local affection; legislators stare at Charlie Russell's painting during sessions and point out to one another minute details of the work that they had not previously noticed.

The Missouri State Capitol is replete with mural art, financed by a surplus remaining in the building fund when construction was completed in 1917. In addition to splendid murals in the rotunda, governor's office, and legislative chambers, the first- and second-floor corridors are decorated with a series of thirty-eight lunettes on historical, landscape, and military subjects. Two are by the famous illustrator N. C. Wyeth and depict

Civil War actions in Missouri: *Battle of Wilson's Creek* and *Battle of Westport.*

In 1935, the eminent Missouri artist Thomas Hart Benton was commissioned to paint in the capitol, and eventually the ambitious, four-sided *Social History of the State of Missouri* covered the walls of the House lounge. Benton's colorful realism shocked Missourians when the room was opened to the public. Instead of portraying Missouri's military heroes and distinguished statesmen, it depicts such scenes as a farmer plowing with a mule, a lawyer arguing before a jury, and a mother swabbing her baby's behind.[6]

Even today, some statehouse art is controversial, although the issue is not proper dignity but political correctness. Paintings of Indian wars hanging in the Minnesota State Capitol, denounced by Native American groups, have been moved from public hallways to back offices. A mural in the governor's reception room of the

Figure 5.12. Charles Marion Russell, *Lewis and Clark Meeet the Flatheads at Ross' Hole*. This object of warm sentiment is in the House chamber of the Montana State Capitol, Helena.

Tennessee State Capitol, painted in 1938, shows an unperturbed Andrew Jackson in the company of slaves. In recent years, the painting has been attacked by civil rights groups, but being fixed to the wall, it cannot be easily taken down. A mural by Edwin Blashfield called *Progress of South Dakota,* glued to the wall of the reception room of the capitol in 1910, shows an Indian being subdued by white settlers. Resisting calls to cover up the mural, state authorities renamed it *Only by Our Mistakes May We Learn.*

In addition to sculptural ornamentation and mural art, Cass Gilbert's vision for the Minnesota State Capitol included fine appointments. He personally designed the building's doorknobs and wastebaskets. For its furniture, he turned to the New York firm Herter Brothers and ordered the manufacture of many hundreds of pieces. Several patterns were prepared by Gilbert, such as ceremonial chairs for judges and legislators, office swivel chairs, legislative desks, office rolltop desks, and heavy tables for the supreme court, governor's office, and governor's reception room. Reflecting an implicit status hierarchy, pieces for high officials were intricately carved in mahogany, while lower-level officials received standard-issue oak.[7]

Associating different woods with different ranks was not unusual in first- and second-wave statehouses. Original furnishings in the Kentucky State Capitol were made of mahogany for important officials on the second floor, but oak for bureaucratic offices on the first (with the exception of the Department of Education, also done in mahogany). The woodwork in the Wyoming State Capitol is maple in the basement, cherry in the rotunda, and oak in the legislative chambers. In the Washington Legislature Building, furniture in the upper house is mahogany, and in the lower house, walnut. The desks in the Senate chamber of the South Dakota State Capitol are built of mahogany, while those in the House are made of oak, with the same distinction applying to the gavels used in each chamber.[8]

Furniture and other appointments receive their greatest attention as objects of taste and prestige in the state reception room, sometimes called the executive reception room or governor's reception room. This ceremonial space is found in most statehouses, usually on an upper floor at a central point in the floor plan. The state reception room is used for important social events and meetings with distinguished visitors as a kind of state parlour. Its lineage can be traced to that mainstay of European palaces, foreign ministries, and town halls: the formal receiving room.

In the United States, the reception room became the perfect space in which to demonstate that even in nonaristocratic democracies, state government is capable of social refinement. This is particularly true in first- and second-wave capitols, where states seem to have tried to outdo one another in degree of opulence. Invariably the room is furnished in elegant, European style,

with period furniture and furnishings assembled as a holistic cultural presentation. In nearly every capitol, it is a main stopping point on the standard public tour, even if visitors must gaze past a roped-off doorway rather than being allowed inside.

The reception room in the Utah State Capitol, a not atypical example of the genre, is called the Gold Room (Figure 5.13). Completed in 1916 and essentially unchanged since that time, the room got its name from the Golden Traverse marble walls, the gold leaf on the furniture, and the gold trimming on the drapes and doorways. French mirrors are mounted at each end of the room, and French chandeliers hang from the ceiling. On the ceiling's center panel is a Rococco-style painting, *Children at Play*, by Louis Schettle of New York. Covering the floor is a 48-foot-long seamless chenille rug, made to order in Glasgow from a design submitted by a Utah artist. Featured also are a large table of Russian Circassian walnut and chairs upholstered in coro-

Figure 5.13. State Reception Room, or Gold Room, in the Utah State Capitol, Salt Lake City. Elegant, European-inspired parlors of this kind are found in most older statehouses.

nation velvet. Tour guides tell visitors the original cost of every item and explain that the room has been used to entertain royalty from Belgium and Sweden, plus four American presidents.

Another example is the state reception room in the Washington Legislative Building. It is decorated in Italian Bresche Violetta marble, known for images of animals that can be seen in the veining with a slight exercise of the imagination. One-ton chandeliers of Czechoslovakian crystal, designed by Tiffany's of New York, hang from the coved ceiling. A 25- by 55-foot rug woven in 1930 by Mohawk, on what is allegedly the largest loom in the world, covers the inlaid teakwood parquet floor. Draperies are French velvet embroidered with gold thread. A round Russian Circassian walnut table placed in the center of the room was donated by the architects. A bust of George Washington is displayed in the room, supplemented in recent times by a bust of Martin Luther King, Jr. The story is told that after President Harry Truman was entertained in the room, he could not resist stopping at a piano outside the door to play the "Missouri Waltz," whose strains thereby entertained the entire building because of the rotunda's echoing acoustics.

Another special space found in many first- and second-wave statehouses is the state library. When capitols were first built, especially in the West, the library was often the only public library in the state. The room evolved into a law library for use by members and staff of the legislature. In some capitols, the library was still later diverted to other purposes or turned into a purely ceremonial space. More than one such room still possesses its original iron balconies and helical stairs (Figure 5.14).

Displays of high taste do not have to be concentrated in single rooms like the state reception room or state library. Elegant objects and decor are often distributed among all public areas of the statehouse, including legislative chambers, member lounges, courtrooms, lobbies, and, of course, the rotunda. Depending on style and era, the wall and ceiling surfaces of these spaces are covered by marble, rich paneling, or molded stucco. Floors are made of marble, terrazzo, encaustic tile, or wood parquet. Some materials are the objects of special local pride, such as Idaho's rotunda columns sheathed in scagliola (imitation marble), Illinois's ceiling moldings created from carton pierre (a combination of paper, glue, whiting, and plaster), and Oregon's "radio black" Vermont marble, so named because it was also used in the lobby of Radio City Music Hall in New York. Other decorative items on display are stained glass, tapestries, metal friezes, brass handrails, elaborate drinking fountains, and ornamented newel posts.

Against this elaborate background decor is encountered the occasional curiosity. Prominent in the rotunda of the Idaho State Capitol is a full-size replica of the renowned Greek statue Nike of Samothrace, popularly known as Winged Victory. Decorating the rotunda in the Washington Legislative Building are four bronze copies of huge Roman firepots. In many statehouses and executive mansions, sets of fine silver table service are on display, complete with tureens, trays, and candelabra. Invariably, these services were individually crafted for the officers' mess in the battleship bearing the state's name, and when the vessel was scrapped, they were presented to the state (Figure 5.15).

REFERENCES TO HISTORY AND CULTURE

In addition to projecting authority, power, and prestige, artifacts can remind citizens of their common heritage and regional culture. Their presentation in the statehouse aims not to inspire awe, but to stimulate more positive emotions, such as local pride and shared interest. However, the inculcation and socialization effects may be just as great, perhaps more so.

One reference of this sort is to important historical personalities. Depicted through portraiture, statuary, and other kinds of representation, these personifications are more individualized and immediate than those found in murals, war memorials, and architectural sculpture. They identify the statehouse with earlier revered figures, anchor the present regime in what is portrayed as

Figure 5.14. Law Library in the Iowa State Capitol, Des Moines. The former gas lamps and intricate ironwork are characteristic of a distinguished government library from a century ago.

Figure 5.15. Silver table service made for the battleship USS *Rhode Island,* on display in the Governor's Reception Room in the Rhode Island State House. The set was created by the Gorham Company.

an honored past, and—more broadly—foster the mythology of history's wise leadership.

Covering the walls of American capitols are innumerable portrait paintings, busts, statues, dedicatory plaques, and stained-glass windows bearing likenesses. Official portraits of past governors hang in the statehouses of Indiana, Nevada, and Virginia, among others. In New York and Utah, the corridor in which these portraits are displayed is called the Governor's Gallery, with new additions ritualistically hung upon each departure from office. In Oklahoma, in celebration of the state's diamond jubilee, busts of all the governors were carved and displayed on pedestals.

Persons other than past governors are honored by these representations. The most common are former Speakers of the House. Their portraits often hang near the House chamber, showing a century of change in men's attire and facial hair. Also displayed prominently in or near the legislative chambers are framed "composites" of individual photographs of the representatives and senators who served in all past sessions. In some states, portrait display is prolific. In South Carolina, for example, visitors to the capitol can inspect the faces of four legislators, two judges, three military heroes, one college president, and four presidents. Vermont's portrait collection includes fifty-two governors, six generals and admirals, three presidents, and thirteen prominent citizens. In the Colorado State Capitol, in addition to stained-glass windows that memorialize thirty-six individuals, are the busts of eight men plus the bronze head of a generic woman, intended to honor all Coloradans of that sex. The Massachusetts State House, no doubt the national champion in honorific display, contains no fewer than 23 busts, 42 plaques, and 116 portraits.[9]

Full-length statues of historical figures abound as well. They are found inside the building, on its portico, or on the grounds. Some statues represent men or women identified with the state's own history and culture, including a marble statue of the Revolutionary War hero Ethan Allen, upright with arm raised on the portico in Montpelier; Wyoming's suffragette heroine Esther Hobart Morris, standing in flowing skirts before the portico in Cheyenne (see Figure 4.4); Mother Joseph, a Catholic sister responsible for social good works in Washington, kneeling in the capitol vestibule in Olympia; General Robert E. Lee, stiffly erect at the exact spot on Virginia's former House floor (now a museum) where he accepted command of what became the Army of Northern Virginia; a dour Mayor Richard J. Daley, mounted solidly on his plinth in the rotunda in Springfield; a heroic Brigham Young, striding purposively in the rotunda in Salt Lake City toward the Mormon homeland; and a larger-than-life Sergeant Alvin C. York, posed on the grounds of the capitol in Nashville, taking careful aim at the enemy (Figure 5.16).

Less famous but revered persons may also be memorialized. Standing in the rotunda of the South Dakota State Capitol is a statue of Briga-

dier General William Henry Harrison Beadle, state superintendent of public instruction from 1879 to 1885. Beadle is credited with laying the basis for South Dakota's public-school system by resisting pressure to sell land-grant property to speculators for $10 an acre. When the state centennial commission sought to remove the statue from the rotunda, letters written by schoolchildren from around the state, plus the accompanying publicity, reversed the decision.

Statuary may also commemorate historic events. A group sculpture behind the Missouri State Capitol depicts the moment on May 2, 1803, when the nation's landmass was doubled through the Lousiana Purchase. It shows Jefferson's diplomats James Monroe and Robert Livingston observing Napoleon's treasurer, François de Barbé Marbois, sign the implementing treaty (Figure 5.17). Bas-reliefs outside the Oregon State Capitol celebrate early exploration and pioneer travel west, tracing in intaglio the routes of Lewis and Clark and the Old Oregon Trail.

Figure 5.16. Statue of Sergeant Alvin C. York, a hero of World War I, on the front grounds of the Tennessee State Capitol. The figure was sculpted by Felix de Weldon and dedicated in 1968.

Standing on the grounds of the Georgia State Capitol is a statue called *Expelled Because of Their Color*, commemorating the explusion of thirty-three black state legislators during Reconstruction.

Former presidents of the United States are memorialized in most capitols. The portrayals often are of native sons who rose to national prominence, such as Harry S. Truman in Missouri, Dwight D. Eisenhower in Kansas, and John F. Kennedy in Massachusetts. The multiple claims for presidential birthplace made by North Carolina inspired a statue popularly known as *Three Presidents*, showing Andrew Jackson on horseback with seated figures of Andrew Johnson and James K. Polk. The remains of Polk and his wife are interred in a tomb on the grounds of the Tennessee State Capitol.

Statues of two presidents, Washington and Lincoln, are found in a large number of statehouses. In Virginia, Washington's native state, the Father of His Country is memorialized in the capitol rotunda by Jean-Antoine Houdon's standing marble figure, carved from life and showing him as an aristocratic Virginian rather than a Roman god. A bronze replica of this work is at the front entrance of the South Carolina State House, with the tip of Washington's cane broken off, reputedly by Sherman's men. Elsewhere, Washington can be found as a classic authority figure from antiquity—for example, clad in a toga in the Doric Hall of the Massachusetts State House and seated in the uniform of a Roman general holding tablet and stylus in the rotunda of the North Carolina State Capitol.

Lincoln's appeal as a subject of statehouse statuary may be even greater than Washington's. In the state of his birth, Kentucky, the huge rotunda space in the capitol is dominated by a large bronze figure of the Great Emancipator, unveiled by President William Howard Taft in 1911. The toe of the left shoe has been rubbed for good luck so many times that the statute is now roped off (Figure 5.18). In Indiana, where Lincoln lived as a child, *Young Abe Lincoln*, by David K. Rubins, was dedicated in 1963 and relocated in 1991. Not unexpectedly, two Lincoln statues are found in Illinois: one on the grounds and the other in the rotunda of the statehouse. In Iowa, a composition memorializing Lincoln on the capitol grounds includes his son Tad. In West Virginia, whose statehood was signed into law by Lincoln, a sorrowful *Abraham Lincoln Walks at Midnight* guards the front approach to the capitol. In Nebraska, another reflective Lincoln stands outside the capitol, sculpted by Daniel Chester French of Lincoln Memorial fame.

Objects that are vernacular in form rather than high art are also on display in the state capitols. Museum displays of Civil War memorabilia, called relic rooms, were once common in both northern and southern statehouses.[10] Contemporary displays include the paintings of regional artists (New Mexico and New York), state animals and minerals (Georgia and Idaho), miniature first lady inaugural gowns (Iowa, Kentucky, and South Dakota), and citizen halls of fame (Colorado, Georgia, Nebraska, and North Dakota). Exhibits found uniquely in single states are annual quilt shows in Denver, a memorial to those who died in the bombing of the Alfred P. Murrah Federal Building in Oklahoma City, a case of Huey Long memorabilia in Baton Rouge, stuffed bison and elk in Wyoming, and a salt-flats racing car in Salt Lake City (Figure 5.19).

Legislative bodies display items that have acquired much sentimental value. On the Senate rostrum in the Connecticut State Capitol is the Charter Oak Chair, carved from the tree in which the colony's charter was hidden from the king's men in 1687. A chair once used by Lincoln stands on the Speaker's podium in the Ohio State House. A stuffed bald eagle, "Old Abe," looks down from his perch in the Assembly chamber of the Wisconsin State Capitol, commemorating a Civil War mascot that flew freely in the capitol for years. Hanging above the House chamber in the Massachusetts State House is the Sacred Cod, a carved wooden fish 5 feet long that dates to at least 1784. In 1933, the statehouse community was shocked and the Boston press delighted when members of the Harvard Lampoon temporarily "codnapped" the fish, but the icon was safely returned within a few days (Figure 5.20).

Figure 5.17. Group sculpture by Karl Bitter depicting the signing of the treaty for the Louisiana Purchase, located on the Missouri River side of the Missouria State Capitol. Robert Livingston and a seated James Monroe observe.

Figure 5.18. Abraham Lincoln stands in the rotunda of the Kentucky State Capitol. Sculpted by A. A. Weinman and dedicated in 1911, the bronze figure's left shoe has been rubbed for good luck.

Figure 5.19. Racing car, the "Mormon Meteor III," on display in the rotunda crypt of the Utah State Capitol. It was driven by David Abbott Jenkins, late Mayor of Salt Lake City, who is portrayed in a bust to the left.

Figure 5.20. Sacred Cod, a 5-foot-long carved fish hanging before the public gallery of the House chamber of the Massachusetts State House. The beloved icon dates to at least 1784.

Figure 5.21. The Oklahoma State Capitol, Oklahoma City. The building was unknowingly placed over a pool of oil, and the now-silent oil rigs on its grounds are objects of enduring affection.

Sentimentalized items are also found on statehouse grounds. Theodore Roosevelt's beloved cabin from his Maltese Cross ranch stood at one time near the South Dakota State Capitol, but was subsequently returned to its original locale. Tablets inscribed with the Ten Commandments, the First Amendment notwithstanding, are implanted in the grass at the capitols of Texas and Montana. On a larger scale, the Oklahoma State Capitol is surrounded by oil derricks, placed as it was on a pool of oil. The wells are now inactive, but the giant rigs remain since they garner much local affection, especially "Petunia Number One," directly in front of the capitol (Figure 5.21).

Some cultural artifacts are found in common on the grounds of many statehouses, as a consequence of artifact-distribution programs. The most common is the Liberty Bell, given to each state in 1950 by the Department of the Treasury as part of a savings bond drive, and in twenty-nine states it is in or near the capitol (see Figure 2.11).

Another is a replica of the Statue of Liberty, presented to several states by the Boy Scouts of America. In the aftermath of World War II, the French government, in gratitude for American support in the war, sent railroad boxcars to the states loaded with gifts for the people of each state. Known variously as the "Merci Train," "Gratitude Train," or "40/8 Box Car," some can still be seen on capitol grounds (Figure 5.22).[11]

SOCIAL MEANINGS OF THE MESSAGES

What are the expressive meanings of the messages sent by the objects and decor of the statehouse? One is reverence for the traumas of war, represented particularly in Civil War memorials on the grounds of capitols associated with both sides of that conflict, with the North's victory arches contrasting pointedly with the South's memorials to Confederate women. Displayed inside the statehouse are regimental banners, the once-common relic rooms and such memory-fixing items as a battlefield tree trunk in Connecticut, a loaded cannon in Rhode Island, and *The Return of the Colors* mural in Massachusetts. Other conflicts are memorialized, too, especially the Vietnam War, whose haunting memorials are found in every state. An oddity of capitol war trophies is a special interest in things naval: Krugg guns in Vermont, seacoast guns in Idaho, a battleship figurehead in South Carolina, a warship modeled in Iowa, and battleship silver services in many states.

A second object of reverence is European culture. While many exceptions exist, to be sure, the irony is that a distinctly American building type is filled with Old World art and culture. In part, the anomaly can be traced to the attraction of Jefferson and other Founders to the symbols of antiquity. More important is the general appeal of Renaissance and neoclassic art at the time the

statehouses were built. Capitol architects were socialized into Continental tastes through connections to the Paris and New York art scenes. They filled their buildings with murals that, while on American subjects, were painted in accord with French or English canons of style. The state reception room, the most concentrated site of European culture, would not be out of place in any eighteenth-century French or German palace.

A third major theme is an interest in state history. Capitol murals tell a story of the past. The busts of past governors and the portraits of former Speakers remind citizens of the legacy of past leadership. More arresting are references to specific state heroes, of which there are many. Ethan Allen, Robert E. Lee, William Beadle, Esther Hobart Morris, and Mother Joseph are enshrined as statues in Vermont, Virginia, South Dakota, Wyoming, and Washington. State his-

Figure 5.22. Boxcar of the "Gratitude Train" on the grounds of the North Dakota State Capitol, Bismarck. Filled with gifts, wagons like these were sent by France as a thank-you for American help in World War II.

tory is relived on capitol grounds by depictions of the signing of the Louisiana Purchase in Missouri, the Lewis and Clark expedition in Oregon, and the expulsion of black Reconstruction legislators in Atlanta. In legislative chambers, links to the past are preserved by such precious memorabilia as the Charter Oak Chair in Connecticut, the Sacred Cod in Massachusetts, "Old Abe" in Wisconsin, and Russell's historical panorama in Montana.

Accompanying this reaffirmation of state historical pride are many national icons. American flags, of course, fly at all statehouses, in a position more honored than that of state flags. Portraits and statues of Washington and Lincoln are found in statehouses across the nation. On capitol grounds throughout the country one sees replica Liberty Bells, miniature Statues of Liberty, and 40/8 boxcars thanking America for invading France. As appropriate to a federal system of government, Americans visiting this locus of state government are coincidentally reminded of their national allegiance.

Having summarized the expressive content of these symbolic displays, what are their effects? This question is raised by the societal lens. The answers must be speculative, but I suspect that surface appeals to respect for authority are less efficacious than implied or subliminal messages. Flags, whether federal or state, are taken for granted as part of the normal civic background—with the important exception of the Confederate battle flag. The same is true with seals, maces, and constitutional documents. What may have a more compelling, hidden impact is the association of state authority with the sacrifices and fruits of war, but whether it registers psychologically is difficult to determine.

Another deeper and less obvious impact may be related to the implicit messages of high cultural taste in the statehouse. From a positive standpoint, the presence of European art and furniture of museum quality in the state government's headquarters—especially its parlor—may foster pride among citizens that "their" state deservedly has the best. Yet a subconscious reaction may be to realize how their own living rooms are so ordinary by comparison. Perhaps citizens are made to feel, without realizing it, inconsequential and alienated from an officialdom whose grand world is so different from their own.

There are however, less elegant and more approachable symbolic artifacts with which to relate. A whittled pine statue surmounts the capitol dome in Vermont. A salt-flats race car reposes in the statehouse crypt in Utah. Stuffed bison and elk stand in the rotunda in Wyoming. Huey Long's final clothes can be seen in the capitol basement in Louisiana. The silent rig of "Petunia Number One" guards the portico in Oklahoma. The emotional valence of these homey items is quite different from that of the statehouse's other objects and decor. Unlike that to flags and maces, the reaction is not indifference; unlike that to cannon and memorials to the fallen, the feeling is not awe; unlike that to grand murals and state reception rooms, the response is not subconscious distance. Instead, such humble articles elicit genuine affection, create memorable images, and permit identification with the state and its past. Paradoxically, they may be the most effective socializing instruments of all.

The Organization of Statehouse Space

The organization of space within the statehouse reveals much about the government components housed in it and the relationships among them. In the early years of this building type, when all headquarter units of state government were under one roof, the organization of statehouse space provided a comprehensive manifestation of intragovernmental relationships. With many units now moved out of the building, a spatial analysis of what remains becomes a study of how its most prestigious parts are ordered.

In using spatial organization to study government, the rankings and relationships among components is especially revealing for a pluralistic, American-style system of separated powers. Its essential concepts of constitutional separation, balance of powers, and mutual checking have spatial counterparts in this spread-out, extended building. Since each branch, house, and elective office of government possesses its own sense of institutional identity, and since this identity is usually tied to a sense of place, it is not surprising that each is consolidated in its own part of the building if possible. Two basic alternatives are available for spatially organizing the building with clear boundaries and distinct separation in mind. Vertical organization—placing different entities on separate floors—is the primary way in which the three branches of government are segregated. Horizontal separation—distributing institutions at the same level, such as in opposing wings of the same floor—is the manner in which legislative bicameralism is usually organized.

THE VERTICAL HIERARCHY OF SPACE

The most common vertical pattern is to place the governor and other elected executives on the lower floors of the statehouse and the legislature on the upper floors, typically the second and third. This "upstairs" placement of the legislature emerged in the old statehouses of Delaware, Connecticut, Kentucky, Mississippi, and Illinois, as well as the early capitols of North Carolina and Alabama. Most of the first- and second-wave statehouses, built after the Civil War and around the turn of the twentieth century, were laid out this way.[1]

Elevating the legislature to upper floors above the executive is one of the most significant features of statehouse spatial organization. Despite the doctrine of separate but equal powers among the constitutional triad of branches, the arrangement implicitly suggests the superiority of the legislative branch, and not just because of the theoretical argument that height bestows superior rank, although that point cannot be ignored.[2] The conclusion is compelling because the hierarchical features of the design of the statehouse correspond to such an interpretation.

To put the matter succinctly, the building's second or third floor is the fanciest, and it is on one or the other that the legislature is found. Its ceilings are typically the highest of any floor, creating an atmosphere of dignity and importance. With a few exceptions, such as the state reception room, the decor—including the opulence and elegance of wall and window treatments, doorways, floors, and ceilings—is the finest in the building. In addition, it is usually the floor with the most wall inscriptions, especially in the rotunda area.

The high status conferred by this special treatment suggests an architectural device made famous by the sixteenth-century Italian villas of Andrea Palladio: the *piano nobile*. This magnificently adorned and furnished "floor of the nobility" is located one story above the villa's lower and very plain floor, which is used by servants and tradesmen. The *piano nobile* is reached by a grand exterior stairway, thereby lending additional status to it. In the statehouse, the corresponding grand stairway is on the inside of the building, in the rotunda. It is itself ornately decorated and carefully integrated in its design with the floor to which it leads (Figures 6.1 and 6.2).

The prestige of the main legislative floor is also expressed on the facade of the building. In Second Empire, Beaux-Arts, and American Renaissance architecture, the outside walls of a major building are not homogeneous fields of worked granite. Rather, they are designed as a series of ascending orders with increased complexity and more expansive window treatment correlated with a rise in elevation. Accordingly, the capitol's ground story is clad in rusticated stone and given simple doors and windows. At its next level, the facade incorporates more intricately carved stone and larger and more amply framed windows. Above that, at the level coinciding with the legislative floor, is an orna-

mental climax of tall fenestration, pilasters with capitals, ornamented cornices, and profiled roof detail just above (see Figure 4.3).

The uppermost story then declines in architectural rank. Without, it may be enclosed by sloping roof lines and hence bear no facade at all. Within, it has low ceilings, simple decoration, and closed stairs. Typically, this lesser upper floor houses ancilliary elements of the legislative branch, such as committee rooms, member offices, and corridor access to the public galleries of the legislative chambers. Combined with the primary floor below, this use of space creates a situation whereby at the very minimum the legislative branch occupies the entire top half of the building, and frequently more.

Hence the rest of state government is "downstairs." Although by no means uniformly plain, from a design standpoint the lower stories, especially the bottom floor, are relatively less impressive than the upper. This creates the impression that the occupants of those floors are less im-

Figure 6.1. Second floor of the Iowa State Capitol, the most ornate of the building. The Senate and House chambers are entered to the left and right of the rotunda, with the Law Library beyond.

portant than those laboring above. In the early years of the statehouse, placement at the lowest level was definitely associated with low rank, for it was there that the administrative departments operated. In the Georgia State Capitol and Indiana State House, the bottom floor also housed the stables, as did that in the Capitol in Washington, D.C.

Sandwiched between the inferior ground floor and the superior legislative floor is the first floor, sometimes counted as the second in American practice. Here are the offices of the governor and other elected officials, a location that persists to this day. Aside from the symbolism of such intermediate placement, this arrangement was not without its logic since it permitted the governor and other full-time officials to operate removed from the street yet only one stairway away from incoming visitors.

Originally, the supreme court was sometimes on the intermediate floor as well, but unlike that of the other two branches spatial placement of the judiciary varied from state to state. In later years, both the bureaucracy and the supreme court tended to move out of the capitol, leaving its lower half to the expanded office of the governor and other constitutional officers, such as the lieutenant governor and secretary of state.

Why is the legislature in the upper reaches of the statehouse, while the executive is in the lower? The practice began in the post-revolutionary Delaware State House and Connecticut Old State House. Its continuation in the early nineteenth century seemed to embody a deliberate decision to place the people's direct representatives philosophically as well as physically above the still weak post-Revolutionary governor. Yet less profound factors also may have been at work, such as a desire to remove legislative deliberations from the dust and noise of unpaved streets. Another practicality was that this arrangement allowed the part of the building that was occupied for only a few months of the year to remain empty and unheated. Then, too, before the invention

Figure 6.2. Grand stairway of the Iowa State Capitol. Elaborate exposed stairs often lead to the main legislative floor of the statehouse, indicating its primary importance in the building.

Figure 6.3. The North Dakota State Capitol, Bismarck. The organization of this statehouse is unusual in that the three branches of government are lined up along the building's facade.

of structural steel and reinforced concrete, it was technically easier to locate long, unsupported spans higher in a building than lower.

In the statehouses built in the 1920s and 1930s, the relationship between legislative and executive space began to change. The first step, taken in Nebraska, Louisiana, Oregon, and North Dakota, was to place the legislature downstairs on the same level as the governor. The second step, taken in the 1960s and illustrated in Hawaii and New Mexico, was to elevate the governor and lieutenant governor to the top floor of the capitol and relegate the legislature to the basement. These changes, which presumably reflect an increasingly positive view of executive power, radically altered the traditional vertical hierarchy of the statehouse. Yet since the many older statehouses that embody this tradition are still in use, the dominant overall pattern remains.

Three nontraditional arrangements warrant mention. The New Jersey State House, which has roots in the eighteenth century, has been altered

and extended several times in its history. In a formal sense, the building is regarded as consisting of two statehouses, even though the two parts are fully joined. The front (or north) half, called the Executive State House, contains the offices of the governor and other officials; the back half, or Legislative State House, serves the General Assembly and Senate. A simple wall opening, equipped with fire door, connects the two branches of government.

In the Nebraska State Capitol, all three branches of government are on the highly ornamented main floor, and hence it constitutes the *piano nobile* for all of state government. Bertram Goodue had planned to have the governor in the front of the building, the judiciary in the rear, and the legislature in the center, but this neat division became blurred after unicameralism was adopted and the bureaucracy moved out. The spatial arrangement of the North Dakota State Capitol is studiously linear, with all three branches lined up across the front of the structure. In its original conception, the governor's office was placed at the base of the tall administrative tower, flanked on the west by a rotunda-like ceremonial space and, beyond that, legislative chambers. In 1981, a large addition was made on the east side of the tower to house the supreme court, with administrative offices provided behind. This change totally altered the building's frontal presentation, but was done because the chief justice insisted on architectural as well as constitutional parity for his branch (Figure 6.3).

THE HORIZONTAL OPPOSITION OF SPACE

In addition to the three branches of government, the American concept of separation of powers refers to the two houses of the legislature. The spatial manifestion of bicameralism is played out in the statehouse not vertically but horizontally, on the main and secondary legislative floors.

Bicameralism in the capitol is spatially expressed along two dimensions: the chambers themselves and the support areas associated with them. To assist in conveying pertinent ideas about each of these dimensions, reference is made to the floor plans of four representative main legislative floors: those of Michigan, Washington, Georgia, and Colorado (Figures 6.4–6.7).

Several interrelated standard features are embedded in the spatial design and placement of the legislative chambers. First, the two rooms are, indeed, clearly separated in a spatial sense, implying autonomy on the part of each body. Typically, the chambers are 100 feet or more apart, a distance that often extends along an axial corridor of the second floor and reaches across the rotunda. This distance is limited by the outer walls of the building, with some marginal space usually provided. In the capitols of Michigan, Washington, and Georgia, line-of-sight distances between the front doors of the chambers are 184, 109, and 121 feet, respectively. In Colorado, where the chambers are perpendicular to each other, the walking distance between the front doors is 130 feet.

It should be stressed that the cruciform shape of the building lends itself to the idea of separated chambers by allowing their placement at the ends

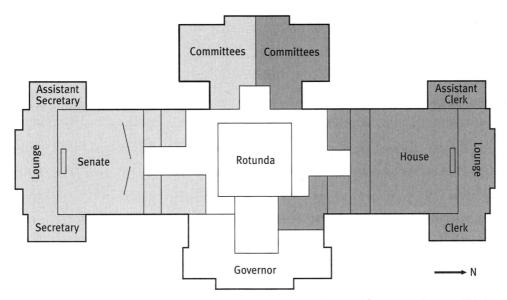

Figure 6.4. Plan of the second floor of the Michigan State Capitol, Lansing. [420 × 274 feet overall: light shading, Senate territory; dark shading, House territory. Building fronts face down.]

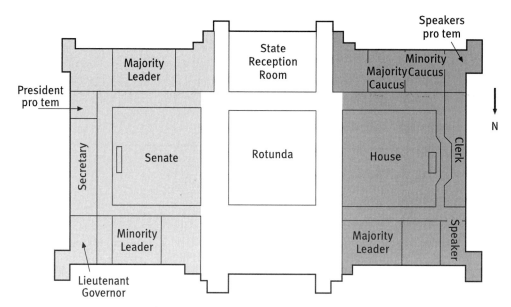

Figure 6.5. Plan of the third floor of the Washington Legislative Building [339 × 235 feet overall]. Note the symmetry of the opposition between the Senate and the House of Representatives, with respect to chambers and ancillary zones.

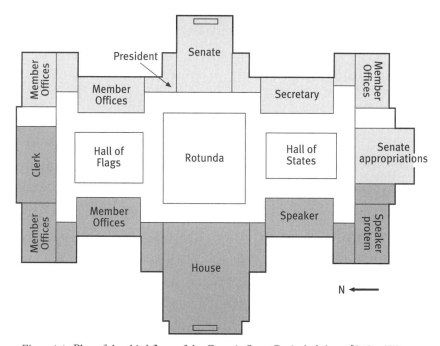

Figure 6.6. Plan of the third floor of the Georgia State Capitol, Atlanta [348 × 272 feet overall]. Bicameral spatial opposition is between the front and rear of the building. Senate Appropriations is in the former supreme court chamber.

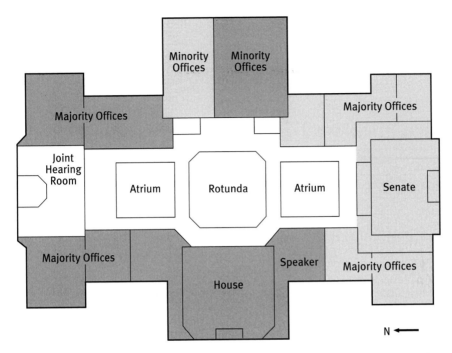

Figure 6.7. Plan of the second floor of the Colorado State Capitol, Denver [383 × 315 feet overall]. Note how the chambers relate to each other at 90 degrees. The former supreme court chamber is now a joint legislative hearing room.

of wings. The chambers usually are the featured spaces in two of the wings, and, hence, the "House wing" and the "Senate wing" often are externally identifiable by observers outside the building. This is the case with the capitols of Michigan, Georgia, and Colorado, but not the more compact Legislative Building in Washington. While in Michigan and Washington the two chamber wings lie along the capitol's long axis, in Georgia they face each other on the short axis.

The second standard feature of bicameral space is the location of the chambers on the same floor of the building; that is, they are horizontally related.[3] This simple but important point means that across the bicameral separation of powers, but not across the branch separation of powers, a common ground exists in the form of a single, connecting floor. In addition to the symbolism created by this bonding surface, the main legislative floor then becomes a place for

intense interbranch interaction and outsider lobbying.[4]

The third spatial feature of bicameralism is that the chambers are evenly matched. This does not mean that they are equivalent; in fact, the Senate is usually smaller than the House because of its fewer members. Furthermore, the two rooms may be shaped, decorated, and furnished in somewhat different ways. Yet the arrangements are comparable—indeed, carefully so. For instance, their locations within the statehouse are of comparable value. They are situated, if possible, at a similar depth in relation to the front of the building and in an equivalent position within their respective wings. If the chambers are two stories in height, which is almost always true, they are the same height. Public galleries for each are not necessarily identical, but are comparable in number and nature. While the two chambers are almost always decorated in different colors,[5] the quality of furnishings and character of decor are evenly matched, except in rare instances. Although this parity corresponds to the constitutional equity of bicameralism, surely equal treatment of the two houses avoids criticism from slighted members of either body.

The fourth spatial feature of bicameralism is spatial opposition, or diametric confrontation, as when two people face each other when sitting at opposite ends of a table. The concept is illustrated by the relationship between Government and Opposition benches in the British House of Commons. In thirty-seven of the fifty statehouses, including those of Michigan, Washington, and Georgia, the presiding officers of the two chambers face each other along a "diameter" or principal axis of the building (see Figures 6.4–6.6).[6]

That the two legislative bodies diametrically face each other implies a relationship of bipolar conflict between the opposing sides. The mental imagery is quite different when the two bodies are on perpendicular axes to each other, as in the Colorado State Capitol (see Figure 6.7).[7] In this alternative pattern, the presiding officers' sightlines do not meet head on, but converge at the center of the rotunda, suggesting in symbolic terms the ability to unite in the people's interest and not just confront each other.

The more typical arrangement—matched opposition of spaces on a common floor—has a ritualistic embodiment: the sine die ceremony at the end of each legislative session.[8] The two bodies are constitutionally required to notify each other that their work is done, so they can adjourn at the same time. In some statehouses, this communication is by messenger or electronic means, but in others it is accomplished visually, across space. The doors of the opposing chambers are opened so that the presiding officers of each body can see their opposite number at the other end of the building. By ringing bells, dropping handkerchiefs, or some other signal the two gavels simultaneously drop for the final time—concluding the work of two separated, equivalent, opposing, but joined bodies.

The second, and complementary, spatial dimension of bicameralism is the organization of the surrounding floor areas associated with the chambers. This ancillary space contains offices, committee rooms, caucus rooms, member lounges, workrooms, rest rooms, and corridors. These areas are considered to "belong to" the House or Senate. But the boundaries of this space are not as definite as chamber walls and, indeed, are sometimes mere invisible lines on the floor. The locations and functions of the territories are, however, quite stable and well known to senior members, and accordingly may be thought of as zones.

The House and Senate zones found on the main legislative floors of the four representative statehouses can be seen in Figures 6.4 through 6.7. The territories are relatively compact and tend to surround their respective chambers. They do not incorporate rotundas or atria and associated circulation spaces, so they are generally separated from each other. As with any kind of political "turf," the zones are taken very seriously; if, for example, members of the two houses must meet jointly, as in a conference committee to reconcile differences between bills, they often seek neutral ground for this purpose, such as a room between the zones, as was the case in the upper arcade of the colonial capitol in Williamsburg, Virginia.

Typically, each house's zone is controlled by the chamber leadership or a space-utilization committee made up of top legislative and party leaders. In the capitols of many states, the boundaries are defended by having separate lock systems on the doors and master keys for each territory. In those of some states, territorial control is taken another step by hiring separate maintenance custodians, security guards, and equipment technicians. In Illinois and Michigan, each house even directs its own remodeling and restoration projects. To illustrate how the existence of these zones enters the consciousness of members of the legislative community, a Senate official, upon taking me into a House zone in one capitol, said with a grin, "We're now entering enemy territory."

Thus, as with the chamber dimension of bicameralism, the zones are separate and autonomous. They also have connections. Points of crossover include behind-the-scenes connecting routes. In the Ohio State House, communication between House and Senate was possible by means of a narrow elevated passageway behind the east portico that only insiders knew. In the Utah State Capitol, a twisting inner hallway connects House and Senate offices, with a nondescript door acting as frontier gate. In the west wing of the Montana State Capitol, unobserved bicameral communication is possible through the back door of a men's restroom—a convenience of little use to female legislators.

With respect to equity of zonal dimensions, two points of view are pitted against each other: one argued by the House and the other by the Senate. The Senate position is that a fair division of scarce statehouse space is a 50–50 split, since the two bodies are of equal standing. According to the House, the only fair division is proportionality based on the ratio of representatives to senators, inasmuch as the more numerous House needs more space. The inherent conflict between these viewpoints fuels ongoing bicameral tension.

Strong feelings on the subject can be expressed in extreme, if not silly, ways. In West Virginia, commitment to the 50–50 principle has created the fiction that the rotunda floor is divided into equal semicircles. During sessions of the New Mexico legislature, a lobby information desk that consists of a single piece of furniture is divided into a House half and a Senate half. In Minnesota, the departure of the supreme court from the capitol opened up a large room for legislative use; the houses could not agree on sharing the space, so it was cut exactly in half by a partition.

Adherence to the proportionality rule can also be carried to extremes. In 1986, the central legislative agency in Colorado facilitated territorial negotiations between the two houses by developing an analysis of six options for dividing the square footage of all available space. Proposed House–Senate ratios ranged from 62.1:37.8 to 64.4:35.6, all of which favored the thirty-two-member Senate over the sixty-five-member House (perfect proportionality would be 67.01:32.99). In Louisiana, mathematical hairsplitting was foresworn in favor of giving four floors in the tower to the Senate for office space and seven floors to the House, but dividing new underground committee space on a 50–50 basis.

Thus space in the statehouse is a hot issue: opposition with respect to space obtains in the sense of contests as well as floor plans. The chronic problem of overcrowding in the capitol sets the stage for conflict. Turf wars can become serious enough to incite strong-arm tactics, as in having locksmiths change door locks at night. This occurred when the new east wing of the Pennylvania State Capitol Building was first being occupied. In Arizona, bicameral jealousies over "turf" can be quite literal, as when the House and Senate could not agree on what varieties to plant in a jointly controlled rose garden, leaving the bed dormant for some years.

THE SPATIAL TREATMENT OF THE GOVERNOR

When the first- and second-wave statehouses were initially occupied, the governor's office was on a lower floor, below the legislature. The residual effect of this "inferior" position, the reverse of the upper placement of the legislature, is still with us. In more than thirty states, the governor's office is on the first floor, with the legislature meeting on a floor above, in either the capitol or a separate legislative building.[9] In eleven states, the governor and the legislature are on the same floor, and in nine, the governor's office is elevated above the legislative chambers, in either the statehouse or a statehouse office complex.[10]

While such floor information seems of almost trivial importance, its symbolic meanings are deeply embedded in the thinking of statehouse habitués. In many capitols, legislators would find it unthinkable for the governor to "come upstairs" without a formal invitation from the Speaker of the House or the president of the Senate. Yet such rules are informal, and more outgoing or activist governors are known to violate them. In his years as governor in Little Rock, a restless Bill Clinton wandered constantly throughout the capitol building, talking to everyone with Styrofoam coffee cup in hand.

Another manifestation of floor consciousness is to refer informally to the chief executive by floor. In Virginia, "The Third Floor" is a euphemism for the governor and governor's office, and the state constitution refers to when the chief executive "sends down" bill amendments to the General Assembly. In Vermont, the governor has a first-floor office in the capitol but seldom uses it, preferring instead a penthouse suite at the top of a five-story building known as the Pavilion. Around Montpelier, the phrase "Fifth Floor" refers to the governor, and an oft-repeated cliché in Vermont political circles is "power comes from the Pavilion."

In some states, including New Hampshire, Rhode Island, and Texas, the governor has been moved higher in the building over time. In some newer capitols, an elevated location for the governor was provided from the start. In the Delaware Legislative Hall, opened in 1933, the governor's office was placed on the second floor, above the legislative chambers; it subsequently was moved to the top floor of the nearby Tatnall office building. In Louisiana, the governor was initially on the same floor as the legislature, but when the supreme court refused to occupy its third-floor courtroom out of hostility to Huey Long, the chief executive moved into its handsome upper space (the court convenes in New Orleans).

In examples of more recent treatment, in the Alaska State Capitol, a five-story territorial office building turned over to the state in 1959 and renovated in 1967, the governor and lieutenant governor are placed on the third floor, directly above the legislative chambers. The governor of Arizona is on the top floor of the nine-story Executive Tower, which was added to the west end of the capitol in 1974. In Columbus, the governor of Ohio has an office on the first floor of the capitol as well as a suite on the top floor of the Verne Riffe building, built across the street from the statehouse. In addition to a second-story office in the capitol in Annapolis, the governor of Maryland is provided a suite on the top floor of a fifteen-story state office building in Baltimore.

Thus the newest state capitols treat the chief executive quite impressively, although we must exempt from the generalization the Legislative Buildings constructed in North Carolina and Nevada, since they were not intended to house the executive. The twenty-one-story central tower of the Florida Capitol, completed in 1977, provides space for various functions of the office of the governor on several floors: the basement, the ground or plaza level (the principal location), and the second, ninth, and twenty-first floors. In New Mexico and Hawaii, the governor is on the top floor and the legislature is in the basement, totally reversing the usual direction of vertical hierarchy.

Regardless of its floor location, in many states the governor's office has received enhanced architectural treatment. The governor of Mississippi was shown little respect in the Old Capitol by being placed at the end of a corridor with almost no special embellishment of the door to his office (see Figure 3.12). When the Mississippi New Capitol was constructed in 1901 to 1903, the governor at the time, Andrew H. Longino, insisted that his position receive more exalted recognition. As a consequence, the current governor's office is entered through a grand primary entrance on the same level as the legislature (Figure 6.8).

More recently the entrance to the gubernatorial office in the Idaho State Capitol was renovated by installing new doors and a vestibule with small shrine (Figure 6.9). Other such renovations include the erection of a carved architrave with broken pediment, as in South Carolina, and the construction of a high glass wall stretching across the entrance to the governor's wing, found in Illinois. Yet, revealingly in terms of political culture, in other states the entrance to the governor's office can be surprisingly modest. In the New Hampshire State House, the governor's door is marked by a small sign reading "Governor's Receptionist, Room 208." In the Wyoming State Capitol, the door is labeled simply "Governor" and at its foot lies the standard "Bucking Horse" fiber doormat used in state offices throughout Wyoming.

Figure 6.8. Principal entrance to the governor's office on the third floor of the Mississippi New Capitol. Compare this treatment with the humble governor's door in the Old Capitol (Figure 3.12).

Figure 6.9. Entrance to the governor's office on the second floor of the Idaho State Capitol, Boise. Several gubernatorial doors have been enhanced, indicating the growing importance of the chief executive.

Figure 6.10. Cabinet room in the office of the governor of Michigan, Olds Plaza Building, Lansing. The table's dimensions are 30 by 10 feet, making communication across it difficult.

Another way to highlight the governor's office is to place it on the front side of the building, which is done in some thirty capitols.[11] While in Egyptian temples, Gothic cathedrals, and Tudor palaces, the highest rank is associated with being farthest back in the structure, this is not the case in democratic America, where power is created by public visibility, not distant remoteness. A side benefit of front location may be a handsome window view, as from the Massachusetts State House, where the windows of the Gold Coast (as the front upper offices in the Bulfinch front are known) look out on Boston Common. Other fine gubernatorial views are of Temple Square from the Utah State Capitol and, from the Montana State Capitol, the Gates of the Mountains through which the Lewis and Clark expedition passed.

Several other aspects of space assignment assert gubernatorial importance. One is the perquisite of a working office in addition to a ceremonial office, already mentioned in connection with Vermont and Ohio. Approximately half the capitols have such an arrangement. In those of Dela-

ware, Florida, Hawaii, Maine, Massachusetts, Michigan, and Ohio, among other states, a conference room is available for meetings of the governor's cabinet (Figure 6.10). In the New Hampshire State House, a special chamber is provided for the Executive Council, a remote descendant of the colonial privy council (Figure 6.11). The five elected members of this group, the only body of its kind in America,[12] share significant executive power with the governor. It, too, has a modest outside door.

Other spatial perquisites of the chief executive include a studio-like room equipped for televised statements and news conferences that is available to the governors of Delaware and New York. In New Jersey and New Mexico, working spaces are set aside for the governor's spouse, called first lady offices in the sexist manner. In all but eight states, executive mansions are provided to the governor, either on the capitol grounds or elsewhere in the capital city.[13] In addition to serving as a home for the governor's family, these residences are used for official entertaining. Although some business meetings are held in them, they are not a combined residence–workplace, as is the White House.

A final spatial reference to gubernatorial importance is room for staff. As with the territorial zones associated with the legislative chambers, the governor controls floor areas in the statehouse in addition to the personal ceremonial and working offices. As one might expect, the contemporary governor requires room for staff professionals of many kinds, as well as offices for such agencies of the executive branch as departments of administration and budget.

The resultant space expansions go in various directions. In the capitols of Nebraska and South Dakota, the governor's staff has moved into rooms across the hall from the governor's office. In those of Iowa, Mississippi, and Utah, the expansion has penetrated the floors below. In the Florida Capitol, as noted, the governor's office operates on several floors of the central tower, including some

near the top. In the Montana State Capitol, the executive zone occupies much of the east wing, and in the California State Capitol, it covers a large part of the first floor (1954 addition).

Expansion of gubernatorial space may reach outside the statehouse as well. In North Carolina, the governor has offices in the State Capitol, but most staff work on the first and fifth floors of a state office building two blocks away. In Michigan, the primary working offices of the governor occupy the first four stories of a former hotel across the street from the State Capitol.

In Arkansas, Rhode Island, and Minnesota, separate buildings have been constructed near the statehouse to accommodate the governor's administrative empire. The relatively new building that houses the Department of Finance and Administration in Little Rock is regarded as an overt indicator of the governor's growing power in Arkansas state government. A similar struc-

Figure 6.11. Chamber of the Executive Council in the New Hampshire State House, Concord. The body has five elected members, and its meetings are chaired by the governor, with whom it shares executive power.

ture has been built across the street from the capitol in Providence to house the Department of Administration. In St. Paul, the Department of Administration occupies a massive structure that looms on Wabasha Hill behind the statehouse (Figure 6.12).[14] These special annexes for executive bureaucracies might be considered as younger counterparts at the state level of the executive office buildings near the White House.

THE SPATIAL TREATMENT OF OTHER EXECUTIVES

Despite the emergence of institutions of gubernatorial control in state government, executive power in the states is not entirely in the governor's hands. Whereas at the national level the only elected executive branch officials are the president and vice president, at the state level a number of elected officials may hold the reins of executive power. Hence in the states, the doctrine of separation of powers extends beyond the three branches and bicameralism to the other constitutional officers, whose offices are created by constitution rather than statute.

One of these constitutional officers is the lieutenant governor. This official, like the vice president at the national level, occupies an ambivalent position in that he or she performs in both legislative and executive roles. In most states, the lieutenant governor is president of the Senate and yet substitutes for the chief executive when he or she is unavailable. The lieutenant governor may also be integral to the administration's political team, as is the vice president of the United States.

The number of additional constitutional officers depends on the state. In some states they are elected, while in others they are appointed. One of the most common is the secretary of state, a title reaching back to Tudor England when the king's personal secretaries evolved into state administrators. This official cares for state documents, records trademarks, commissions notaries public, and administers election and incorpora-

Figure 6.12. Building occupied by the Minnesota Department of Administration, St. Paul. In several states, the increasing power of central executive agencies is reflected by an imposing building.

tion laws. Another is the state treasurer, who is in charge of protecting, disbursing, and investing state funds. Before the advent of computers and modern bank accounts, treasurers kept physical possession of gold, silver, and cash belonging to the state in vaults within the statehouse, many of which can still be seen as an architectural relic of the past (Figure 6.13).

Another common constitutional officer is the state auditor, who analyzes the expenditures and operations of state agencies and oversees local government finance. The attorney general is the state's lawyer and often implements consumer and monopoly laws. In some states, additional constitutional officers administer individual administrative departments—for example, the superintendent of public instruction and commissioners for agriculture, land, insurance, labor, taxation, and elections. If these officials are elected, separate executive fiefdoms are created that pluralize the executive from a public-administration standpoint. Yet they may also add continuity and access to state government.[15]

At one time, all these executives had their principal offices in the statehouse, usually on its lowest floors. Many remain in the capitol, even if their administrative operations have been moved elsewhere. Because of the attorney general's law-enforcement role, this official is frequently housed in a separate justice or law building, sometimes in conjunction with the supreme court.

An analysis of the spatial treatment of these executives uncovers two general patterns. One is a "quadrangle" arrangement, whereby the offices of the governor and three other constitutional officers are located at the four corners of the first or second floor of the statehouse. The arrangement, found especially in the West and South, creates in effect a four-way relationship of equity, comparable to the two-way equity inherent in the organization of bicameralism. By implying that all four officers are of equal importance, the quadrangle pattern both downplays the governor as "chief" executive and subordinates the elected executive officers not included in the quartet.

An early example of the quadrangle arrangement is in the North Carolina State Capitol, built in 1840. Its first-floor office space is divided into four quadrants, each of which contains two rooms. Although the occupants of these spaces varied over the years, for a long time they were divided among the governor, secretary of state, auditor, and treasurer. Eventually, the governor took over three of the quadrants, leaving the fourth to the lieutenant governor.

Another pre–Civil War statehouse, that of Ohio, exemplifies a variation of the four-part arrangement. Not all the first-floor space fits neatly into four quadrants, but the corner spaces of the floor are assigned to four officials: the governor, secretary of state, auditor, and attorney general. Most of the staff members working for these officials are housed in nearby office buildings. A similar situation obtains on the ground floor of the Wyoming State Capitol, whose four corners are filled by the governor, secretary of state, treasurer, and auditor. The corners of the second floor of the Washington Old Capitol Building are occupied by the same four officials.

The step taken in North Carolina—modifying the quadrangle arrangement at a later time in order to increase the governor's space—has occurred elsewhere. The corners of the first floor of the Tennessee State Capitol were originally occupied by the governor, the treasurer, the supreme court, and a federal court. Today, the corresponding tenants are the governor, treasurer, secretary of state, and governor's staff. Gubernatorial staff in Tennessee also occupy most of the basement, excavated from the crypt to create more room. In the Utah State Capitol, where the four-corners approach is generally in effect, the governor also acquired territory downstairs. In Kentucky, another quadrangle statehouse, the governor's office was moved to the center of the building to be near the rotunda and its statue of Lincoln.

The second overall model of the distribution of executive space is less structured than the quadrange approach. It derives from individual situations of historical precedent and space rivalry that are peculiar to each statehouse. Yet some patterning is evident. One of two constitutional officers, the lieutenant governor or the secretary

Figure 6.13. Former vault of the state treasurer of Montana, now part of the secretary of state's office. Such vaults, now used for storage, once held cash, gold, silver, warrants, and other valuables.

of state, is given elevated status more often than the others. This is done by associating one or the other spatially with the governor's office, by equivalence or proximity or both.

In the South Carolina State House, the lieutenant governor's office is directly across from the governor's, and it bears an identical broken-pediment architrave. Similarly, as one enters the front of the Kansas State Capitol and reaches the second floor, the governor's office is on one side of the hall and the lieutenant governor's is on the other, although behind the scenes the chief executive commands more floor space. A parallel situation obtains in the Michigan State Capitol. The lieutenant governor of Hawaii occupies the capitol's favored fifth floor along with the chief executive, in an equivalent penthouse on the other side of the roof.

Elsewhere, proximity alone rather than design similarity obtains. In the capitols of California and Montana, the lieutenant governor is the only other official located in the governor's part of the statehouse: the first floor of the east wing in Sacramento, and the second floor of the east wing in Helena. In North Dakota and Massachusetts, two states where the lieutenant governor has in recent years become a close political ally of the governor, this official was moved from more distant points in the statehouse to the governor's immediate vicinity. In both cases, the shift was widely seen as a sign of increased political collaboration between the top two executives and heightened power for the lieutenant governor.

In an approximately equal number of other states, the secretary of state benefits from equivalence or proximity to the governor. A prime example of both exists in the Georgia State Capitol, where, along the primary corridor of the second floor, the governor's office is on one side and the secretary of state's is on the other. Although, again, the governor controls more total space in the building, the doorways, anterooms, and head offices of the two officials are of equal size and layout.[16] In the Illinois State Capitol, the two officials occupy equivalent spaces on the second floor along the prestigious front of the building. A corner sitting room in the secretary of state's office is one of the most splendidly decorated areas in the building (Figure 6.14).

In several other statehouses, the tie to the governor is by proximity alone. The governor and secretary of state of Iowa occupy first-floor center positions at the front of the capitol. The secretary of state's office is small, but its rich decoration has earned it the appellation Arabian Jewel Box. The governor and secretary of state of Rhode Island each occupy a row of front offices on the second floor of the capitol, one on each side of the governor's reception room. In the statehouses of Indiana, South Dakota, and Texas, the two officials are also side-by-side along prime corridor space, and in New Jersey the secretaries of state and the treasury together occupy the front, or "A Wing," of the Executive State House, while the governor and counsel are in the "B Wing" behind it. In many states, then, the contemporary spatial setting of the secretary of state seems to honor the office's Tudor origins.

SOCIAL MEANINGS OF STATEHOUSE SPACE

The organization of space in the statehouse carries a number of social meanings. The expressive lens invites us to consider how several ideas introduced when the statehouse building type was created have since fared. The post-Revolutionary development of placing the two representative bodies in the upper story became, particularly in the first- and second-wave statehouses, a pattern whereby the upper half of the building is dominated by the legislative branch. The main legislative floor became a kind of legislator *piano nobile,* possessing the highest ceilings and most elaborate interior and facade ornamentation and attained by a grand staircase. On this floor, the principle of bicameralism is emphatically stated by the diametrically opposing and equivalent legislative chambers.

The rest of government in the traditional statehouse is housed downstairs, where ceilings are lower and decor is less ornate. The governor, often placed one level above the ground story, is treated in a spatial sense far better than his or her

Figure 6.14. Corner room in the office suite of the secretary of state of Illinois. Paul Powell, a longtime incumbent of the office, was a legendary figure who amassed great power.

predecessor in the late eighteenth century, but still subordinate to the legislative branch. Yet some perquisites are possible, such as placement on the side of the building with a view. In later years, further enhancements have occurred, such as making the front door more ornate and providing a separate working office. Exponential growth in gubernatorial staff is reflected in the addition of behind-the-scenes floor space and, in some states, the construction of a new building to house departments of administration or budget.

In nontraditional statehouses built in the 1920s and later, a noticeable adjustment in the legislative–executive relationship is spatially reflected. The first pattern to emerge was the placement of both branches on the same floor, on a downstairs *piano nobile*. A subsequent pattern is to give the legislature a building of its own or to radically inverse the traditional vertical hierarchy by locating the governor at the top of the capitol

and the legislature in the basement. Yet most states had by this time constructed their permanent statehouses, so this revisionist concept is found in only a minority of capitols. Meanwhile, the third branch of government, the judiciary, is treated variously. In the minority of statehouses where the supreme court remains in the building, it is ambiguously placed either up- or downstairs. Elsewhere, the judges have moved from the capitol to a courthouse of their own.

Examining the capitol's organization of space through the behavioral lens identifies the underlying force for conflict over "turf" in the building: a continual growing demand for more room within an essentially fixed quantity of space. The capitol can be added to only so much, and when that level of feasibility is reached, there is no way to alleviate further space pressures except to go underground, an option taken in some states. This means that the remaining occupants of the statehouse engage in ongoing struggles over space.

Extreme turf consciousness and boundary sensitivity are signs of the resulting tension. It is not unusual for each house of the legislature to have its own master keys and security and custodial forces. Territorial feelings run sufficiently high that neutral ground is needed for bicameral negotiation, and hidden connecting passages are useful for border crossings. An unresolved argument between the chambers concerns the "fair" allocation of space between them. Meanwhile in the executive branch, attempts by the governor to find more office space for growing staff causes the other constitutional officers to be always on the lookout for raids on their territory.

The perspective of the societal lens invites recognition of the most fundamental lesson taught by statehouse spatial organization: state government in the United States is not a single centralized system, but a pluralistic collection of separated powers. It is not mere semantics that in America the term "the state" does not mean, as in European political discourse, a unitary apparatus for ruling population and territory. Rather, it refers to one of fifty jurisdictions of the federal union—whose competing sovereignties of state and national government rival the separation of powers itself as a hallmark of governmental pluralism.

Even when looking at the statehouse from the outside, one witnesses disaggregation. The capitol is not an architecturally compact palace, but a sprawling structure with wings and additions, most particularly an identifiable House wing on one side and a comparable Senate wing on the other. A third wing may have been devoted to the judiciary.

Inside, the visitor discovers not a uniform degree of elegance, but a curious upstairs–downstairs distinction between the more ornate upper half of the building and the plainer lower half. Moreover, it is downstairs that the chief executive is housed, which in most government headquarters of the world would be unthinkable. Also difficult to imagine outside the American states is the presence downstairs of a rival set of executive offices, occupied by autonomous constitutional officers. Meanwhile upstairs, an even more important spatial pluralism operates, between the opposing legislative chambers. Viewed as a whole, then, the statehouse may be seen in spacial terms as a kind of matrix of major contending powers, with the executive and legislature confronting each other vertically and the House and Senate horizontally.

7 | Features of Statehouse Interiors

Two general types of interior are evident in the statehouse: civic and private space. Civic space refers to governmental interiors dedicated to ceremonial use before the observing public.[1] Examples of such rooms are the chambers of the House and Senate, the courtroom of the supreme court, and legislative committee rooms. The second type of interior in the statehouse is more private and exclusive, departing from the concept of civic space to one degree or another. These are offices of executives and legislators and rooms for privacy and relaxation.

Another distinction relates to whether features of the room are fixed or semifixed. Fixed features are items that are physically nonmovable (without intervention by carpenters, for example) because they are attached to floor or walls. Examples are partitions, large platforms, and heavy railings or balustrades. Semifixed features could conceivably be moved, but are assumed to be fixed because of their weight, character, or association with authority.[2] Many desks, chairs, and tables fall into this category. It is noteworthy because the social meanings attached to the objects become so firmly established over time that the existing arrangement is considered an unquestioned "given" in the room's interpretation and effects.

INTERIORS FOR CONFLICT AND DELIBERATION

The legislative chamber is the official meeting place of the upper and lower houses of each state. There are ninety-nine such spaces in the fifty states because Nebraska's legislature is unicameral.[3] The legislative chamber is an important civic space from several standpoints. Architecturally, it is in the most distinguished part of the capitol building. Legally, the space is given added cachet because it is the subject of specific prescription in many state constitutions.[4] Semantically, it has importance because a reference to the chamber is incorporated, with a few exceptions, into the very name of one of the two bodies: the "house" of representatives.[5]

Finally, the legislative chamber is significant in a broad political sense. It is the place where representative government is exercised. Along with the voting booth and courtroom, this interior functions as the crucial cockpit for the resolution of societal conflict. The space can be said to substitute for the violent streets and fields of battle where society's struggles would otherwise be settled. In constitutional democracies, the legislative chamber thus becomes the scene for debating issues, enacting statutes, passing resolutions, confirming appointments, and hammering out public policy—with all that these activities imply for raucous discourse, solemn ceremony, and tension-breaking tomfoolery.

The design and contents of the ninety-nine state legislative chambers vary, of course. Differences among the rooms can themselves be revealing, not only among the states but between the House and Senate. Yet the degree to which the individual rooms are unique is less significant than the several characteristics that most share. These commonalities are quite striking and set the American legislative chamber apart from its parliamentary counterparts in Europe and elsewhere. It is not too much to say that the physical interior of the state legislative chamber incorporates what might be thought of as a distinctively American approach to the legislative function.

We begin with spatial composition. The legislative chamber in the statehouse is not long and narrow, like a cathedral, suitable for processions and worship. Nor is it a large auditorium, built for major assemblages or massive audi-

Figure 7.1. Chamber of the Wyoming Senate. The room illustrates the typical features of the American state legislative chamber, such as flat floor, low rostrum, and recessed public gallery.

ences. Rather, the legislative chamber tends to be a room rather modest in size for a significant public space—between 3,000 and 7,000 square feet. Moreover, its floor plan is typically a relatively compact rectangle. That is, its breadth and length are not too dissimilar. Thus occupants of the room find themselves closer together than would be true with a more extended or dispersed design (note the chamber proportions in Figures 6.4–6.7).

Actual measurements of illustrative chambers add concreteness to this picture. In the Iowa State Capitol, the dimensions of the lower house are 74 by 91 feet. The lower house in Pennsylvania is 80 by 100 feet; in Missouri, 70 by 78 feet; and in Vermont, 67 by 70 feet. In the Rhode Island State House, the chamber of the lower house measures 56 feet square. The Senate chambers of these states are smaller because the body has fewer members: Iowa, 58 by 91 feet; Pennsylvania, 60 by 65 feet; Missouri, 68 by 70 feet; Vermont, 38 by 46 feet; and Rhode Island, 44 by 56

feet. In contrast to these relatively small rooms is the Texas House, which at 95 by 137 feet is the biggest legislative space in the country. Not even the chambers of the United States Congress are that large: 65 by 113 feet for the House, and 48 by 85 feet for the Senate (including upstairs galleries, 80 by 135 feet and 75 by 115 feet, respectively).

In addition to its compactness and limited size, the state legislative chamber is relatively horizontal. Using analogies from outdoor landscape, the room's fixed and semifixed features are like a flat plain or perhaps undulating farmland, with no mountains in sight.

The rostrum, or ensemble of semifixed furniture that minimally includes a front bench for clerks and a back bench for the presiding officer, tends to be about 5 feet above the floor at the presider's reading surface (Figure 7.1). The presiding officer's platform or podium is usually reached by two to four steps (Figure 7.2). As for members' desks, their tops are approximately 30 inches from the floor, a height suitable for writing while seated. Moreover, they are not placed on stepped platforms that rise above the empty floor space directly in front of the rostrum, which by tradition is called the well of the House. Indeed, in most chambers, the room's floor is perfectly flat (Figure 7.3). In a minority of chambers, there is a slight angle of incline of 1 or 2 degrees, sloping downward toward the rostrum. Even in such sloped rooms, the result is still a basic horizontality, with the writing surfaces of the front rostrum and rear row of desks at an approximately equal elevation (Figure 7.4).

This essentially horizontal topography contrasts markedly with the landscape of most of the world's parliaments. At the front of the French Chamber of Deputies, one of the classic models of such a room, is not a low rostrum but a high tribune, rising at least 15 feet above the well of the house. It incorporates four separate levels and requires stairways with handrails to surmount. Similarly high tribunes are found in

the parliamentary chambers of, for example, Austria, Belgium, Finland, Germany, Japan, and Portugal.

Moreover, in most parliamentary chambers, the topography of member seating is very different from that of the statehouses. Instead of being horizontal or slightly sloped, the floor consists of a series of rounded, concentric, stepped platforms ringed with mounted benches or desks. The curve of these rows of seating is often semicircular or U-shaped, creating essentially an amphitheater design. (In Britain and some Commonwealth countries, Government and Opposition benches are placed in straight, raked rows, facing each other.) The overall consequence of the high tribune and raked seating, separated by an intervening void formed by the well of the house, is a very uneven topography. Again using landscape metaphors, a sizable mountain juts up in the front of the room, a steep hillside rises in the rear, and between the two lies a valley of separation.[6]

Figure 7.2. Chamber of the Utah House of Representatives. The room exemplifies the two-bench rostrum, ganged yet individual desks, shallow-arc seating, radial aisles, and close-in well.

Figure 7.3. Chamber of the Michigan House of Representatives. A single aisle penetrates the shallow-arc seating on a flat floor. Note the common-use lecterns with microphones along the aisle.

Figure 7.4. Chamber of the Pennsylvania House of Representatives. The room's 80- by 100-foot dimensions force the 203 members into a deeper arc than is usual. The floor slopes downward toward the rostrum.

Furthermore, the members of most parliaments do not sit at individual desks, as do legislators in almost all the states (and the United States Senate, but not the House). Rather, they sit on common or joined benches, in some instances without assigned seats. In most parliaments, little or no writing surface is provided to individual members. The result is a setting that emphasizes mere attendance and voting rather than deliberation and influence. Indeed, the situation is close to conditions in the auditorium or sports arena, where merely occupying a seat is what counts.

In short, the horizontality of the American state legislative chamber is quite unusual. A comparatively flat topography prevails all across the country, with only Nevada and New Mexico constituting modest departures in terms of raked floor as well as continuous benches (Figure 7.5). The United States Congress deviates modestly from this model in that the floors of both chambers have concentric steps built into them, but each step is only a few inches high.

The expressive and behavioral significance of an essentially flat chamber is considerable. In a physical and therefore psychological sense, all legislators are "on the same playing field." When the presiding officer and members address one another, they do so across the room, not down from a superior height, up from a lowly position, or across an empty void. Members occupy individual desks or desk spaces that give them personal importance and meaningful work space. With the desks mounted on a horizontal floor, members can move in and out of their seats and approach colleagues and rostrum officials without difficulty. The design facilitates member mobility and interaction, on the one hand, and symbolizes member individuality and equality, on the other.

In addition to horizontality, a significant characteristic of statehouse chamber design relates to the arrangement of desks. Instead of a semicircle, U-shape, frontal opposition, or full circle, the arrangement constitutes a shallow arc. The same is true in the United States Congress, where, as

Figure 7.5. Chamber of the New Mexico Senate. Successive arcs of member benches rise on a raked floor, creating an exception to the flat room topography. The room is located below ground level.

in many state chambers, this curve arcs across the length rather than the width of the room. This feature makes the distance from rostrum to back row relatively short, sometimes as little as 25 feet (see Figure 7.2). Even when the arc is across the width rather than the length of the room, the space's compact composition keeps members at rear desks from being too distant from the rostrum (see Figure 7.3).

When seated in a shallow arc, all legislators face in the same general direction. They are not divided into two halves that face each other head-on, as in the House of Commons. Unlike those sitting in the semicircular, circular, or deep-U pattern, no member directly faces a colleague, even at the ends of rows.

A related point is that the shallow arc lends itself to an understated rather than a dramatic separation of the political parties. Democrats and Republicans may be on the opposite sides of a center aisle (not a universal practice, however), but they do not face each other from opposite sides of "The Floor," as in England, or sit in a continuum of pie-shaped wedges, as results from the multiparty systems of Europe. Although American politics has adopted the terms "right" and "left" from the practice, there is no equivalent in the United States of the Chamber of Deputies in Paris, where the monarchists or neo-Nazis sit on the presiding officer's extreme right and the Communists on the extreme left, with the other parties spread out between in a fan of ideological factions. In short, the American legislative floor not only emphasizes interaction and equality, but deemphasizes factionalism and partisanship.

At the same time, the centered and symmetrical nature of the shallow curve fixes attention on the rostrum. This focus is reinforced by the converging aisles that transect the arc at various intervals. The point of convergence is the well of the chamber. Because of the flatness of the room, the well is not a cleft of separation, but a visual and behavioral commons. This is analogous to the spatial commons that obtains when the sightlines of the House and Senate presiding officers converge in the rotunda when the chamber

spaces relate to each other at 90 degrees, not in opposition.

The overall effect of the shallow arc, then, together with the compactness and flatness of the room, is to produce a generally nonhierarchical setting. Leaders of the body, whether positioned on the rostrum or on the floor, are at about the same elevation as one another and the membership. Except in the very large chambers, such as the lower houses of Pennsylvania and Texas, no one is ever very far away from anyone else, physically or psychologically. Furthermore, very few prestige differentials exist in shallow-arc seating, from either front to back or side to side. In fact, members with high seniority who have first choice of available seats prefer to sit at many different points in the arc, for different reasons, suggesting the absence of an inherently "elite" location.

Departures from shallow-curve seating can be found. In the House chamber of North Carolina and both chambers of Delaware, Oklahoma, South Dakota, Texas, and Wyoming, the desks are aligned in straight rows, classroom style. In the Vermont House and both New York chambers, desk placement assumes a rather deep U-shape. The Senates of Connecticut, Florida, Massachusetts, and Wisconsin impart a rounded or circular image, because of either the shape of the room or the arrangement of the desks. The perfectly round Senate arrangement in Hartford, with an inside diameter of 25 feet, is known as "the circle," and the phrase "sitting in the circle" refers to being a member of the body (Figure 7.6). Whether or not the furniture is a factor, the Connecticut upper house has a reputation for goodwill and camaraderie.[7]

With respect to desk design, two general types of furniture are found. In many statehouses, old and even original wooden desks are still used, with matching chairs. These revered antiques are intricately carved and often finished with brass fittings (Figure 7.7). Desks once occupied by a well-known historical figure are so remembered and may be marked with a commemorative plaque. In many chambers, it is fondly recalled, each desk once had a polished spittoon beneath it.

Figure 7.6. Chamber of the Connecticut Senate. Its thirty-six members sit around a 25-foot circle, without segregation by political party. The body is known for its informal collegiality.

Figure 7.7. Member desks and chairs, Georgia House of Representatives. These antiques, from the 1880s, bear brass fittings for desk number, mail slot, and identification plates.

The second general type is the contemporary desk and chair, inspired by modern office equipment and built from the latest and most durable materials (Figure 7.8). The desk is equipped not with spittoon, but with console for electric voting and perhaps hook-up of telephone and computer as well. The comfortable executive-style chair accompanying the desk typically swivels 360 degrees, a not inconsequential factor in encouraging floor interaction around the room.

When a chamber is furnished with "modern" furniture, departing members are often allowed to purchase their chairs, to take home as a souvenir; since the furniture is made in a factory rather than hand-carved, replacements can easily be ordered. If the chairs are upholstered in leather, as they often are, the color and patina of the leather covering each piece will vary slightly with age and use. Variations in this surface give the keen observer of the assembly subtle evidence

by which to assess each member's seniority and hence colleague status.

Typically, each desk bears the name and district of a legislator, in print large enough to read at a distance and on television. This clear designation publicly affirms that this piece of furniture belongs to the member—it is his or her legislative home and "seat" in the sense of constitutional representation. In the smaller states where legislators are not provided with offices, the chamber desk also becomes an important place for doing business while in the capitol. The larger point is that these parliamentarians do not just sit at a common bench or occupy an unassigned place, but have their own individual semifixed feature by means of which they can create a sense of personal and political identity. With time, moreover, the association between member and desk grows; after the death of Jesse Unruh, long-time Speaker of the California As-

Figure 7.8. Member desks and chairs, Arizona Senate, Arizona State Capitol, Phoenix. Dating from the 1960s, they are typical of the "modern" floor accommodations for state legislators. Such desks often contain electronic equipment.

sembly, his floor desk was set to the side of the chamber and his chair was shrouded, with the understanding that no one would ever occupy it again (Figure 7.9).

In some chambers, desk individuality is slightly compromised by paired or ganged furniture (Figures 7.10 and 7.11). This step is sometimes taken in small chambers to save floor space. Even so, individual writing surfaces and storage drawers are clearly demarcated. Such multiple arrangements can create behavioral consequences. Close personal and political ties often form among seatmates, and in debate members sometimes refer to one another on this basis. Neighbors along a row have been known to vote for one another in electrically recorded ballots when they temporarily leave the chamber, although in some bodies this practice is much frowned upon.

The lower house in New Hampshire is an interesting exception to several of these generalizations. Every second year, it convenes in Representatives Hall, whose theater-style seats have no writing leaves (Figure 7.12). At 400 members, the New Hampshire House is the biggest state legislative body in the country, with each of its members representing fewer than 3,000 constituents. These citizen-solons proudly earn only $200 per biennium, a figure unchanged since 1889.

A final design feature of the distinctive statehouse chamber is its public galleries. Seating areas for the public were installed in colonial legislative rooms as early as 1766. Some early galleries were at floor level, but by the nineteenth century they had moved upstairs, removing citizens from the immediate scene of legislative action, but allowing them to look down onto the chamber floor. Except in the capitols of Oregon and Ohio, where some provision is made for downstairs seating, citizens climb up back stairs to an inferior architectural level of the building to view their representatives at work.

Figure 7.9. Desk of Jesse Unruh, former Speaker of the California Assembly. Placed to one side of the chamber with the chair shrouded in black, it is left unused in his honor.

Figure 7.10. Chamber of the South Dakota Senate. The rolltop desks, paired but self-standing, are made of mahogany. Those in the House are constructed of oak. Note the recessed public galleries.

Figure 7.11. Chamber of the Idaho House of Representatives. The multiple member desks are divided into individual work spaces. Note the gooseneck microphones on each desk.

Figure 7.12. Chamber of the New Hampshire House of Representatives. Its 400 citizen members sit in theater-style seats. The chamber was enlarged twice to accommodate the body's growing size.

For the most part, these galleries are unsegregated. This differs from English and European practice, by which separate galleries exist for members of royalty, civil servants, diplomats, former members, and the press. Only the "strangers' gallery," as it is customarily called, is open to the general public. During the nineteenth century, some American states placed women in separate galleries, but that practice went out with the Nineteenth Amendment, if not before. The only exception to unsegregated galleries is a few instances where special seating areas are reserved for VIPs or members of legislators' families.

American state legislatures do not label observing citizens as strangers, yet from a spatial viewpoint their treatment in the room is far from dominant. Public galleries are frequently restricted to the back of the room or are obscured by columns or pillars (see Figures 7.2 and 7.5). Another pattern is to place them in a kind of recessed wall cavity (see Figure 7.1). In only two

states, Oklahoma and Texas, are the galleries built out from the walls and around all four sides of the room, as in the House of Commons and the United States Senate (notice how this is not done in Michigan, Figure 7.3). A further restriction on public galleries occurs in the lower houses of Arkansas, Pennsylvania, and Wyoming and in both chambers in Florida: the fronts of the galleries are partly or entirely glassed off, isolating the public further from the legislative process (see Figure 7.4).

INTERIORS FOR HEARING AND JUDGMENT

The legislative chamber, whose floor is relatively nonhierarchical and egalitarian in design, contrasts with two other statehouse civic spaces: the courtroom used by the supreme court and hearing rooms used by legislative committees. These interiors are elitist, not egalitarian. They differentiate between key officials, on the one hand,

Figure 7.13. Courtroom of the Pennsylvania Supreme Court. Separate zones for appellant attorneys and observers are divided by a balustrade. The murals were painted by Violet Oakley.

and lesser players or observers, on the other. Moreover, all of those in authority are placed at a common semifixed feature, thus presenting an image of collective rather than individual power and authority.

At one time, state supreme courts convened in the capitol, with exceptions.[8] The space given the court tended to include a courtroom, robing room, conference room, law library, and offices for the justices. In recent decades, most of the courts have moved out of the statehouse, either to their own building or to a justice or law center containing other elements of the judicial branch, plus sometimes the office of the state attorney general. In some states, including Arizona, Nevada, and New Jersey, the separate judicial building is palatial in size and far more intimidating than the statehouse.

Twelve supreme courts still meet in the statehouse: those of Indiana, Iowa, Kentucky, Minnesota, Nebraska, North Dakota, Oklahoma, Pennsylvania, South Dakota, Utah, West Virginia, and Wisconsin. The Minnesota Supreme Court alternates sessions between its statehouse chamber and a courtroom in its own building down Wabasha Hill. The Pennsylvania Supreme Court, which claims to be the oldest court in North America, meets in three places: Pittsburgh, Philadelphia, and the chamber in Harrisburg decorated by Violet Oakley (Figure 7.13).

The central focus of the courtroom is the bench. It is a single, massive piece of furniture fixed to the floor. Typically, the bench is straight, long enough (often 20 to 25 feet) to reach across much of the courtroom, and fronted with a skirt that rises 4 to 5 feet from the floor. Behind it, a platform about 1 foot high elevates the judges above others in the room. The bench's writing surface lies a few inches below the top edge of its front skirt, providing a parapet to hide the justices' hands and papers. The symbolic importance of this piece of furniture for the court's members is enormous; indeed, the word "bench" is a synecdoche for the court itself.

Supreme court benches are built to fit integrally into the decor of the courtroom as a whole. They are constructed of fine woods and are paneled or ornately carved. Mounted lamps or other appurtenances create an overall impression of elegance, solemnity, and high significance (Figure 7.14). Members of the Oklahoma Supreme Court make their way to their positions at the bench through the curtained doors of a reredos or screen.

Chairs for the justices are also ornate, with cushions bound in leather and high backs that protrude well above the bench. In some, but not all, courtrooms, the center chair, reserved for the chief justice, is noticeably higher and more ornate than the chairs of the associate justices. It is important to note, however, that the chief justice is not given a special table or even a raised reading surface, let alone rostrum, as is the presiding officer of a legislative body. Although the court's highest official enjoys special status, he or she is treated as a member of a collegial body.

Since the single bench and chairs behind it must accommodate all the members of the court, constitutional changes that create additional justices can lead to a shortage of seating positions at the bench. On more than one occasion, following amendments to the constitution that enlarged the court, skillful joinery has been required to extend the ends of the bench in a way that no one will notice. Before the Arkansas and Texas Supreme Courts left their respective statehouses, the bench was expanded from five to seven seats in Little Rock and from three to nine in Austin, although the restored bench now seen in the Texas State Capitol is back to three. The present supreme court bench in the Minnesota State Capitol has been enlarged twice, from five to seven positions and then from seven to nine. When the number of justices was later cut back to seven, two unnecessary end chairs were removed. The Iowa Supreme Court bench was also enlarged, by its original craftsman.[9] These changes show how the built environment of government can reflect

Figure 7.14. Bench of the Supreme Court of Kentucky. The ornate brass lamps and mahogany paneling are imported. The presiding judge has a distinctive chair and raised parapet, but not a separate writing surface.

Figure 7.15. Courtroom of the West Virginia Supreme Court of Appeals. Cass Gilbert later designed an almost identical courtroom for the United States Supreme Court, substituting a frieze for the inscription.

governmental practice in an immediate and direct way.

The floor of the courtroom is flat, like that of the legislative chamber. One of its prime characteristics is its division into zones by means of fixed and semifixed features. The most important zone is the bench and its immediate environs. It is here that unquestioned authority rests. Customarily, no one but the justices themselves and officers of the court are allowed in this area. The national and state flags repose in the corners of the bench zone.

The area of secondary importance beyond the bench is the appellants' zone, marked off by a balustrade for exclusive use by attorneys arguing a case. A lectern facing the bench may rest on the balustrade separating the justices and attorneys, but the lawyers use it from their side. The principal furniture in the secondary zone is a set of two heavy tables, one for each party of litigants. In the tertiary zone, reserved for observers and members of the public, benches or simple chairs

are available. The arrangement of seating in the two lesser zones assumes that their occupants will be watching the justices seated behind the bench.[10]

One state supreme court chamber is of particular interest because it became the model for the United States Supreme Court. In the latter 1920s, when the West Virginia State Capitol was being erected, architect Cass Gilbert was selected, at the urging of his friend Chief Justice William Howard Taft, to design the new Supreme Court building being planned across from the Capitol. As it turned out, this neoclassic structure became the final project for the famous but passé designer, and Gilbert died before the building was completed in 1935. The courtrooms in Charleston and Washington, D.C., are almost identical, except for a higher ceiling in Washington decorated by a wide frieze rather than an inscriptive band (Figure 7.15). Even the skirt of the bench of the Supreme Court duplicates its West Virginia ancestor, although in 1972 it was bent forward at each end to facilitate communication among the justices.

The legislative hearing room resembles in some ways the courtroom. It, too, presents the official body—in this case, the legislative committee—as a corporate group. Members of the committee sit around a single table or dais (Figure 7.16). The chairperson, like the chief justice, receives very little, if any, special attention, although he or she is usually placed in the middle of the room's furniture centerpiece. In addition, floor space is segregated and hierarchical, although separating balustrades are uncommon. The exception is when committees meet in former supreme court chambers, which occurs fairly often because many state supreme courts have abandoned their courtrooms in the statehouse, only to be snatched up by the space-hungry legislative branch.

A comparison of the hearing room and the courtroom is revealing. Zonal and furniture differentiations are not as sharp in the hearing room, giving it a somewhat more egalitarian air. Members of the committee sit in relatively plain chairs. They are grouped around not a high or an ornate bench, but a standard 30-inch writing surface, without parapet. This piece of furniture usually is angled or curved in a concave manner, conveying the idea that diverse viewpoints are appropriate around it, not a unified or an official opinion.

The other major difference between courtroom and hearing room is the treatment of nonofficial players. Unlike in the courtroom, in the hearing room there is no clear zonal distinction between those who possess inherent status, such as litigating attorneys, and members of the observing public. Everyone who is not on the committee is treated equally and seated together, in a relatively up-front position.

There is, however, provision for giving a rotating series of individuals a temporary place in the spotlight: the witness desk or lectern. Its design varies from a simple elevated reading surface

Figure 7.16. Committee hearing room of the Ohio Senate, Ohio State House, Columbus. The angled dais is raised 6 inches. Note the lack of highlighting for the chairperson and the central witness lectern.

to a form of secular pulpit. The latter is substantial in size and weight and is outfitted with numerous electronic controls; by means of a console, the witness operates sophisticated audiovisual equipment, a kind of technological substitute for the arcane legal argumentation used by attorneys in the courtroom. After stepping up to the stand, the individual appearing—whether legislator, bureaucrat, lobbyist, or citizen activist—is the official center of attention (Figure 7.17). Immediately after giving testimony, he or she returns to the general audience, not to a privileged zone, immediately leaving the spotlight. This arrangement emphasizes the function of giving testimony, not the status of the person testifying.

Each house of the legislature has numerous committees and subcommittees, and making space available for them in the chronically overcrowded statehouse is a tedious exercise in the allocation of scarce resources. In the process, some committees win out over others, making the outcomes of such competition an index of relative commit-

tee status. In almost all statehouses, the clear winners are the "money" committees—those that write appropriation bills and tax legislation. Such committees tend to be large, have much paper to process, and are automatically deferred to because they hold the power of the purse. In many capitols, the money committees control all the permanently assigned hearing rooms, an advantage in terms of not only stability, but also accommodation of the needs of committee staff. Other committees make do with sharing rooms on a rotating, assigned basis.[11]

INTERIORS FOR DISPLAY AND WORK

The offices of elected state officials serve as both civic and private space. They perform a ceremonial function in that the officeholders who occupy them are on display before the visiting public and press. Yet they are also places where much practical work is accomplished on a daily basis.

Figure 7.17. Meeting of the House Appropriations Committee in the Morris Hearing Room, House of Representatives Office Building, Florida Capitol. The witness is standing behind the lectern.

To a surprising degree, perhaps, statehouse offices tend not to be of great size or elegance. They are quite utilitarian for the most part, even simple in many cases. The chronic crowdedness of the capitol is one factor, but there appears to be a tradition in American state government to present officials in populist, not regal, settings. With the exception of very few—such as the governor of Missouri, the Speaker of the California Assembly, and the secretary of state of Illinois— top state officials operate in surroundings far less impressive than those given America's major corporate executives.

The generalization applies to the governor, despite this official's top executive rank, media fame, and symbolic headship of state government. The governor's personal office suite tends to be dignified, but restrained. Typically, three or four individual rooms are clustered for a reception anteroom, a formal gubernatorial office, sometimes a private working office, and space for immediate staff.

The formal office is of considerable but not extravagant dimensions—for example, 25 by 25 feet in the Ohio State House, 26 by 26 feet in the Nevada State Capitol, and 20 by 30 feet in the Texas State Capitol. Typical decor is dark period furniture and walls decorated with historical portraiture or regional landscapes. The desk is a handsome piece of furniture, yet of reasonable size and in active use. It tends to face outward into the room, toward visitor seating. Family photographs, paperweights, and mementoes adorn its top, together with files, binders, and often a computer. Remarkably absent are overt trappings of power, such as red telephones or rows of buttons by which to summon aides. Almost all the visible symbols of authority in the room are depersonalized, such as the state and national flags or state seal mounted on the wall or woven into the carpet.

Not all governor's offices are the same, of course. The office of the governor in the Maryland State House, when occupied by William Donald Schaefer, was obviously a place of intense activity (Figure 7.18). In the Nebraska State Capitol, the governor's office is outfitted with a splendid fireplace and fine antiques, but it constitutes a relatively small corner of the building. The governor of Kansas occupies a spacious room in the capitol on whose walls large paintings hang, yet the desk itself is simple (Figure 7.19).

By contrast, the office of the governor of Missouri is splendid. Elliptical in shape, it is 50 feet long and 35 feet wide, substantially larger than the 36- by 28-foot Oval Office occupied by the President (Figure 7.20). Like the Oval Office, it curves outward from the building in the form of a rounded, bay portico to secure additional light internally and architectural prominence externally. The interior walls are paneled with carved oak and feature painted panels that celebrate Missouri educational and literary figures, such as Mark Twain. The explanation for its opulence is that the room once served as the state reception room, called in Missouri the governor's reception room.

Sometimes the formal office is supplemented by a private office. In the nineteenth century, a back office was essential because visitors, including office seekers, would walk in unannounced, a problem later obviated by modern buffering techniques. In the late twentieth century, the protective function of the private office was supplemented by a presentation function performed by the front one. It is here that television interviews are often conducted, and thus a controlled rather than a messy backdrop is essential. In some statehouses, the front office is exclusively for show; it is emptied of all working papers and prettied up with historic artifacts (as in Illinois) or coordinated period furniture (as in Oregon), thereby becoming a permanent stage set. Its primary purpose is to serve as a regular destination point on the public capitol tour. Without disturbing the work of the office or threatening its security, visitors are offered the thrill of "being in the governor's office."

Another display associated with the governor's office is the exhibition of desks used by past holders of the office. While these pieces of furniture are often unremarkable from a design standpoint, state history has in effect been writ-

Figure 7.18. Office of former governor William Donald Schaefer of Maryland. A working rather than a ceremonial space, the room is crowded with files and mementoes.

Figure 7.19. Office of former governor Joan Finney of Kansas. The office is large and decorated with regional paintings, but the furniture is simple. Note the positions of the American and state flags.

Figure 7.20. Office of the governor of Missouri. This elliptical room, larger than the Oval Office in the White House, was once the Governor's Reception Room. The windows look out on the Missouri River.

ten on them, creating keen sentimental interest. They are on view in the governor's suite or elsewhere in several capitols. For example, in the Red Room of the New York State Capitol is the mammoth partner desk used by both Governors Roosevelt on their respective ways to the White House. In New Jersey, after a long search, Woodrow Wilson's gubernatorial desk was uncovered at Princeton University; it was moved back to Trenton and now serves the current governor.

The issues are quite different in relation to the offices in the statehouse that are used by members of the legislative branch. With rare exceptions, such as the Speaker's office in the California State Capitol, the intended audience of the legislative office is not the outside public, but other capitol insiders. One of its striking features is the degree to which it memorializes the personal political career of its occupant. Campaign posters, photographs of handshakes with famous party figures, and toy donkeys or elephants are ubiquitous. In the offices of veteran

leaders who have gone through many electoral campaigns and legislative sessions are displayed an incredible proliferation of banners, gavels, cups, gifts, awards, and other political memorabilia (Figure 7.21). In the governor's office, by contrast, the artifacts presented carefully display an allegiance to only the state as a whole.[12]

As for the location of legislative offices, their layout and assignment sheds light on the collegial and interactive nature of legislative activity. An office considered "good" for a legislator, in addition to size and such perquisites as a private toilet and back door by which to escape lobbyists, is one that is well located. A desirable location puts its occupant close to political colleagues and is handy to the chamber. The issue is more than mere convenience; physical proximity is crucial for political operators who strive to be at the center of the action. Hence the best offices are on the main legislative floor and along a hallway that leads to the chamber, particularly near a door that leads to the rostrum. Conversely, offices con-

Figure 7.21. Office of Thomas B. Murphy, Speaker of the Georgia House of Representatives. Elected to the House in 1961 and to the speakership in 1974, Murphy became dean of the nation's House Speakers.

sidered inferior are on the level above or below the legislative floor or, even worse, in another building from which getting to the chamber takes several minutes.

For the top chamber and party leadership, office selection is a stable and known matter. Good spaces are permanently set aside for those holding such positions as Speaker of the House, president of the Senate (or president pro tem if the lieutenant governor is a Senate figurehead), majority floor leaders, minority leaders, and, sometimes, caucus chairs and whips. The same is true for the full-time administrators of each chamber, customarily called the clerk in the House and the secretary in the Senate. Again, the proximity criterion operates in these permanent assignments, as can generally be seen in Figures 6.4 to 6.7.

Legislators not in central leadership positions receive varied office assignments. Chairs of committees, especially the money committees, often have offices in or near their hearing rooms or committee offices. The office location of everyone else is decided by informal rules that form part of the legislative culture. Although members typically are invited to submit requests with respect to office space, final assignments tend to be made personally or at least approved by the chamber's top political "boss": the operative presiding officer. This power is a potent weapon to reward friends and punish enemies, and it is sometimes overtly employed for that purpose.[13] The same can be true with respect to assigning parking places in the capitol garage or reserved lots on the statehouse grounds.

Yet space assignments are usually more than a personal or dictatorial act. Several customary rules of the game condition the process. One is the benefits of seniority. Members who have the longest tenure and are in the good graces of the leadership usually receive priority. Another rule is that a member is never "bumped" from an occupied office; involuntary eviction is reserved for extreme situations, such as retaliation for attempting to organize a leadership coup. The consequence of the nonremoval rule is that few office assignments are up for reconsideration at the beginning of a given session; thus the selection process centers on filling only the occasional vacancy, not on reallocating en masse.

Another consideration in the calculations is party affiliation. In less partisan legislatures, the offices of Republicans and Democrats may be mixed together, but this is unusual. In states where party identification is crucial and party discipline is expected, strict office segregation of the two parties is the order of the day—probably because of the intuitive feeling that keeping the faithful physically close helps keep them politically close.

Partisan segregation usually results in members of the minority party receiving inferior offices. For example, in the highly partisan Pennsylvania House, offices of majority members are located on the preferred first floor of the capitol, while minority members are relegated to the fourth. In Oregon, where party control can alternate, the majority party is housed on the second floor and the minority on the third. In the event that party control shifts, everyone moves. The same is true in the Stratton office building in Illinois, where majority members of the House occupy the south wing and minority members the north, an arrangement derived from the closer location of the south wing to the House wing of the capitol.

The extent to which a legislature is "professionalized" in terms of heavy staffing and long sessions greatly affects office availability and distribution. In statehouses like that of New Hampshire, where the part-time, citizen legislature is a matter of civic religion, there are no offices for members, only lockers in the basement. Another solution is to crowd many members into single rooms, such as the chaotic "bullpens" endured by minority members of the Colorado legislature. By contrast, in states like Georgia, Illinois, Maryland, Michigan, Minnesota, Nevada, New York, North Carolina, and Washington, every member, minority or majority, of each house has an individual office and sometimes a suite of offices

for staff. In order to accommodate such largesse, however, one or more legislative office buildings separate from the capitol are required. Legislative work then becomes more professionalized, but members are taken far from their chambers, with a consequent reduction in the intimacy of the legislative process. Such office buildings also highlight the power of staff and staff agencies by creating large physical structures separate from the capitol that are dominated by other legislative actors than the elected representatives of the people.[14]

INTERIORS FOR PRIVACY AND RELAXATION

Space that is fully closed off to the public is the conceptual opposite of civic space, since it is not used to hold ceremonies and outsiders are seldom present. Although in proportionate terms, such space is scarce in the statehouse, it can yield interesting insights. Its private, inward nature reveals features not intended for the public eye. Three types of private space revealing to the legislative function are the caucus room, the member lounge, and the chamber rest room.

The caucus room is where a chamber's legislators of one party can meet alone—for example, before voting on major legislation. During these confidential discussions—which are sometimes bruising battles—reporters, lobbyists, and usually even staff are kept out. Guards may even be posted outside the door to ensure privacy.

The very existence of special caucus rooms is a significant datum, for many capitols do not have such spaces. Instead, empty committee hearing rooms, multipurpose conference rooms, or even the chamber itself are called into use. The presence of designated caucus rooms indicates the existence of a militant partisan culture, particularly if each party has its own. In Pennsylvania, whose legislative bodies are very partisan, the Democratic and Republican caucuses for each chamber possess not only their own rooms, but their own clerks, staffs, and pages. In addition, each caucus maintains separate systems of duplication, computing, and security. In many states caucuses are composed of members grouped by characteristics other than party—for example, legislators who are female, African-American, or from urban or rural districts. Unlike on Capitol Hill in Washington, D.C., these "demographic" caucuses rarely have their own staffs or offices in state government.

Caucus rooms fall into two categories with respect to the relationship between the parties. In one category, the majority party is assigned a much larger and more favorably located room than the minority party. In the event of a turnover election, the rooms are switched. This arrangement operates in Delaware, where the majority caucus rooms for House and Senate are immediately adjacent to their respective chambers on the first floor. By contrast, the Senate minority caucus meets on the second floor of the capitol, and the House minority caucus convenes in a corner of the basement.

The other arrangement gives the two parties equal caucus space regardless of which is in power. Rather than the notion of majority rule, this pattern evokes the concepts of fair play and minority rights. In practical terms, it means that election turnovers do not require physical moves; with permanent occupancy possible, the caucus space can become, in addition to a meeting room, a party office or even a kind of political clubhouse. Examples are found in Hawaii, the Senates of Connecticut and Indiana, and the House in Washington (see Figure 6.5).

The member lounge, unlike the caucus room, is for the exclusive use of not the members of one party, but the members of one chamber. It is a kind of back room for the legislators, used for relaxation and frank talk. Usually found just off the chamber, the lounge is fitted out with comfortable seating, facilities for light refreshment, telephones with privacy booths, and, sometimes, television sets and card tables (see Figure 6.4).

During sessions, members of both parties and all political factions circulate into and out of the lounge, where they are removed from the public scrutiny of the chamber and the party discipline of the caucus. In this neutral sanctuary, matters in contention can be discussed and negotiated without fear of being overhead by reporters or lobbyists. Of the ninety-nine legislative chambers, thirty-seven limit the lounge to member-only use and another twenty-seven allow visitors if they are accompanied.[15]

With respect to the character of lounge interiors, in newer or renovated capitols, the room is similar to the lounge of any contemporary men's club. In older capitols, however, the lounge may be formally and richly appointed in the manner of a European drawing room. The House Retiring Room in the Minnesota State Capitol, for example, features French windows, velvet draperies, oak wainscoting, and a forest mural by Elmer Garnsey (Figure 7.22). Particularly luxurious old-style lounges are also found in the statehouses of Arkansas, Nebraska, and Pennsylvania. While these accommodations are no more pretentious than those of the state reception room, it must be remembered that—unlike the reception room—the member lounge was always meant for legislators only. Hence its elegance reflects (or did) the legislature's elitist view of itself, not a desire to impress citizens.

The chamber rest room is also capable of yielding insights. Its exclusivity is based not on institutional membership, of course, but on gender. The significance of this interior for our discussion lies in the unequal facilities afforded men and women. The imbalance in favor of men is in keeping with the American state legislature's historically male-dominant culture. Only in recent decades have steps been taken to correct the imbalance, in the wake of feminist pressure and the growing number of women members, who compose more than 20 percent of state legislators.

Until the 1970s, rest-room facilities were typically provided for men along the hallways and lounges immediately adjacent to the legislative chamber. But women had to find staff areas meant for secretaries or descend to the public restrooms on the ground floor. The situation was innately irritating to female legislators and forced them to miss debates and votes.

But constructing new facilities near the chambers was not a simple task in the interior of these old, overbuilt stone structures. In some state-

Figure 7.22. House Retiring Room, Minnesota State Capitol. It is decorated with velvet draperies, oak wainscoting, and a forest mural by Elmer Garnsey. (Shown: Chief Clerk Edward A. Burdick)

houses, attempts were made to solve the problem by partitioning the men's room into a dual facility, but this solution did not work because of the absence of soundproofing. Then entirely separate women's facilities were built by converting existing office or meeting spaces (Figure 7.23).

Yet the earlier sexist mentality that led to the problem in the first place did not quickly die, as manifest by pranks or comments related to the new arrangements. In the Oklahoma Senate, a condom machine was surreptitiously installed in the new women's facility. In Maryland, the female member of the House of Delegates who had pressed for change was publicly presented by the Speaker with a muskrat-covered toilet seat.[16] Nicknames for the newly built facilities referred to the first members to use them: "Lottie's Potty" (Illinois House), "Rose Room" (California Senate), "Pat Regan Room" (Montana Senate), and "Barbara Jordan's Room" (Texas Senate). Once again, physical space records social attitudes.

SOCIAL MEANINGS OF STATEHOUSE INTERIORS

The perspective of the expressive lens provides insights into the organizational cultures of the institutions housed in the statehouse. With respect to the legislature, the flat topography of the room expresses an egalitarian rather than a hierarchical concept of the legislative body. The presiding officer is not raised high on a tribune, each member is given an equivalent desk of substance, and all players operate on the same flat floor. Furthermore, a shallow arc of desks depicts a relatively common focus of purpose and understates party differences, especially when compared with the opposed benches in London or the ideological seating in Paris.

At the same time, separate caucus rooms, the partisan segregation of member offices, and the plethora of campaign mementoes within them reveal that political parties remain an important element of state political life. When, in the strug-

Figure 7.23. Chamber of the Virginia Senate, showing the door to the former office of the lieutenant governor, converted into a lounge for female members.

gle for scarce space, it is primarily the money committees that are assigned permanent hearing rooms, the universal power of the purse is underscored. Traces of past cultural values now disappearing from the legislative culture are member lounges decorated like elitist men's clubs and the absence, until recently, of rest rooms convenient to female members.

The interiors of other rooms in the capitol are also culturally revealing. The elegant and hierarchically zoned supreme court chamber reflects the majesty of the law as well as the adversary system of justice. The high bench, which is the central focus of the room, and the differentially backed chairs behind it express the august status of the court and its tradition of colleagial leadership. If the state constitution is amended to enlarge the membership of the court, a physical lengthening of its bench directly reflects the change.

The governor also occupies dignified interiors, but they are of reasonable size, modest decor, and not filled with overt symbols of power or partisanship. Hence the chief executive, regardless of impressions given by grand murals and European furniture elsewhere in the statehouse, is presented in the gubernatorial suite itself as a leader of all the people.

The behavioral lens leads us to consider how the composition of interiors and the design of their fixed and semifixed features affect statehouse conduct. The legislative chamber's compact shape, moderate size, flat topography, shallow seating, accessible well, desk separation, and swivel chairs all contribute to the ability of American state legislators to interact with one another freely and intimately. In those chambers where desks are ganged and in the few Senates where desks are arranged in a circle, an additional degree of collaboration is probably fostered.

Legislators who occupy offices near their chamber perceive proximity as affording an advantage in exercising influence. Yet because of the crowded conditions in the capitol, many cannot have private offices in the building. When offices are assigned in separate buildings, it distances members significantly from the action. At the same time, it creates an opportunity for expanded influence on the part of individual staff and staff agencies that also occupy these separate buildings.

The examination of statehouse interiors through the societal lens presents ambivalent impressions from the standpoint of the public. Legislative chambers contain unsegregated public galleries open to the citizenry, but they are spatially withdrawn from the center of the room and, sometimes, sealed off with glass. Legisla-

tive committee hearing rooms are egalitarian in public seating and treat all witnesses alike, from hired lobbyist to citizen activist. By contrast, supreme court chambers provide chairs for the public only in the inferior back zone. Moreover, when the judiciary moves into a building of its own, it tends to be truly palatial. In those state capitols where an antiseptic show office, rather than the governor's dignified but modestly furnished working office, is used to receive tour groups, members of the public are probably not fooled, but a few may take an interest in a former governor's desk displayed in the room that helps bring alive the state's history.

8 | Conduct in and around the Statehouse

The statehouse and the areas within it, especially the legislative chamber, function as "behavior settings," to use the term coined by Roger G. Barker.[1] When this happens, the physical structure and its surroundings act to condition and frame human conduct. One type of conduct, the exercise of power, is pursued in a number of venues of influence both inside and outside the building.

THE STATEHOUSE AS BEHAVIOR SETTING

The statehouse, like all buildings, exercises initial control over behavior within its spaces by determining who can enter and when. The issue of access to government buildings in a democracy is complex because they serve, at the same time, as symbols of democratic governance, on the one hand, and symbols of hated authority (at least to some) on the other. Citizens can rightfully demand ready access to them in fulfillment of the democratic ideal. Yet, increasingly, government buildings are the targets of shootings, bombings, and other forms of violent disruption. This makes it difficult to determine an appropriate balance between security and openness. The resolution of this dilemma is the most fundamental way in which the statehouse influences human behavior.

For the most part, access to the American statehouse *appears* exceedingly open and free. The grounds of very few capitols are fenced, and when they are, the effect is purely ornamental. Unlike at the White House and Capitol in Washington, D.C. (and federal offices all over the country), sidewalk barriers rarely stand in front of the building.[2]

The doors of most capitols are unlocked between 6:00 and 8:00 A.M. each business day and remain open until 5:00 to 7:00 P.M. When entering the buildings, visitors seldom encounter armed checkpoints or magnetometer gates.[3] All citizens, as well as visitors from abroad, enter and depart without signing in or out or wearing security badges. In one extreme case, the Hawaii State Capitol, the atrium-like rotunda at the heart of the structure is never closed to foot traffic.

At the entrances to legislative and judicial chambers, metal-detection equipment is not generally used except in tense circumstances. Uniformed guards are not regularly observed in the corridors or around critical areas like the governor's office or computer room. In short, along with the rural county courthouse, the statehouse is the most unfortress-like public building type in America. International visitors often express amazement over the absence of obvious security measures in comparison with those they encounter at parliamentary buildings back home.

This does not mean, however, that disguised or less noticeable security measures are not taken. In most statehouses, guards or police officers dressed in civilian clothes keep a general watch on the building's grounds and entrances. They also linger in crowded areas, monitor the movements of public personalities, and walk the halls at night. Closed-circuit-television security cameras are mounted around the capitols of approximately half the states. The windows of sensitive rooms, such as the legislative chambers and governor's office, are either blocked off from outside view or fitted with bullet-resistant glass. In legislative chambers, sergeants-at-arms and their staffs keep main entrances and public galleries under careful observation. Silent alarm buttons are installed on many chamber rostra and courtroom benches in case quick calls for help are needed. In a few instances, Kevlar bullet-resistant shields are built into the skirts of supreme court benches.

Thus the statehouse is not a fortress, but a carefully, if unobtrusively, monitored building. Security gaps exist, but are minimized to the extent that is possible in a substantially open building. Steps are taken to avoid danger or property damage during protests or demonstrations, but no attempt is made to remove protesters summarily or prohibit noisy conduct. Although this general pattern of low-key but concerted security measures is implemented to varying degrees, depending on the individual capitol, in general a combination of apparent openness and hidden observation achieves an effective balance between the needs to celebrate and protect democracy.

Like many public behavior settings, the statehouse does not condition conduct within it in a uniform way over time. The setting changes, depending on the time of year. The overall milieu of its public and ceremonial spaces shifts rather predictably over the political cycle. A rhythm of roughly five phases recurs annually in the building, the exact dates of which depend on the timing—in the years they are held—of legislative sessions and election campaigns.

The first phase is the legislative session, which starts in early January and continues to March or April. This is the building's busiest time, and it is crowded with legislators, lobbyists, members of the media, constituency groups, and demonstrators. The second phase is when early-spring filings take place for reelection of incumbents holding state office and seats in the state congressional delegation. At this point, the formation of campaign organizations and the raising of campaign funds create a behind-the-scenes stir. The third phase, which occurs in the late spring and summer, is when hoards of schoolchildren and tourists visit the capitol. Although the building is quite full then, little policymaking takes place and the civic spaces are empty. The next phase begins with the onset of fall campaign activities, bringing to the capitol staged campaign speeches, news conferences, and visits by national political figures. The final phase is Thanksgiving through New Year, when the great building stands largely empty except on festive days. Enjoyed particularly by state employees and capital residents is the annual lighting of the state Christmas tree in the capitol rotunda.

During the first, or legislative, phase of the year two kinds of behavior can be observed that are affected by the distinctive design of the capitol's circulation spaces. One springs from traffic flows; the other, from visual sight lines.[4]

At the center of the statehouse interior is, of course, the rotunda, which is not far from the building's main entrances. Leading from it are the wings, which, at each floor level, are bisected by public corridors that pass to the chambers, offices, and other operational spaces of the capitol. This design funnels most foot traffic in and out and around the statehouse through the rotunda, up and down the stairways that connect the rotunda to the corridors, and then along these common corridors.

These pathways, because of their defined and common-destination nature, become "political venturis" of the kind Grady Clay discovered near busy street intersections in the business heart of the city.[5] Everyone in the building is channeled together, creating a continual process of spontaneous social interaction (Figure 8.1). Unplanned encounters occur whereby friends greet one another and strangers rub shoulders. Much of this interaction is, of course, perfunctory, but because of the setting's political intensity at the legislative time of year, brief contacts may be used to good purpose, such as thanking an ally for support or recognizing a hometown constituent. Since this spontaneous interaction occurs on neutral ground, partisan opponents can appropriately exchange words and clerical personnel can chat with high officials without violating the barriers of status and hierarchy. In short, the political venturi effect enhances both the efficiency and the directness of verbal communication within the building, making it into a giant social mixing bowl for the statehouse community.[6]

It would be wrong to assume that all foot traffic in the capitol flows through these common venturis. There are stairs at the ends of wings and back doors on the ground floor. Yet a major proportion of the pedestrian flow converges, much more so than if the building were designed differently. If all statehouses, like Florida's, incorporated high-rise towers instead of being low structures with only three or four floors, people would move vertically in closed elevator cars instead of on open stairways. Similarly, if the floors on each wing consisted of sealed units with external doorways, the social mixing bowl would be replaced by segregated ingress and egress, as in a motel. Much interaction would also be lost if the hallways on each floor simply intersected in the middle of the building instead of emptying onto a public rotunda.

The second general pattern of conduct to spring from the design of statehouse circulation space has to do with visual sight lines. The rotunda's sizable height and breadth allow people to see one another at a distance inside the building. Standing on one of the balconies that ring the rotunda, people would find it difficult not to notice others standing at the rail opposite (Figure 8.2). Moreover, it is impossible to miss people standing on the balconies of other floors, not to

mention those on the rotunda floor. Similar visibility is, of course, possible in the opposite direction along these sight lines, causing balconies to be not just a place from which to view, but a place to be viewed—from above, below, and at the same level.

Additional wide-angle sight lines are available in the open courts or atria that supplement the rotunda in many statehouses, such as those in Colorado, Connecticut, and Georgia. Still another place for noticing and being noticed is on the grand stairways that descend into the rotunda or the atria. Tunnels to and escalators in attached legislative office buildings function in the same way.

Within the highly charged political space of the statehouse, these visual conditions fulfill a purpose: the need of naturally gregarious politicians to be visibly on stage. Those who have already reached the heights of power revel in the receipt of public attention; those who are aspiring to power enhance their reputations by

Figure 8.1. Rotunda corridor leading to the chamber of the South Carolina House of Representatives. Such "political venturi" passageways, used by statehouse occupants of all kinds, act as a social mixer.

Figure 8.2. View across the rotunda on the second floor of the Michigan State Capitol. Such lengthy, wide-angle sight lines allow political display and reconnaisance in the statehouse.

being seen with the famous. In addition, it is good for any politician to be noticed by newspaper reporters who shape his media image and corporate lobbyists who finance her campaigns. Then, too, observing the dynamics of interaction on the part of other, rival politicians provides a form of political intelligence on who is doing what.

Thus the wide sightlines of the capitol's central circulation spaces create display racks for visual self-presentation and elevated platforms for political reconnaissance. That the interior design of statehouses makes such display and reconnaissance possible no doubt encourages their taking place. In the Hawaii State Capitol, the habit of frequently gazing to and from those standing along the rotunda's balcony rails has led one political insider to describe the practice as "government by rail."

Some behavioral consequences of statehouse design are less obvious, more complex, and cannot be detected by simple observation. A method

to ferret out hints on this subject is to inquire about any changes that may have taken place in the aftermath of physical moves within and from the statehouse. When a group or an office moves from one location to another, clues about the influence of an environment on behavior can be gathered by asking those affected to describe the differences experienced in the former and current settings. If the social dynamics of the unit changed noticeably between the locations, it is possible that the changed setting had something to do with the altered behavior. It did not necessarily "cause" the outcome in a deterministic way, but in some direct or indirect manner may have facilitated it. In social science research, this would be called a quasi-experiment: the independent variable—the behavior setting, in this case—is altered for a reason other than experimentation, yet the aftermath can be observed.

Behavioral consequences were much in evidence after the majority party caucus of the Iowa House of Representatives moved its meeting place. For years, the caucus had met in one of the large caucus rooms on the second floor of the capitol. In that setting, the fifty-plus members of the caucus had plenty of room and, because of the physical separations thus possible between people, got into the habit of breaking into private conversations during the meeting.

The legislators were, in effect, subcaucusing, a practice that annoyed the Speaker because it delayed business and made it difficult to control the group and call for final votes. So the Speaker had the site for caucus meetings shifted to his personal conference room, a much smaller space. The members were forced to sit either around a center table or in a second ring of chairs along the walls of the room. Under these much more crowded conditions, there was no space or opportunity for private conversations. Suddenly, according to reports, the meetings became quieter and more easily controlled by the leadership.

Another revealing alteration of the physical setting occurred in the Oregon State Capitol, to which an extensive wing was added in 1977. It contained six new committee hearing rooms, each equipped with ample audience seating. Soon after the wing was opened for use, public attendance at committee hearings significantly increased. One reason cited for this was that now there was plenty of room to sit down; committee rooms in the older part of the capitol were small and contained few chairs for the audience. According to observers of the Oregon state political scene, a general expansion of citizen interest and involvement in state government seemed to flow from the change in the physical environment.

The construction of the new statehouse in Florida seems to have set off more than one behavioral consequence. The Old Capitol, constructed in several stages beginning in 1845, had since the 1950s been a rabbit warren of small rooms and twisted, narrow hallways. The new statehouse, built just behind the old one between 1973 and 1977, is a massive complex of several interconnected structures whose interiors are large and clearly organized.

When the legislators left their meager old offices to move into the spacious new office buildings, they acquired unprecedented office space for both themselves and their staffs. Each senator and representative now had an office suite with room for personal aide and secretary. Soon the number of individual legislator staff began to grow, eventually exceeding that of committee staff, who previously predominated. This shift, some argue, led to a significant transfer of power away from the legislature's committee structure and into the hands of its general membership.

Another major change that resulted from opening the new Florida capitol was the creation of substantially more room for political interaction. In the Old Capitol, only a narrow passageway connected the House and Senate wings, and the back recesses of the wings were so confusing that few could navigate them. In the new capitol is a central area for bicameral interaction: the fourth-floor lobby. This space was originally meant to be closed to nonmembers, but following lobbyist agitation it was opened to the public. This created an immensely active senator–representative and legislator–lobbyist meeting ground, or "political commons," between the two chambers at floor level. Large closed-circuit-television monitors were set up in the lobby so the proceedings of each body could be easily followed by everyone present. An information desk for documents and messages was positioned along one wall. Since the main doors to the chambers empty into the lobby, lobbyists and reporters find it convenient to wait there so they can buttonhole members when they recess (Figure 8.3). The very creation of this space, and the subsequent decision regarding access to it, significantly affected the legislative process in Florida.

In North Carolina, a new capitol was not built, but the legislature left the State Capitol in 1963 for the new and much larger State Legislative Building. Persons around the North Carolina Senate and House who remember life in the old capitol recall many changes that were set in motion by the move. For example, the governor's office was no longer immediately accessible downstairs, which in the old building had permitted continual, informal negotiations over legislation. With the construction of the new capitol, the

Figure 8.3. Fourth-floor lobby of the Florida Capitol, located between the two legislative chambers. Legislators and lobbyists interact in the "political commons" when recesses are called.

governor was located some blocks away, inevitably making legislative–executive interaction more formalized.

Relations among members of the North Carolina legislature became more distant as well. In the State Capitol, the House and Senate had met in tiny, overcrowded chambers on the second floor. The members were on top of one another, and the seating was uncomfortably close. But camaraderie was high, and the high jinks that took place during and after sessions became legendary. In the State Legislative Building, the chambers were the ultimate in spaciousness and accommodation, as were the individual members' offices. Every committee had space for its own hearing room and staff. The legislative service agencies, too, had plenty of room, especially after a supplemental legislative building was added in 1990. But, say some who experienced both worlds, the old feelings of closeness and esprit de corps have disappeared, replaced by a sense of distance, impersonality, and alienation.

Removal to new and more spatious quarters can, however, have more positive consequences. Many state supreme courts have departed from the capitol. In Arizona, for example, a new state court building was constructed in 1990. This structure provided a new behavior setting for the state supreme court that, according to reports, augmented its institutional independence from the political branches that still sat in the statehouse. Located on the other side of Wesley Bolin Memorial Plaza from the capitol, the state court building, however, because of its size, cost, color, and expansiveness, earned the sobriquet "Taj Mahal Across the Mall" (Figure 8.4).

Indeed, the new courts building became something of a political football. Legislators and fiscal conservatives questioned its enormity and opulence. The Speaker of the House and president of the Senate checked to see if the offices of the justices would be larger than theirs. Environmental lobbies protested the use of mahogany in the decor because of the destruction of the Ama-

Figure 8.4. View toward downtown Phoenix from the Arizona State Capitol, with dome, dating from 1901, in the foreground. Across the plaza on the right is the Arizona State Courts Building, controversial for its cost.

zon rain forest. The justices were, however, able to get their building, and they claim that, as a result of having left the capitol, they feel less obliged to compromise their decisions in the direction of gubernatorial and legislative demands. Their generous fourth-floor office windows give them a beautiful view of the capitol and, politically, an ability to see it in perspective. Their feelings of autonomy are reinforced by a separate building security force, cleaning staff, and parking facility. To avoid blurring the constitutional separation of powers, the judges insisted that the state attorney general not be housed in their palace but in a separate law building.

THE LEGISLATIVE CHAMBER AS BEHAVIOR SETTING

The design of the legislative chamber, like that of the statehouse as a whole, affects behavior within it. The floor of the room frames, in a physical way, the ongoing proceedings of the bodies and the conduct of their members. While legislators no doubt see themselves as unhampered in their conduct, the physical setting conditions what transpires.

With respect to access to the floor, for example, two conditioning patterns obtain. One is to regard the entire floor of the room—on a wall-to-wall basis—as constituting "The Floor" in connection with the application of the formal rules on floor access. Typically, lobbyists and other outsiders are excluded from The Floor during sessions and, frequently, thirty minutes before and after. This means that such onlookers must retire to the upper galleries at such time. But if a balustrade or rail mounted on the floor surface sets off the legislators' desks on one or more sides, this opens the possibility of designating The Floor as consisting of only the area within that boundary. In this situation, lobbyists can observe what takes place from the room's periphery and even pass notes to members, producing a quite different social dynamic. An

Figure 8.5. Chamber of the Louisiana House of Representatives, Louisiana State Capitol, Baton Rouge. Since the balustrade defines the body's legal floor, nonmembers can observe the proceedings from the perimeter of the room, with lobbyists at the rear.

example of this arrangement is the Louisiana House (Figure 8.5).

Aspects of the material environment that condition access to the legislative process need not be limited to fixed feature design. In this age of information technology, ways other than physical presence are available to observe and "pass notes." In Louisiana, legislators at one time were also "watched" by the governor by means of a remote display of voting tallies located in his office.[7] In most statehouses, for many years, a live audio signal of debates was distributed throughout the building by means of "squawk" boxes. More recently, this is accomplished by television monitors, and in a few states the signal is fed to public or commercial broadcasters.

The installation of electronic equipment at members' desks has opened up a succession of new issues regarding floor access. Some years ago, telephones were installed in desks in some states. This had two consequences: the sight of mem-

bers talking on the phone during sessions gave the impression that they were not paying attention to the proceedings; and the perception grew that telephones provided a new opportunity for lobbyist access and pressure, although the phones were often fixed so only outbound calls could be made. Nowadays, lobbyists carry cellular phones and use them continually in and out of the building. To prevent the reality or appearance of lobbyists phoning down instructions from the gallery, many states forbid the use of cellular phones inside chambers.

More recently, computers have been installed at some legislators' desks. They were initially designed to give members access to data banks containing information on current legislation under consideration. The development of portable laptop computers has opened up the possibility of sending and receiving e-mail as well, not to mention obtaining data from the Internet. To the extent that modem connections are introduced into the legislative chamber, instant and unregulated computerized access to and from the floor seems inevitable. Even if laptops are outlawed in the galleries, with live audio and television transmission of proceedings outside the chambers, there is nothing to prevent the electronic transmission of instructions to legislators on the floor at any time.

Returning to issues of floor design, the extent of furniture congestion can affect members' activity. Although space around desks generally facilitates mobility in the American legislative chamber, a lack of room between rows can result from crowding created by a body's membership growth due to constitutional amendments. This restricts mobility for all, except those sitting in the front or back or on aisles. If only one center aisle cuts through the arc of desks, the problem is exacerbated. In a chamber of that design, desks at the periphery of the two blocks of seating are favored by the leadership and others seeking high levels of influence. Within the seating blocks, it

is difficult to get out except during recesses. The lower house in Maine is a good example of such a tight chamber (Figure 8.6).

Physical arrangements can also affect the ability of members to speak on the floor. While in some of the smaller state senates no microphones are used, in most chambers all remarks are amplified by the public-address system. Hence in order to speak, one must have access to a microphone. Furthermore, the microphone must be activated, which is often accomplished by means of a control panel at the disposal of the presiding officer on the rostrum.

Two patterns of placing microphones on the floor are used, each with its own behavioral implications. One is to give each member an individual instrument at his or her desk, mounted on an arm or a gooseneck or possibly attached to a long cord (see Figure 8.6). The other is to make microphones available on only certain lecterns located around the floor that everyone uses (see Figure 7.3). With desk microphones, a more

Figure 8.6. Floor of the chamber of the Maine House of Representatives. Tight quarters such as these restrict members' mobility, thereby affecting the dynamics of the legislative process.

organic or evolving style of debate is facilitated, since there is no need to line up physically behind a common lectern to take one's turn. Speakers are more likely to talk without initially planning to do so, and there is less reason to follow the order of those wishing to speak in a mechanical manner.[8]

Dependence on common lecterns not only reduces the flexibility of debate, but also influences its structure. In bodies where members of the two parties sit on opposite sides of a central aisle and a lectern-microphone is given to each side, a back-and-forth duel between opposing partisan positions is encouraged. Even when the center aisle does not segregate the parties, the existence of two separated microphones can set into motion a dichotomous interaction. In Alabama, it is the practice for the "pro" position to be taken at the lectern nearest the desk of its chief supporter, with the second lectern going by default to the "con" forces. In the Texas House, it was the custom for many years to have the initiators of a measure speak at a lectern in the front well, with the opponents relegated to a lectern located 100 feet to the rear of the chamber.[9]

The American state legislature differs from most parliaments of the world in assigning each member his or her own desk. Interesting behavioral implications flow from how these desks are assigned.

In most chambers, it is the practice to select certain desks for permanent use by the majority floor leader and the minority leader, regardless of who holds the position. Two desk sites are popular for these individuals: the front row, which affords easy access to the rostrum while being visible to the rank-and-file behind, and the back row, from which the leader's flock can be easily observed and movement around the room is relatively unobtrusive. The first position has embedded within it a strategy of working closely with the presiding officer while showing the party faithful what to do. The second is good for leaders who wish to observe what their followers are doing and be able to move about inconspicuously in order to instruct them or conduct negotiations. As for other members of the leadership team,

assistant floor leaders or whips tend to sit at the sides of the room, and committee chairs, on the aisle. Each location is helpful for mobility. Speakers of the House often retain a desk on the floor, even though they are usually presiding on the rostrum.

With respect to desk assignments of members in general, in a few bodies seating is tied to geography through the electoral system. In both chambers in Florida and the Senates of Connecticut, New Hampshire, and Vermont, desks are permanently assigned by district number to the person representing that district. This system makes the concept of holding a "seat" meaningful from the standpoints of both district representation and a concrete piece of furniture.

In at least thirty-three of the ninety-nine bodies, the assignment of desks occurs within a framework of partisan segregation.[10] In these chambers, the center aisle divides, at least roughly, the two political parties. In about two-thirds of these bodies, Democrats sit on the presider's right and Republicans on the presider's left, with the remainder the other way around. The Democrats-right, Republicans-left pattern is also employed by the United States House and Senate. If one considers Democrats to be politically to the left of Republicans, this practice is the opposite of European parliamentary seating, where the Communists are generally on the presider's far left and the monarchists and neo-Nazis or other extreme conservatives on the far right.[11]

One of the consequences of partisan seating is that if the aisle is placed at the midpoint of the arc of desks, and if all majority members are seated on one side, the majority side of the room automatically becomes more crowded with desks than the minority. If the majority's margin is not great, this does not create a problem. If it is large, there may not be room for all the majority desks on that side, making adjustments necessary. In Delaware, where the approach is a national exception, the desks are shifted as the proportion demands, making the pathway of the main aisle changeable and irregular. In other words, the assumption is dropped that semifixed furniture cannot be moved (Figure 8.7).

The more common solution to the problem of an overloaded majority side is to seat some members of the majority party with the minority. This is done in the United States Congress by placing some of the majority's surplus in the rear of the minority's area. On Capitol Hill, this back zone is called the Cherokee Strip, a reference to a thin band of land along the northern edge of Cherokee territory that was ceded to the United States in 1866. A similar arrangement has been made in the New York Assembly, but its version of the Cherokee Strip is at the front of the chamber. Two schools of thought obtain on who should occupy such alien territory. In the Michigan House, freshmen are sent there because the area is deemed less desirable, but in the Washington legislature, veterans are assigned to such seats, with the reasoning that they are less susceptible to partisan contamination.

In most party-segregated chambers, each party is permanently assigned to its side. Thus after a turnover election, the side from which the cur-

rent leadership speaks is simply switched. In a minority of chambers (at least eight), the majority party, whether Democrat or Republican, is permanently assigned to one side.[12] This more structured approach requires that after a turnover election, a complete change of desks is needed —and sometimes offices as well.

In approximately two-thirds of the legislative chambers, seating is not formally structured, a finding that will surprise many political scientists. Members may seek assignments freely, depending on the availability of vacancies made possible by departures or reassignments, with the caveat that more senior members have first choice. In this situation, various idiosyncratic factors come into play, such as whether one likes to be on an aisle for mobility or in the middle of the action. Smokers often migrate to the rear of the chamber so they can easily get out for a cigarette. The location of personal friends is also a factor; indeed, some years ago, Samuel C. Patterson found that in state legislative bodies seating pro-

Figure 8.7. Chamber of the Delaware House of Representatives, as seen from the rostrum. Members' desks are moved from left to right as the ratio between minority (left) and majority (right) requires.

pinquity correlates quite well with both friend-
ship and voting behavior.[13]

Less known is the way legislators gather in
certain seating clusters on the basis of such factors as ethnicity, faction, and geography. In the
Missouri House, for example, at the time of my
fieldwork, African-Americans sat together in
the center of the majority side. In the Michigan House, a "Polish Corridor" crossed the back
of the chamber. In the Rhode Island House, dissident Democrats grouped behind opposition
Republicans. In the Texas Senate, a coalition of
Republicans, conservative Democrats, and members representing rural interests sat on the presider's left, while urban liberals sat on the right.
In the Texas House, the back middle of the north
side of the chamber was known as Red Square,
an appellation derived from its many "liberals" (in
the Texas sense of the word) from Dallas and
Houston.

Clustering can also occur by geographic area
without reference to ideology. Delegations from

certain counties, metropolitan areas, or rural regions tend to sit together. The pattern occurs in
the lower houses of several states, but not in the
upper houses, a difference presumably due to
their less finely divided electoral districts. Examples are the Louisville delegation in the Kentucky House, the northern urban Democrats in
the Virginia House, and rural members in both
states. In 1995, the floor of the Tennessee House
was composed of five geographic "islands": the
Nashville, Memphis, and Chattanooga areas,
rural-central, and rural-west.

PHYSICAL SETTINGS OF INFLUENCE

The exercise of power is at the heart of politics,
yet it is an elusive and intangible subject. Power
usually is place bound, however, and the statehouse is the most important, although not the
only, place for wielding power in state government. Even within the largely open statehouse,

Figure 8.8. Decorative fireplace at the rear of the chamber of the New York Senate. Designed by Stanford
White, the fireplace, with its 13- by 6-foot opening, is used for private conversations on the floor.

there are private and public settings of influence. In the first, activities are carried on individually, informally, and out of the glare of publicity. In the second, activities of a coordinated and externally observed nature are undertaken.

The legislative chamber is the key political space of the statehouse. It is the locale of not only the formal legislative process, but much behind-the-scenes politicking. Serious political discussion and deal making can take place most anywhere in the room, yet in many legislative chambers one or two physical domains become traditional locales for the quiet, informal, but often very tense exertions of pressure that precede legislative compromise.

In the New York Senate, for instance, a favorite site for engaging in private politics is in the huge Stanford White fireplaces located in the back corners of the room (Figure 8.8). In the Mississippi Senate, a small table located in an alcove at the side of the chamber serves this purpose, and in the Ohio Senate, a side room known as the Smoker did the same. A glass-enclosed room called the Bubble is used in the Florida House. In the New Jersey General Assembly, small rooms

or loggia line one side of the chamber. They are equipped with an audio signal and glass windows facing the room; considered legally part of The Floor, they are the site of much strenuous private debate (see Figure 5.1).

Other locales for private political conversation are hideaways and small service facilities located away from the chambers in the capitol. In the West Virginia State Capitol, a hidden, windowless room just off the rotunda known as the Crow's Nest is used for making deals as well as enjoying a glass of good whiskey (Room 274, whose outside door reads "House Bookkeeping and Payroll"). In the Pennsylvania State Capitol Building, male senators are accustomed to talking over pending legislation while getting a haircut in the building's barbershop. Mississippi senators buttonhole one another at their chamber shoeshine stand. Its chief porter, John Henry Davis, was for decades an invaluable source of advice on upcoming votes (Figure 8.9).

Restaurants and coffee shops in the statehouse are also sites for informal politicking, and since they are open to the public, they are a magnet for lobbyists as well. Much statehouse business is

Figure 8.9. Shoeshine stand adjacent to the chamber of the Mississippi Senate. (Shown: Chief Porter John Henry Davis, whose advice was sought for years on pending bills and who retired in 1993.)

transacted over morning coffee and lunch. If conversations are sensitive, restricted dining rooms are usually available. Food and politics are a convenient mix in the basement cafeterias in the Oregon and West Virginia State Capitols and the ground-floor cafeteria in the Iowa State Capitol, situated at the bottom of the rotunda.

Even the lowly snack bar has a political function. Before the restoration of the Texas State Capitol, one of the main locales of insider conversation in Austin was the Linoleum Club, a snack bar named after its type of flooring. Chicken's is a popular lunch counter on the ground floor of the Virginia State Capitol, operated for a half century by the generous and outspoken Lonis Oliff; statehouse habitués of every kind continue to convene there daily to grab a bite and exchange gossip.[14] In the Colorado State Capitol, the ground-floor snack bar, affectionally known as the Roachateria, has a "Power Table" where the state's lead politicians take morning coffee and welcome others to join.

Moving outside the building, in most state capitals nearby bars and restaurants serve as frequent hangouts for legislators, lobbyists, reporters, and political junkies. Examples around the country are Barnaby's in Albany, the Golden Dome in Boston, Lorenzo's in Trenton, Clyde and Costello's in Tallahassee, Flamingo Joe's in Atlanta, the Profile in Denver, and Ike and Jonesy's in Indianapolis. These political watering holes are witness to a mix of spontaneous and planned political interaction, particularly after the workday and into the evening hours. They are the venue for the persuasion, promising, pressuring, negotiation, and deal making that become the basis for state public policy.

As might be expected, the role of each watering hole is a bit unique. The Galleria in Columbus is where for years the Speaker of the Ohio House held court each afternoon beginning at 5:00 P.M., at which time he was approached by all lobbyists attempting to get a bill killed and all administrators seeking to get a budget passed. Until an FBI sting operation sent several lawmakers to jail, Flynn's in Frankfort was known as the headquarters for small-time bribery in

Kentucky government. Doe's Eat Place in Little Rock was a favorite haunt of Bill and Hillary Clinton in their Arkansas years. Frank Fat's in Sacramento is a Chinese restaurant where major compromises in California lawmaking are traditionally worked out; in one legendary case, the details of a medical-malpractice bill were written out on a table napkin and signed on the spot by the affected parties.

The political hotel was at one time an important venue of private power brokering. This institution has a long history in American politics, extending back to the taverns frequented by Revolutionaries in colonial capitals and the boarding houses resided in by members of Congress in the early years of the republic.[15] Especially in rural states, where legislatures met for only a few weeks a year, lawmakers booked rooms in a local hotel for the duration of the session. Lobbyists moved in as well, creating a veritable informal capitol. Examples of such classic political hotels were the Adams in Phoenix, the Cornhusker in Lincoln, the Eagle in Concord, the Exchange in Montgomery, the Jay Hawke in Topeka, the Marion in Little Rock, the St. Charles in Pierre, and the St. Nicholas in Springfield.

This venerable institution's time has now passed, however. With modern roads and cars, most legislators can commute home at night, and those who must remain in the capitol are less interested in carousing than in guarding their personal privacy. Lawmakers who cannot commute tend to take up residence in separate hotels, rent rooms in private homes, or invest in local condominiums.

In public, rather than private, settings of influence, group-sponsored activities and functions openly take place, as distinct from the private efforts of individuals to wield influence. Right in the legislative chamber itself, quite tangible evidence of the presence of lobbyists may be evident right on legislators' desks. In a number of states, interest groups publish the body's legislative directory, pocket manual, and membership roster. The sponsoring organization's name is prominently displayed inside the document, along with the identity of its lobbyists and leaders.

In Missouri, Montana, Rhode Island, Tennessee, and Wyoming, these publications are produced by petroleum associations, electrical cooperatives, and telephone companies. In North Dakota, the motor carriers' association puts out a pictorial directory of the legislature, the grocers' association provides it with desk pads, and the bankers' association gives out a seating chart. To make the chairs of the North Carolina House more comfortable, a mattress company provides seat cushions and a chiropractor association, back cushions. Legislative desks in Indiana receive blotters from the trucking association, scratch pads from the health-care industry, and vases of roses from the state right-to-life lobby.

During the initial legislative phase of the statehouse year, the lobbyists themselves are, of course, much in evidence. In some capitols, it is obligatory for them to wear name badges as part of a color-coded system of identification. Hundreds of lobbyists and lawyers representing every trade association, interest group, and advocacy movement conceivable swarm in and around the chambers. Although the term "lobbyist" suggests that a specific room is used for buttonholing, group representatives are found everywhere in the capitol, including members' offices and along all political venturis of the building.

As working professionals, lobbyists have special needs of their own within the statehouse. They must be able to receive messages from clients, have documents duplicated, and use telephones if they do not possess cellular phones. As a consequence, many statehouses have created de facto lobbyist service centers that provide phone banks and a message desk. In the Wyoming State Capitol, a staffed, basement facility is called the Wyoming Capitol Club. In the Washington Legislative Building, the service desk adjacent to the rotunda is known as Ulcer Gulch. As might be expected, the lobbyists serve multiple clients, know one another, and have much in common as colleagues. While awaiting a chance to do business, they tend to gather in favored hallway niches or on corridor benches to chat and exchange information.

Another public venue of political interaction and influence is around the catered buffet meal. This is a well-established institution during session time. For most of each day, a heavily laden buffet table is set up in the corridors of the second or third floor. Interest groups rotate in sponsoring these meals, and their identity is known to capitol insiders. Variations on this practice include the provision of coffee and doughnuts in areas behind the chambers (South Dakota), catered lunches where legislators and lobbyists dine privately together (Utah), and beer-and-pizza sessions outside the Speaker's office on Friday afternoon (Rhode Island).

Free food and drink are also made regularly available around town. Legislators receive multiple invitations to breakfasts, luncheons, and, most important, evening receptions called hospitality suites. The last are sponsored by trade associations or other groups and often are held in local hotels. The ambitious legislator plans to visit several hospitality suites each night in order to be seen, make contacts, and save out-of-pocket expenses for food and drink.

Hospitality suites are also held at buildings that associations or corporations maintain in the capital city. One of the advantages of entertaining at this site is that members are brought on to the interest group's own turf, so to speak. Food and drink are so plentiful at the headquarters of the poultry association in Little Rock, a couple of blocks from the capitol, that the phrase "the chicken house is open" is universally understood to mean that the organization's bars are serving.

In a broader sense, such local facilities maintained by associations are useful because they place lobbyists near the capitol and give the groups an overt, obvious presence at the physical center of state government. I conducted an analysis of the list of registered lobbyists in Nebraska and determined that nearly 400 were located within five blocks of the statehouse. In a remarkable number of states, the state education association maintains its headquarters building right across the street from the statehouse. This location not only offers convenience to the corridors of power for the group's lobbyists, but is a continuing reminder to politicians of the association's political clout.

A final category of public social activity that takes place in and around the state capital is the many "big events" of the session that are attended by all the leading players in state government. It is at these functions that the statehouse community comes together most visibly, strengthening the personal bonds that underlie the networks of influence. Two of the most important annual events are the opening-day ceremony of the legislative session and the closing sine die ceremony. Another is the annual softball or basketball game between House and Senate or between lobbyists and the press corps. Other popular activities are campaign fund-raising banquets, prayer breakfasts, social dances, talent contests, and a variety of roasts and skits. In Arkansas, an elaborate "Farkleberry Follies" is put on by the press corps each year, complete with tuneful parodies and a lampooning newspaper. An event unique to Massachusetts is the "Long Walk," a practice begun in 1884 whereby a governor departing from office walks from his office through the building to the front door, running a gauntlet that combines well-wishers and hecklers.

PHYSICAL SETTINGS FOR IMAGE FORMATION

Several physical settings exist in and around the statehouse for the purpose of influencing mass opinion. Some of these areas are not different from those described for statehouse insiders. Capitol correspondents assigned to the statehouse frequent the same corridors, snack bars, buffet tables, watering holes, and social events that bring together politicians and lobbyists. Generally speaking, print journalists circulate freely in the building, although while on the legislative floor during sessions, they are usually required to stay at press tables and not conduct interviews. In most statehouses, reporters are given rent-free office space by the state. Typically, the capitol press room is dingy, crowded, and isolated in basements or back areas, giving rise to much good-natured humor about the fourth

estate's second-class citizenship (Figure 8.10). But when journalists are offered fancier quarters outside the statehouse, they usually decline, much preferring to be close to the action.

Electronic journalism increasingly dominates coverage of the statehouse scene. Television images emanating from the capitol are, in fact, the single most important shaper of public opinion regarding state government and politics, especially outside the capital. The physical settings for the creation of television images from the statehouse fall into three categories. One is the legislative chamber, where television cameras are often running. The same is true in committee hearing rooms (see Figure 7.17). A second point of origin for television images is the staged news conference, held in the capitol or a nearby building. Depending on the phase of the political cycle, governors, legislators, candidates, and activists are eager to secure footage for the evening news programs that feature themselves against a backdrop of a capitol interior (Figure 8.11). In some states, such as Delaware, Louisiana, New York, and Pennsylvania, executive officials have at their disposal permanent stage sets or media studios for this purpose.

The third setting for television images of state government is the building as a whole. Many news anchors and capitol commentators speak in front of a large photograph of the capitol dome. The statehouse's real dome is the backdrop for many televised interviews conducted on the grounds. Its image is also shown in the opening moments of some television news programs, not to mention on the mastheads of statewide newspapers. Because of this enormous mass exposure, the building's familiar facade is presented for cultural absorption to a degree infinitely greater than seeing it in person could ever generate.

Since the capitol and its dome are so well known and so symbolic as a center of state life, they are an enormously attractive backdrop for the politics of mass demonstration. The portico, with its traditional temple front acting as proscenium arch, is a popular setting for political theater. Groups of every imaginable type appear

Figure 8.10. Legislative Press Room in the New York State Capitol. Typically, press rooms are cramped, messy, and difficult to find, but reporters like to be near the statehouse action.

Figure 8.11. Televised news conference in front of the entrance to the Florida House of Representatives. Members of the Black Caucus are criticizing a pending congressional redistricting plan.

in front of the capitol, almost daily in good weather. The principal strategy of demonstrators is to draw sufficient supporters to create a crowd-filled television picture and then make news-worthy statements before the cameras (Figure 8.12). Sponsors may attempt to incorporate visually compelling actions into the event in order to draw more media attention. In Wisconsin, for example, farm groups have poured milk on the capitol steps to protest low dairy prices. A modern-day Boston Tea Party was celebrated against antismoking laws by Kentucky tobacco farmers who dumped bales of leaf into the Kentucky River. In Massachusetts, in behalf of AIDS research, members of ACT-UP have thrown condoms filled with red dye on the sidewalk. Sometimes mass entertainment is used to swell the crowd; on the first anniversary of the Three Mile Island incident, an antinuclear demonstration outside the east wing of the Pennsylvania State Capitol Building featured Pete Seeger and

Linda Ronstadt, drawing more than 5,000 people.

Political theater can also be performed inside the building. In Rhode Island, when a financial crisis closed credit unions, frustrated depositors dumped boxes of petitions on the floor of the Speaker's office. In Colorado, a group of physically disabled protesters banged tin cups on the rotunda's brasswork to push for greater state spending. In Montana, Native American groups have conducted war dances in the rotunda, and in Washington, schoolteachers have stamped on legislators' desks to reinforce their demands. Single outraged individuals also publicize their causes, by such techniques as camping on the grounds, carrying signs in the corridors, or sitting for days at the governor's door (Figure 8.13).

The reaction of state officials to these demonstrations is usually to accept them as part of the contemporary political scene and live with them as well as possible. Everyone realizes that precipitous action would simply invite a spate of bad

Figure 8.12. Rally of Americorps Volunteers on the front steps of the Tennessee State Capitol. Statehouses are the scene of daily rallies and demonstrations, which are governed by permits issued by the states.

publicity. The goals of security officials and facilities managers are not to suppress or counter demonstrators' oratory, but to avoid bloodshed and minimize destruction of state property or interference with state business. Hence demonstrations outside the statehouse are generally not stopped unless violence is likely, as when opposing hate groups confront each other. On these occasions, the usual strategy is to separate the groups rather than disperse them. Demonstrations inside the building and even occupations of it are, within reason, tolerated as well. A favorite way to deal with them is to take passive action, such as cutting off water and air-conditioning.

Political demonstrations are so common and predictable at statehouses that written rules are developed to deal with them on a routine basis. Most states have instituted a permit system, which endorses the holding of public events, provided that sponsors agree in writing not to nail posters on trees or carry placards mounted on sticks inside the capitol. Alcohol and drug use are also prohibited. In return for compliance to the rules, the authorities assist demonstrators in such ways as lending them sound equipment, laying electric cables, diverting traffic around the site, and cleaning up afterward. In two states, North Dakota and Rhode Island, speaker platforms are permanently built into the steps of state buildings (Figure 8.14); whether or not used, they stand as silent symbols of free speech in a democratic society.

SOCIAL MEANINGS OF STATEHOUSE SETTINGS

Viewed through the perspective of the behavioral lens, two general design features of the interior of the statehouse have important behavioral consequences. One is the common and intersecting pathways of pedestrian movement. They facilitate spontaneous interaction across all sectors of state political life. The other is wide-angle sight lines created by large volumetric spaces. The balconies and platforms within these spaces are used by political figures to display themselves and conduct political reconnaisance. These two global background features of the capitol's circulation space have such deep effects on state governance that their presence can easily go unnoticed.

Figure 8.13. Michael Wade, a protester in behalf of rights of divorced parents, outside the office of the governor of Massachusetts. He had been there for eleven days when photographed.

Figure 8.14. Speaker podium built into the front steps of the Rhode Island State House for use during outdoor public meetings. A similar podium exists at Liberty Memorial Building in Bismarck, North Dakota.

Changes in physical setting that resulted from moves in or from the statehouse or additions made to the statehouse influenced behavior. The behavioral consequences included making a caucus more controllable by convening it in a smaller room; encouraging public participation in lawmaking by enlarging committee rooms; increasing the influence of personal staff by augmenting its office domain; fostering interaction among members of the two houses and with lobbyists by creating an interaction floor; decreasing the intimacy and camaraderie of political life by transfering the legislature to large, separate, and impersonal quarters; and increasing the self-image of political independence awakened in the supreme court by moving it out of the statehouse and into an imposing building of its own.

Conduct in the statehouse can also be affected by design variables operating within the legislative chamber itself. Balustrades demarcating the floor permit lobbyists to surround legislators in session. Bringing television cameras and laptop computers into the chamber expands access to the legislative process. Causing chamber floors to become crowded by desks and absence of aisles limits mobility and hence member participation. Selecting desk rather than lectern microphones influences the character of debate. Providing two separated lecterns fosters two-sided debate.

The chamber's horizontal layout of rostrum, aisles, and desks, while expressing a nonhierarchical and deliberative legislative process, also frames conduct in the room in certain compelling ways. In order to lead, party floor leaders sit in either the very front or the very back of the room. Legislative bodies that emphasize partisanship in their proceedings segregate the parties on either side of the center aisle. Large majorities and turnover elections can lead to crossing that aisle. Members seeking colleagues with similar interests, like-minded viewpoints, or common constituencies pick neighboring desks. The physical setting is not mere background, but an active element in conduct in the chamber.

The concept of physical setting is, as well, a useful tool for exploring the subtleties and pervasiveness of political influence. The places for influence are numerous and include private and public venues, many of which come alive only during legislative sessions. Private settings consist of isolated portions of the chamber suitable for conducting sensitive negotiation, hideaways in the capitol appropriate for persuasion, eateries in the statehouse that permit informal conversation and networking, and watering holes outside the capitol where less inhibited entertainment is a medium of influence.

Public venues of influence consist of donated publications and artifacts that remind legislators of their corporate friends, corridors and meeting places near the chamber that are frequented by lobbyists, buffet tables within the statehouse that are sponsored by interest groups, hospitality receptions thrown in hotels and nearby association headquarters, and annual social events that bring the statehouse community together for comradeship and connection.

Insights into conduct-related meanings of statehouse settings are discerned by means of the societal lens as well. A number of measures are taken to ensure the capitol's security, but they tend to be unobtrusive rather than obvious in order to avoid giving state government the image of operating from a bunker. Citizens of all kinds, from sophisticated lobbyists to earnest activists to strangely dressed demonstrators to legions of schoolchildren, freely enter and move about. Depending on the time of year, the atmosphere shifts from political madhouse to tourist site to locale for press conferences to auditorium for holiday concerts. The relative openness of the building matches the openness of its grounds, reinforcing the portrayal of open, democratic government.

It is important to realize that the way the statehouse is presented to the general public is not limited to the citizen's direct experience. In the age of television and the Internet much—perhaps most—of the public's experience with government is indirect, filtered through electronically transmitted pictures and information. Politicians use the electronic media to project their personas and shape public opinion. Government officials rely on them to communicate policy, and political activists seek as much media attention as possible for their causes.

As a large, architecturally impressive, and widely known public symbol, the statehouse lends itself to these mass-communication efforts. Its dome and portico, in particular, are perfect visual backdrops for much of society's political activity. Hence the capitol's familiar images of authority and governance carry far beyond its physical surroundings. The symbolic meaning of the building, whether intimidating or attracting, permeates the society.

The Statehouse Socially Interpreted

Recalling that fine day in July 1898 in St. Paul when the cornerstone of the Minnesota State Capitol was laid, what have we since learned about the American statehouse? Let us endeavor to bring together the contentions, discoveries, and interpretations of this study.

THE EVOLUTION OF A BUILDING TYPE

The fifty state capitols, while, of course, individual in many ways, can be described and analyzed as more than an aggregate of fifty different structures. The statehouse is a type of building with certain largely common characteristics: an elevated, prominent site, often on the banks of a river; a surrounding of open, parklike grounds that sets the structure off and gives it a softened image; a contradictory configuration of low, horizontal cross with rounded dome pointing skyward from the center; a temple front with grand steps, columns, and triangular pediment; and a lavishly decorated interior central space, or rotunda, located just below the dome. While some statehouses depart in particularistic ways from this model, our analysis addresses the building's conceptual ideal type in the Weberian sense of that term.

As Henry-Russell Hitchcock and William Seale have pointed out, this building form is distinctly American.[1] Yet it has deep roots in antiquity and the Renaissance. The basic features of cruciform ground plan and temple front are derived from concepts of classical and neoclassic architecture and became standard elements in the vocabulary of eighteenth- and nineteenth-century European public architecture. These borrowed forms were first used to construct early government temples inland from the Atlantic seaboard. Later, under the influence of a relatively small group of Establishment statehouse architects, the form was brought to maturity in two great waves of construction following the Civil War. The United States Capitol was evolving at the same time and in the same directions, under the same architectural influences. Although statehouses built in the late twentieth century rejected the European mold, even they exhibit signs of the past, such as cruciform plan, central rotunda, and nascent dome.

In short, these buildings, while constituting an original New World convergence of architectural elements, are essentially Old World in origin. The building type is domestic in manufacture, yet foreign in its roots and spirit, making it an arresting feature of this country's physical and political landscape. Just as Jefferson's great capitol on the James River startled eighteenth century observers with its towering "antique appearance," the statehouses that grace the skylines of our state capitals appear arcanely old-fashioned against the modern commercial structures that surround them.

This is part of their charm, perhaps. It is certainly one reason why state capitols are known by resident and visitor alike as a notable landmark and tourist attraction. While today their physical size is less overwhelming than at the time they were built, these structures are powerful symbols on the American scene, in part because of their uniqueness. The tall columned entrances, pointed dome, cavernous yet empty rotunda, lavish stairways and corridors, and ornately furnished reception rooms become identified with something "special": the authority and presence of state government.

The American statehouse has, as we have seen, evolved over time. The first change was that the original functional concept of the statehouse, providing a headquarters for all of state government, had to be abandoned. As public responsibilities grew during the Progressive era, state governments outgrew their capitols. One by one, the administrative departments of government had to depart for other quarters. Over time, these departmental buildings came to form the basis of a state office complex that took on a life of its own as a small politico-administrative city surrounding the original statehouse.

The second major change was that the core constitutional bodies of government had to expand outside the statehouse as well. The first to leave was the supreme court, which looked elsewhere for its own temple of justice, itself an imposing structure. The same occurred in the nation's capital in the 1930s. Later, when legislatures became less part-time and more professionalized, they required more office space, which called for separate buildings. The bodies themselves continued to meet in their original chambers, except in a handful of states where new legislative buildings were constructed. The governor, too, needed more space to house a growing staff, and separate buildings gradually were erected to accommodate central control bureaucracies associated with the chief executive. Many of the other elected constitutional officers of state government also had to relocate outside the capitol, at least to house the operations they supervised. The statehouse thus became largely a space for the official public meetings of the two houses of the legislature and its committees, plus the headquarters offices of executive officials. It continued, however, to remain the symbolic heart of state government. This structure of "antique appearance" never relinquished its position as the target of attention for all players in the political game who seek opportunities for influence and fame.

The third great change to occur as the centennial of the traditional American state capitol has passed is its transformation from a handsome physical "house" for state government to an electronic image. Because of television, the building has become a stage set for mass political persuasion and visual manipulation. The articulated dome, a quaint architectural device borrowed from Renaissance churches, has long been the central symbol for state government, appearing in cartoons and on newspaper mastheads across the land. Now the dome and temple front serve as backdrops for television cameras. Activists and advocates of every stripe use the building as a tool for media coverage of demonstrations held before it. Thus this old-fashioned, European-style edifice is not only the permanent home of representative government and the separation of powers in America, but also the focus for the emerging, American-style form of electronic politics.

SOCIAL MEANINGS OF THE BUILDING

Three "lenses," or ways of looking at and interpreting public architecture—the expressive, behavioral, and societal—illuminate the social meanings of the American statehouse. Each of these perspectives converges on the building type from a different angle (Table 9.1).

The expressive lens examines architecture and design to derive from the physical structure the ideas and values that have been embedded in it by its builders, whether consciously or unconsciously. Hence the view of this lens tends to be retrospective, although the statehouse, like most buildings, is continually altered and adapted over time. Attempts to analyze what is being expressed are, of course, matters of interpretation, not a simple "reading" of an architectural text. Such meanings are subjective, hidden, and culture-bound, and thus must be stated with caution. My strategy in approaching this task has been to coordinate the ideas of others with my own from a theoretical standpoint and, with respect to empirical study, develop relatively conservative judgments from a vast quantity of field data.

That the American statehouse still stands and is in good working order indicates that it is a building that has become revered for its own sake. Unlike most other "out-of-date" structures, it was not torn down when it could no longer accommodate a growing state govern-

Table 9.1
SOCIAL MEANINGS

Summary of principal insights (by chapter)	Expressive	Behavioral	Societal
Building type (chapter 2)	Openness of grounds implies open government; later nearby structures trace contextual changes	Site and dome identify building; portico clarifies entrance; rotunda helps circulation	Statehouse size, facade, and dome assert power, but parklike setting is disarming
Creation (chapter 3)	Position of governors declined, then improved; that of legislatures rose and bicameral equity emerged	State government made more intimate because all parts brought under one roof	Symbols of antiquity assert authority; reminders of the past form bonds
Construction (chapter 4)	Emphasis on historic preservation shows how statehouse is valued for its own sake	Magnitude and wide ramifications of construction projects affected many lives	Act of construction became a public founding ritual of state governance
Objects (chapter 5)	Reflect reverence for traumas of war and European culture; show interest in local and American history		War symbols underscore state power; high culture fosters awe; homey objects promote pride
Space (chapter 6)	Dominance of building by legislature; continued rise of governor; departure of supreme court	Overcrowding in statehouse creates space rivalries among its institutions	"The state" is presented as not unified but a pluralist set of institutions
Interiors (chapter 7)	Legislature depicted as egalitarian; supreme court, as authoritarian; governor, as populist and nonpartisan	Design of legislative chamber encourages close interaction among legislators	Public given spaces in ceremonial rooms, but they send ambivalent messages
Conduct (chapter 8)		Movement and sightline patterns and physical changes shape political dynamics	Unobtrusive security measures prevent alienation; TV images amplify symbolic impact

ment. Rather, millions of taxpayer dollars are spent on its preservation and restoration.

Another major expressive theme centers on the openness of the unfenced statehouse grounds, not to mention that of the building itself. Foreign visitors who are used to barricaded parliaments and palaces in less democratic countries marvel at this degree of accessibility, and, indeed, this feature serves as a physical analogy to the relatively transparent nature of American government.

Neither the grounds nor the interior public spaces are left empty, however, but are filled with numerous artifacts and items of decoration. Many of them commemorate the wars in which the state's sons and daughters fought and died. This reverence for the traumas of war, which intensifies the sacred aura of the capitol, is accompanied by displays and decor that reiterate the building's ancestral link to European tastes in art and architecture. Yet presentations of American culture also are found in abundance, particularly those that celebrate the state's own history and heroes.

The organization and use of space within the building comment on a perceived status, relative to one another, of the three branches of state government. Following the Revolutionary War, the position of governor was reviled by the builders of the new republics because of its association with the Crown's representatives under colonialism. This feeling was expressed by initial inferior treatment of that official from a space standpoint. In later times, as executive power became more enhanced and accepted in state government, the chief executive ascended to higher stories of the building and received more favored decor. Yet the governor's office never became the center of attention in the capitol. Its relatively modest and nonpartisan decor portrays an official who wishes to maintain common bonds with the people, not overawe them.

The legislative branch, by contrast, was, from the very beginning, given the most honored architectural treatment in the statehouse. The representatives of the people are and always have been the building's stars. They convene on an upper floor that is presented as a Palladian *piano nobile*, attained by a grand public stair. Its decor is the finest in the building, both inside and on the external facade.

The legislature's two chambers are equal in weight and opposed in diametric fashion, mirroring the constitutional intent of making bicameralism an integral part of the separation of powers. The design and furniture arrangement of the chambers depict bodies composed of equally important, independent-minded representatives who are prepared to talk face-to-face in an interactive manner about the affairs of state, rather than simply listen to speeches and vote as instructed.

Other physical spaces associated with the legislative chamber are also expressive. The tendency to provide designated committee rooms to only appropriations and revenue committees speaks to the power of the purse in making public policy. The presence or absence of special caucus rooms for the political parties points to the degree to which the legislative culture is partisan in character. The existence of ornate private member lounges and the initial absence of women's rest rooms adjacent to the chambers reveal residual elitist and sexist streaks in the legislative culture.

The third branch of government, the judiciary, was for many decades represented by the supreme court chamber. It was variously located in the capitol, but always in honored space. Unlike the egalitarian legislative chamber, the supreme court's room stresses the authority of the judges and the subordinate roles of litigants and observers. The court's bench embodies judicial authority in a remarkably full sense, and when the state constitution is amended to alter the size of the court, the carpenters must be called in to modify its furniture.

The behavioral lens examines the ways that the physical setting shapes or conditions the conduct of people. Because of the dynamic, mutually interactive, and subjective nature of the built environment, its influence on people is complex and unpredictable. I am certainly not an environmental determinist and do not offer my interpretations in this light. Rather, my conclusions stem from the reports of others, plus my own observations and speculative comment.

Insights from this perspective point in various directions. One is the behavioral implications of the building type's primary characteristics. That the statehouse is placed on a hill or river bluff and is topped by a dome makes it easy to identify and find. The classic temple front marks the front door unmistakably. The rotunda within, at the intersection of all circulation streams, helps to create an efficient social mixing bowl and effective arena for political display and reconnaisance.

The magnitude of the capitol has, over time, shaped people's experiences. Building it with nineteenth-century technology was a giant under-taking. The lives of many ambitious politicians and architects, profit-seeking landowners and suppliers, and work-hungry artisans and day laborers were profoundly affected. Originally, the structure was designed to be big enough to house all of state government, which for a time created within its walls a degree of face-to-face interaction and informality across all branches of government that has been lost. As state government grew with time and departments and offices left for the growing state capitol complex around the building, the behavior consequences were considerable. What was originally a gemeinschaft relationship of intimate community under one roof became a gesellschaft social model of distant communication between separated buildings.[2] While fax, e-mail, and the telephone help to make up for this physical separation, the informal intimacy of a century ago cannot be re-created.

The design of the ceremonial rooms of the statehouse conditions behavior within them. The American legislative chamber, because of its flat topography, shallow arc seating, and capacity for mobility, is by world standards extraordinarily facilitative of low-key debate and private negotiation. If the room and its features were instead cavernous, isolating, and oppositional, we would, I am convinced, have a quite different legislative tradition in this country.

Our confidence in the capacity of space to affect behavior in the statehouse is not derived from theory alone. A number of physical changes were reported by observers to have set off important behavioral consequences. These consequences were often unintended, such as the deterioration of legislative community that followed a move out of a small capitol and the high level of interaction that emerged when a new legislative floor was opened up as a commons.

Legislative conduct is importantly influenced by physical space. If legislators have their offices near rather than far from the chamber floor, they have more opportunities for influence there. If the floor's legal boundaries are formed by a balustrade rather than its walls, legislators can be closely watched by lobbyists rather than observed from afar in the gallery. If microphones are positioned on each legislator's desk rather than at a few common floor lecterns, the nature of debate becomes more fluid.

The arc of desks, seemingly unmovable as semifixed features of the room, acts as a physical framework in which individual desk selection is worked out. The determination of seating assignments has an enormous effect on the chamber's social climate. Partisan seating separated by a center aisle, used in only a minority of states, creates one mood. Another results from seating by geographic district. With the most common method, unsegregated seating where choice is (subject to seniority considerations) individual, ad hoc social friendships and ideological clusters form.

Finally, space is an important medium for understanding the exercise of political influence in and around the statehouse. While the official venues of policymaking are the chamber floor and committee hearing rooms, numerous unofficial places are seized for attempts at persuasion, negotiation, and deal making. Near the chambers themselves, side rooms, fireplaces, and shoeshine stands are used. Elsewhere in the capitol, snack bars, cafeterias, and semisecret hideaways are deployed. Well-healed interest groups put on buffet luncheons in the corridors and sponsor hospitality suites in hotels. Also, found in every state capital, are the favored downtown watering holes in which after-hours business is transacted.

The societal lens draws attention to the effects of the statehouse on the public at large. Citizens do not notice the capitol's detailed embedded expressions or subtle behavioral effects, but they do experience the structure as a whole, in important ways. Often these are symbolic ways, which by their very nature are ambiguous and subjective.

A major school of thought within architectural theory entertains innate suspicions about the intent and capacity of monumental public buildings to overwhelm the populace. Yet other commentators see possibilities also for the ability of public architecture to foster community spirit, create collective identity, and maintain links with the past.

Certainly, the capitol's great size, stone facade, and identification with government and history are capable of inspiring awe, if not intimidation. The long process of constructing the statehouse, often consuming many decades, may, indeed, be thought of as a kind of founding ritual for the state, achieving in physical form its fulfillment as a part of the federal union. The construction project's long duration, consuming struggles, and highly public nature would, then, in line with this interpretation, secure a sacrosanct status for its physical product.

The most defining feature of the capitol, the dome, may be viewed symbolically as a great archetypal head of authority. The temple front below the dome, imprinted on the Western mind as a universal sign of government power, was taken deliberately from classical antiquity to generate symbolic support for the new American republics. The facade's broad length and columned, bilateral symmetry impute an implicit order to the government regime housed within.

Upon entering the statehouse, citizens encounter a proliferation of authority symbols. Cannon, battle flags, and war memorials seem to consecrate state authority with the blood of war. Opulent reception rooms, giant murals, and sculpted pediments create an elegant domain much removed from the citizen's more humble world, creating what is perhaps an intimidating disjuncture. In the rotunda at the heart of the statehouse, the vast height, celestial ceiling, and suspended egg of creation cause the individual below to feel small and insignificant. The capitol is unmistakably an abode of sovereign authority; moreover, the hardness of the marble with which it is made suggests that this authority is indestructible.

Yet there is another side to the picture. The statehouse is placed in a serene park in the middle of what is often a small town. Security measures in and around the building are not overtly visible, and the visitor can walk in the front door without passing a metal detector. The rambling

ground plan of the building, with great wings pointing in opposite directions, suggests a government of multiple institutions rather than centralized power. Inside, the citizen is put at ease by displays of state flora, fauna, and culture, including such homey artifacts as race cars and stuffed bison. Outside are familiar icons, like the Statue of Liberty and Liberty Bell, along with such appealing oddities as an abandoned oil rig. If the visitor signs up with a tour group, the legends of history are heard—for example where Huey Long was shot and where Martin Luther King, Jr., led the civil rights movement.

Perhaps the most important part of the citizen's experience at the statehouse is the opportunity to wander freely through its public spaces. Famous politicians may be spotted and greeted while walking across the rotunda. The visitor's own senator or delegate may be encountered in the capitol cafeteria. It is possible to visit the governor's office, where the tourist is warmly greeted and asked to sign a guest book. If the legislature is in session, access to either House or Senate gallery is an easy matter.

Those members of the public who are political activists already know the capitol and will avoid the public tour. But they, too, find their movements within it relatively unencumbered. They know how to find the offices of key legislators and officials for the purpose of securing appointments. They make plans to testify before committees in behalf of their cause or group and, when doing so, stand before the same lectern used by everyone. If truly strong convictions are held, it is possible to hold a political rally in the statehouse or on the grounds; if a few basic rules are agreed to, state authorities not only grant permission to demonstrate, but assist in the arrangements.

In sum, the American statehouse is both an imposing and an open edifice. It represents sovereign power, on the one hand, and constitutional restraint on power, on the other. It is controlled by government officials, but crowded with ordinary people. It is a building whose symbolism is rooted in remote antiquity, yet still contains the

Figure 9.1. La Etoile du nord, inlaid in glass and brass in the center of the rotunda floor of the Minnesota State Capitol, is symbolically sacred, but for Minnesotans a curiosity.

symbols and history of one of the fifty American states.

The exact center of the building, the midpoint of the rotunda, is the sacred heart of state government, and the bas-relief or stained-glass seal embedded in the floor is roped off, as if untouchable. And yet this place is also a simple curiosity to show a child on the way to the capitol gift shop, a splendid contradiction in terms that the young Cass Gilbert may have had specifically in mind for the Minnesota State Capitol (Figure 9.1). As Hitchcock and Seale point out, the American statehouse is not just a temple—of the state—but a temple of democracy—of the people.

Notes

1. INTRODUCTION TO THE STATEHOUSE

1. Information on the ceremony and events surrounding the laying of the cornerstone is from Neil B. Thompson, *Minnesota's State Capitol: The Art and Politics of a Public Building* (St. Paul: Minnesota Historical Society, 1974), chaps. 1–4.

2. Thompson, *Minnesota's State Capitol*, 35.

3. Geoffrey Blodgett, "Cass Gilbert, Architect: Conservative at Bay," *Journal of American History* 72, no. 3 (1985): 615–36. For an overview of his work, see Sharon Irish, *Cass Gilbert, Architect: Modern Traditionalist* (New York: Monacelli Press, 1999).

4. Henry-Russell Hitchcock and William Seale, *Temples of Democracy: The State Capitols of the USA* (New York: Harcourt Brace Jovanovich, 1976), 3.

5. Hitchcock and Seale, *Temples of Democracy*.

6. Hitchcock and Seale, *Temples of Democracy*, 59–63.

7. Murray Edelman, *The Symbolic Uses of Politics* (Urbana: University of Illinois Press, 1964); Cortus T. Koehler, "City Council Chamber Design: The Impact of Interior Design upon the Meeting Process," *Journal of Environmental Systems* 10, no. 1 (1980): 53–79; J. A. Laponce, *Left and Right: The Topography of Political Perceptions* (Toronto: University of Toronto Press, 1981); Harold D. Lasswell, with Merritt B. Fox, *The Signature of Power* (New Brunswick, N.J.: Transaction Press, 1979); David Milne, "Architecture, Politics and the Public Realm," *Canadian Journal of Political and Social Theory* 5 (1981): 131–46; Lawrence J. Vale, *Architecture, Power, and National Identity* (New Haven, Conn.: Yale University Press, 1992); James Sterling Young, *The Washington Community, 1800–1828* (New York: Columbia University Press, 1966).

8. Charles T. Goodsell, *The Social Meaning of Civic Space: Studying Political Authority Through Architecture* (Lawrence: University Press of Kansas, 1988). Chapter 2 of this book includes an extensive multidisciplinary literature review pertinent to "civic space," by which I mean indoor, publicly accessible ceremonial spaces of government. Other of my pertinent publications are "The Architecture of Parliaments: Legislative Houses and Political Culture," *British Journal of Political Science* 18 (1988): 287–302; "Political Meanings of the American State Capitol," *Journal of Architecture and Planning Research* 10, no. 4 (1993): 294–30; "Public Architecture as Social Anchor in the Postmodern World," *Public Voices* 3, no. 1 (1997): 89–97; and "The Statehouse: Elite Space in Conflict," *Journal of Architectural and Planning Research* 15, no. 1 (1998): 6–23.

9. George Kubler, *The Religious Architecture of New Mexico During the Colonial Period* (1940; reprint, Albuquerque: University of New Mexico Press, 1990); Nikolaus Pevsner, *A History of Building Types* (Princeton, N.J.: Princeton University Press, 1976); Karen A. Franck and Lynda H. Schneekloth, eds., *Ordering Space: Types in Architecture and Design* (New York: Van Nostrand Reinhold, 1994).

10. For a brief description of Weber's idea, see S. M. Miller, *Max Weber* (New York: Crowell, 1963), 27–31.

11. Bill Kinser and Neil Kleinman, "History as Fiction," in *Drama in Life: The Uses of Communication in Society*, ed. James E. Combs and Michael W. Mansfield (New York: Hastings House, 1976), 402–3.

12. Amos Rapoport, "Sociocultural Aspects of Man–Environment Studies," in *Mutual Interaction of People and Their Built Environment: A Cross-Cultural Perspective*, ed. Amos Rapoport (The Hague: Mouton, 1976), 7–35, and *History and Precedent in Environmental Design* (New York: Plenum Press, 1990), 92. On the concepts of superiority of height and importance of centrality, see Laponce, *Left and Right*, and Barry Schwartz, *Vertical Classification: A Study in Structuralism and the Sociology of Knowledge* (Chicago: University of Chicago Press, 1981).

13. Juan Pablo Bonta, *Architecture and Its Interpretation: A Study of Expressive Systems in Architecture* (London: Lund Humphries, 1979).

14. Lasswell, *Signature of Power*.

15. Goodsell, *Social Meaning of Civic Space*.

16. This distinction is made by others. In a comment on physical artifacts in business firms, Pasquale Gagliardi says they serve as not only "remains and markers," but also "pathways of action" ("Artifacts as Pathways and Remains of Organizational Life," in *Symbols and Artifacts: Views of the Corporate Landscape*, ed. Pasquale Gagliardi [New York: Aldine de Gruyter, 1990], 3–4).

17. For the full text of Churchill's speech, see *Winston S. Churchill, His Complete Speeches, 1897–1963,* ed. Robert Rhodes James (New York: Chelsea House, 1974), 7: 6869–73. In 1924, Churchill expressed the same idea more generally before a group of British architects: "There is no doubt whatever about the influence of architecture and structure upon human character and action. We make our buildings and afterwards they make us. They regulate the course of our lives" (quoted in Stewart Brand, *How Buildings Learn: What Happens After They're Built* [London: Phoenix Illustrated, 1994], 3). Possibly in these comments, Churchill took inspiration from Montesquieu's words: "At the birth of societies, the rulers of republics establish institutions; and afterwards the institutions mold the rulers."

18. Roger C. Barker, *Ecological Psychology: Concepts and Methods for Studying the Environment of Human Behavior* (Stanford, Calif.: Stanford University Press, 1968). A revision and extension of this pioneer work is Phil Schoggen, *Behavior Settings* (Stanford, Calif.: Stanford University Press, 1989). Another relevant work is W. Bruce Walsh, Kenneth H. Craik, and Richard H. Price, eds., *Person–Environment Psychology: Models and Perspectives* (Hillsdale, N.J.: Erlbaum, 1992).

19. For a discussion of this literature, see Goodsell, *Social Meaning of Civic Space,* 44–47.

20. Amos Rapoport, *The Meaning of the Built Environment: A Nonverbal Communication Approach,* 2nd ed. (Tucson: University of Arizona Press, 1990), 80–86.

21. John W. Black, "The Effect of Room Characteristics upon Vocal Intensity and Rate," *Journal of the Acoustical Society of America* 22, no. 2 (1950): 174–76; Tom Porter and Byron Mikellides, *Color for Architecture* (New York: Van Nostrand Reinhold, 1976); Edward T. Hall, *The Hidden Dimension* (London: Bodley Head, 1969).

22. Koehler, "City Council Chamber Design."

23. For commentators on civic space who do not make the expressive–behavioral distinction, see Paul Goodman, *Utopian Essays and Practical Proposals* (New York: Random House, 1952), 168–72 (on parliamentary space), and John N. Hazard, "Furniture Arrangement as a Symbol of Judicial Roles," *ETC: A Review of General Semantics* 19 (1962): 181–88 (on courtroom space).

24. For an example of this approach, see Andrew Baum and Stuart Valins, *Architecture and Social Behavior: Psychological Studies of Social Density* (Hillsdale, N.J.: Erlbaum, 1977).

25. Grady Clay, *Close-Up: How to Read the American City* (New York: Praeger, 1973), 52–61.

26. See, for example, Mark Wigley, *The Architecture of Deconstruction: Derrida's Haunt* (Cambridge, Mass.: MIT Press, 1993); Henri Lefebvre, *The Production of Space* (Oxford: Blackwell, 1991); Bill Hillier and Julienne Hanson, *The Social Logic of Space* (Cambridge: Cambridge University Press, 1984); and Denis E. Cosgrove, *Social Formation and Symbolic Landscape* (London: Croom Helm, 1984). With respect to Bentham's Panopticon concept, the French philosopher Michel Foucault's commentary has been influential: "Panopticism," in *Rethinking Architecture,* ed. Neil Leach (London: Routledge, 1997), 356–67. Less known is Bentham's proposal for an observational spatial arrangement whereby citizens could watch government ministers in their offices, thereby making them accountable to public scrutiny: see *Works of Jeremy Bentham,* ed. John Bowring (New York: Russell and Russell, 1962), 9: 325–33.

27. David Milne, "Architecture, Politics and the Public Realm," *Canadian Journal of Political and Social Theory* 5 (1981): 131–46; Murray Edelman, *From Art to Politics: How Artistic Creations Shape Political Conceptions* (Chicago: University of Chicago Press, 1995), 76–77; Michael Parker Pearson and Colin Richards, *Architecture and Order: Approaches to Social Space* (London: Routledge, 1994); Ron Robin, *Enclaves of America: The Rhetoric of American Political Architecture Abroad, 1900–1965* (Princeton, N.J.: Princeton University Press, 1992).

28. Per Olof Berg and Kristian Kreiner, "Corporate Architecture: Turning Physical Settings into Symbolic Resources," in *Symbols and Artifacts: Views of the Corporate Landscape,* ed. Pasquale Gagliardi (New York: Aldine de Gruyter, 1990), 41–67.

29. James P. Armstrong, Jeffrey M. Coleman, Charles T. Goodsell, Danielle S. Hollar, and Keith A. Hutcheson, "Social Meanings of Public Architecture: A Victorian Elucidation," *Public Voices* 3, no. 3 (1998): 7–28.

30. Thomas A. Markus, *Buildings and Power: Freedom and Control in the Origin of Modern Building Types* (London: Routledge, 1993), 23, 25.

2. THE STATEHOUSE AS BUILDING TYPE

1. S. M. Miller, *Max Weber* (New York: Crowell, 1993), 27–31. For added discussion, see editor's introductions to H. H. Gerth and C. Wright Mills, eds., *From Max Weber* (New York:

Oxford University Press, 1946), 59–60, and Talcott Parsons, ed., *Max Weber* (New York: Free Press, 1947), 11–13.

2. Such a book has been written: Vaughn Cornish, *The Great Capitals: An Historical Geography* (London: Methuen, 1923). Cornish, a geographer, concluded that important national capitals on a worldwide basis tend to be located in one of three sites: natural storehouses near productive agricultural areas, crossways of communication, and points useful as strategic strongholds. A more recent volume on capitals (but not just their location) is John Taylor, Jean G. Lengellé, and Caroline Andrew, eds., *Capital Cities: International Perspectives* (Ottawa, Ont.: Carleton University Press, 1993).

3. States whose capitols are sited on a rise are Alabama, Arkansas, Colorado, Connecticut, Iowa, Maine, Maryland, Massachusetts, Michigan, Minnesota, Missouri, Montana, Rhode Island, South Dakota, Tennessee, Utah, Virginia, and Washington.

4. Coloradans take pride that one of their capitol's front steps is exactly 1 mile above sea level. When, using modern technology, a slight error was discovered in an earlier calculation, a brass medallion was added three steps higher to correct it.

5. States whose capitols are sited on the banks of rivers are Iowa, Louisiana, Maine, Missouri, New Jersey, New York, Pennsylvania, Virginia, and West Virginia. Those whose statehouses are close to, but not on, a river are Arkansas, California, Idaho, Indiana, Kentucky, Michigan, Minnesota, Mississippi, New Hampshire, New Mexico, North Dakota, Ohio, Oregon, Rhode Island, South Dakota, Tennessee, Texas, and Vermont. Statehouses near lakes, sounds, or oceans are those of Alaska, Hawaii, Maryland, Massachusetts, Washington, and Wisconsin.

6. Another aspect of siting is directionality. Interestingly, American statehouses disproportionately face south: twenty-one are oriented in that direction or nearly so. No other point on the compass is so honored, not even the traditionally sacred east (origin of the term "orientation"). Rather than suggest a deeply significant reason for this alignment, my guess is that it is due to the desire of architects to have their front facades in the sun as much as possible.

7. James Holston, "On Reading and Writing Streets: Political Discourse in Two Models of Brazilian Urbanism" (Department of Anthropology, Yale University, n.d., Manuscript); Michel Foucault, "Of Other Spaces: Utopias and Heterotopias," in *Rethinking Architecture,* ed. Neil Leach (London:

Routledge, 1997), 350–56; Denis E. Cosgrove, *Social Formation and Symbolic Landscape* (London: Croom Helm, 1984), pp. 192–96; Bill Hillier and Julienne Hanson, *The Social Logic of Space* (Cambridge: Cambridge University Press, 1984), 21–22; Lawrence J. Vale, *Architecture, Power and National Identity* (New Haven, Conn.: Yale University Press, 1992), 43.

8. By convention, the pavilion entrance between the east and south wings of the Wisconsin State Capitol is considered to be the front door, making a Main Street address logical. In another example of an unclear front, the Hawaii State Capitol faces in two opposing but equally meaningful directions, toward the mountains (*ma'uka*) and the sea (*ma'kai*).

9. On the *axis mundi* concept, see Mircea Eliade, *The Sacred and the Profane: The Nature of Religion* (New York: Harcourt, Brace & World, 1959).

10. Amos Rapoport, *The Meaning of the Built Environment: A Nonverbal Communication Approach,* 2nd ed. (Tucson: University of Arizona Press, 1990), 219–25.

11. E. Baldwin Smith, *The Dome: A Study in the History of Ideas* (Princeton, N.J.: Princeton University Press, 1950), 77–79.

12. William L. MacDonald, *The Architecture of the Roman Empire,* vol. 2, *An Urban Appraisal* (New Haven, Conn.: Yale University Press, 1986), 241.

13. MacDonald, *Architecture of the Roman Empire,* 2: 133–42, 167–68.

14. W. R. Lethaby, *Architecture, Mysticism and Myth* (1891; reprint, London: Architectural Press, 1974), 260–63.

15. For a book entirely devoted to such ceilings, see Eric Oxendorf and William Seale, *Domes of America* (San Francisco: Archetype Press, 1994).

16. States whose capitols incorporate all six elements are Alabama, Arizona, Arkansas, California, Colorado, Florida, Georgia, Idaho, Illinois, Indiana, Iowa, Kentucky, Maine, Maryland, Michigan, Mississippi, Missouri, Montana, New Jersey, North Carolina, Ohio, Pennsylvania, Rhode Island, South Carolina, South Dakota, Utah, Washington, West Virginia, Wisconsin, and Wyoming. States whose capitols are missing one or two elements are Connecticut, Louisiana, Massachusetts, Minnesota, Nebraska, Nevada, New Hampshire, Oklahoma, Oregon, Tennessee, Texas, Vermont, and Virginia.

17. Certain wings of the Florida Old Capitol were torn down in the late 1970s, but the oldest parts of the building were kept and restored.

3. THE CREATION OF
THE AMERICAN STATEHOUSE

1. J. K. Shishkin, *The Palace of the Governors* (Santa Fe: Museum of New Mexico, 1972).

2. George W. Hodgkins, "Naming the Capitol and the Capital," *Records of the Columbia Historical Society* 60–62 (1960–62): 39–43.

3. For the floor plans, see Marcus Whiffen, *The Public Buildings of Williamsburg: Colonial Capital of Virginia* (Williamsburg: Colonial Williamsburg Foundation, 1968), 44–45.

4. Pamela Scott, *Temple of Liberty: Building the Capitol for a New Nation* (New York: Oxford University Press, 1995), 22–23.

5. Sara B. Chase, "A Brief Survey of the Architectural History of the Old State House, Boston, Massachusetts," *Old-Time New England* 68, nos. 3–4 (1978). [Reprinted as brochure by Bostonian Society, n.d.]

6. Patrick T. Conley, Robert Owen Jones, and William McKenzie Woodward, *The State Houses of Rhode Island: An Architectural and Historical Legacy* (Providence: Rhode Island Historical Society and Rhode Island Historic Preservation Commission, 1988), 8–13, 23–41.

7. William H. Pierson, Jr., *American Buildings and Their Architects: The Colonial and Neoclassical Styles* (New York: Anchor Books, 1976), 105–8; Henry-Russell Hitchcock and William Seale, *Temples of Democracy: The State Capitols of the USA* (New York: Harcourt Brace Jovanovich, 1976), 9–13.

8. *The Pennsylvania Capitol: A Documentary History* (Harrisburg: Heritage Studies for Pennsylvania Capitol Preservation Committee, 1987), 3:1–7.

9. An argument can be made that the New Jersey State House is oldest, on the grounds that one of its present wall fragments, buried deep within the existing structure, dates from 1792. Yet even so, the Maryland State House was initially occupied in 1779 while unfinished, making it the oldest existing site of state governance in the country.

10. John W. Reps, *Tidewater Towns: City Planning in Colonial Virginia and Maryland* (Williamsburg: Colonial Williamsburg Foundation, 1972).

11. For the details of its construction, see Morris L. Radoff, *The State House at Annapolis* (Annapolis, Md.: Hall of Records Commission, 1972), and Hitchcock and Seale, *Temples of Democracy*, 17–26.

12. Scott, *Temple of Liberty*, 46.

13. Sara B. Hanan and Edward C. Popenfuse, *The Maryland State House, Annapolis* (Maryland Commis-sion on Artistic Property of the State Archives and Hall of Records Commission, 1984); Maryland Heritage Committee, *Bicentennial Celebrations* [brochure], 1984.

14. John M. Bryan, *Creating the South Carolina State House* (Columbia: University of South Carolina Press, 1999), 6–9.

15. James Hoban's authorship of the first South Carolina State House is questioned by Hitchcock and Seale, *Temples of Democracy*, 50–51.

16. *The Delaware State House: A Preservation Report* (Dover: Department of State, Division of Historical and Cultural Affairs, 1976).

17. Newton C. Brainard, *The Hartford State House of 1796* (Hartford: Connecticut Historical Society, 1964); Joan W. Friedland and Wilson H. Faude, *Birthplace of Democracy* (Chester, Conn.: Globe Pequot Press, 1979); Hitchcock and Seale, *Temples of Democracy*, 37–38. Space analysis is based on drawings from the Historical American Building Survey (1934), Library of Congress, Washington, D.C.

18. Fiske Kimball, *The Capitol of Virginia* (Richmond: Virginia State Library and Archives, 1989), 40–44, 52–59.

19. Benjamin Latrobe's sketches are reproduced in Kimball, *Capitol of Virginia*, 52, 55, 59; William Smith, quoted in Reps, *Tidewater Towns*, 275.

20. The Pennsylvania State Capitol designed by A. Stephen Hills combined for the first time the basic clustering of symbols—dome, rotunda, portico, and balanced houses—outlined by Hitchcock and Seale, *Temples of Democracy*, 59–63. On the relationship of the Pennsylvania State Capitol (1810–1821) and the Missouri State Capitol (1837), both designed by Hills, see Marian M. Ohman, *The History of Missouri Capitols* (Columbia: University of Missouri Extension Division, 1982), 22–26.

21. Bayless E. Hardin, "The Capitols of Kentucky," *Register of the Kentucky State Historical Society* 43, no. 144 (1945), 173–90; Hitchcock and Seale, *Temples of Democracy*, 77–83.

22. Hitchcock and Seale, *Temples of Democracy*, 110–20.

23. Quoted in "Capitol of Indiana," in *Library of American History* (Cincinnati: James, n.d.), 130, a transcribed copy of which was examined at the Indiana State Library, Indianapolis; Hitchcock and Seale, *Temples of Democracy*, 86–89.

24. Hitchcock and Seale, *Temples of Democracy*, 93–96.

25. Hitchcock and Seale, *Temples of Democracy*, 90–93.

26. John Ray Skates, *Mississippi's Old Capitol: Biography of a Building* (Jackson: Mississippi Department of Archives and History, 1990).

27. Sunderine Temple and Wayne C. Temple, *Illinois' Fifth Capitol* (Springfield, Ill.: Phillips Brothers, 1988); Hitchcock and Seale, *Temples of Democracy,* 107–10.

28. McDowell Lee, H. E. Sterkx, and Benjamin B. Williams, *The Role of the Senate in Alabama History* (Troy, Ala.: Troy State University Press, 1978), chap. 3; Hitchcock and Seale, *Temples of Democracy,* 125–26.

4. THE CONSTRUCTION OF THE AMERICAN STATEHOUSE

1. Daniel Robbins, *The Vermont State House: A History and Guide* (Montpelier: Vermont Council on the Arts and Vermont State House Preservation Committee, 1980), 16, 18, 31.

2. Earle G. Shettleworth, Jr., and Frank A. Beard, *The Maine State House: A Brief History and Guide* (Augusta: Maine Historic Preservation Commission, 1981).

3. Stan Cohen and Richard Andre, *Capitols of West Virginia: A Pictorial History* (Charleston, W.Va.: Pictorial Histories, 1989), 9–16.

4. Harold H. Schuler, *A Bridge Apart: History of Early Pierre and Fort Pierre* (Pierre, S.D.: State Publishing, 1987), 104–16.

5. Ellen Roy Jolly and James Calhoun, *The Louisiana Capitol* (Gretna, La.: Pelican, 1980), 9–13, 117–24.

6. Mike Fowler and Jack Maguire, *The Capitol Story: Statehouse in Texas* (Austin, Tex.: Eakin Press, 1988), 36–38.

7. Stanley H. Cravens, "Capitals and Capitols in Early Wisconsin," in *State of Wisconsin Blue Book, 1983–1984* (Madison: Wisconsin Legislative Reference Bureau, 1983), 103–68, esp. 111–33.

8. Margaret Coel, *The Pride of Our People: The Colorado State Capitol* (Denver: Colorado General Assembly, 1992), 4–6.

9. Henry F. Wade, *Ship of State on a Sea of Oil* (Oklahoma City: Oklahoma Historical Society, 1975), 11.

10. Henry-Russell Hitchcock and William Seale, *Temples of Democracy: The State Capitols of the USA* (New York: Harcourt Brace Jovanovich, 1976), 174.

11. For biographies of these two important figures, see Paul Goeldner, "The Designing Architect: Elijah E. Myers," *Southwestern Historical Quarterly* 22 (1988): 271–87, and Geoffrey Blodgett, "Cass Gilbert, Architect," *Journal of American History* 72, no. 3 (1985): 615–36. A more extended treatment of Gilbert's work is Sharon Irish, *Cass Gilbert, Architect: Modern Traditionalist* (New York: Monacelli Press, 1999).

12. Eldon Hauck, *American Capitols: An Encyclopedia of the State, National and Territorial Capital Edifices of the United States* (Jefferson, N.C.: McFarland, 1991), 78. For a discussion of technical aspects of the construction of the Nebraska State Capitol, see Charles F. Fowler, *Building a Landmark: The Capitol of Nebraska* (Lincoln: Nebraska State Building Division, 1981).

13. Frank Lloyd Wright, *An Autobiography* (New York: Horizon, 1977), 75–76.

14. Norman J. Johnston, *Washington's Audacious State Capitol and Its Builders* (Seattle: University of Washington Press, 1988), 19.

15. Christie Zimmerman Fant, *The State House of South Carolina: An Illustrated Historic Guide* (Columbia, S.C.: Bryan, 1970), 14–32.

16. Robert W. Richmond, "Kansas Builds a Capitol," *Kansas Historical Quarterly* 38, no. 3 (1972): 249–67.

17. Fowler and Maguire, *Capitol Story,* 53–63.

18. John Alfred Treon, "The Building of the Arkansas State Capitol, 1899–1915" (M.A. thesis, University of Arkansas, 1964), esp. 57–59, 138, 149.

19. Wayne C. Temple, "Alfred Henry Piquenard: Architect of Illinois' Sixth Capitol," in *Capitol Centennial Papers,* ed. Mark W. Sorensen and John Daly (Springfield: Illinois State Archives, 1988), 18.

20. James R. McDonald, *Historic Structure Report: Montana State Capitol Building* (Helena: State of Montana Architectural and Engineering Office, 1981), 16–19.

21. *The Pennsylvania Capitol: A Documentary History* (Harrisburg: Heritage Studies for Pennsylvania Capitol Preservation Committee, 1987), 3:chap. 6.

22. Some states—for example, Arkansas, Louisiana, South Carolina, and South Dakota—still use convict labor around the statehouse, mainly for grounds maintenance.

5. OBJECTS AND DECOR AT THE STATEHOUSE

1. David C. R. Heisser, *South Carolina's Mace and Its Heritage* (Columbia: South Carolina House of Representatives, 1991).

2. Neil B. Thompson, *Minnesota's State Capitol: The Art and Politics of a Public Building* (St. Paul: Minnesota Historical Society, 1974), 19–20, 36. On Cass Gilbert's sentiments on the place of art in capitols, see Cass Gilbert to Governor George W. Donaghey of Arkansas, 12 October 1914, in George W. Donaghey, *Building a State Capitol* (Little Rock, Ark.: Parke-Harper, 1937), 368–76.

3. Daniel Robbins, *The Vermont State House: A History and Guide* (Montpelier: Vermont Council on the Arts and Vermont State House Preservation Committee, 1980), 125.

4. Thompson, *Minnesota's State Capitol,* 65–70.

5. *The Pennsylvania Capitol: A Documentary History* (Harrisburg: Heritage Studies for Pennsylvania Capitol Preservation Committee, 1987), 3:334–35, 340–67.

6. Nancy Edelman, *The Thomas Hart Benton Murals in the Missouri State Capitol* (Jefferson City: Missouri State Council on the Arts, 1975).

7. Carolyn Kompelien, Kendra Dillard, and Sherri Gebret Fuller, *Attention to Detail: 1905 Furniture of the Minnesota State Capitol* (St. Paul: Minnesota Historical Society, 1989); Wade Alan Lawrence, "Herter Brothers and the Furniture of the Minnesota State Capitol, 1903–1905" (M.A. thesis, University of Delaware, 1987).

8. Showing how conscious of types of wood the builders of the statehouses could be, the doors to the Senate chamber in the South Dakota State Capitol are a sandwich of mahogany on the interior side and oak on the exterior side, presumably to recognize the chamber's superiority to the rotunda corridors outside.

9. *Memorials and Art in and Around the Colorado State Capitol* (Denver: Colorado Legislative Council, 1992); *Art in the Massachusetts State House* (Boston: Massachusetts Art Commission, 1986).

10. Such displays are not extinct. In the California State Capitol, by statutory requirement, cases of Civil War memorabilia stand in a public hallway. The Oklahoma Historical Society maintains, at least in name, two Civil War museums, one for each side of the conflict.

11. The "40/8" is a reference to the stated capacity of these cars: forty men or eight horses. They can also be seen on the grounds of the Montana State Capitol and the Louisiana Old State Capitol.

6. THE ORGANIZATION OF STATEHOUSE SPACE

1. First- and second-wave capitols that have the executive offices below the legislative chambers are those of Arkansas, Colorado, Connecticut, Georgia, Idaho, Illinois, Indiana, Iowa, Kansas, Kentucky, Michigan, Minnesota, Missouri, Montana, New York, Oklahoma, Rhode Island, South Dakota, Texas, Utah, Washington, West Virginia, Wisconsin, and Wyoming.

2. An anecdote from St. Paul reveals how important height differentials can become between branches. Leaders of the Minnesota legislature became alarmed when in the 1980s the justices of the supreme court proposed to build a new supreme court building up Wabasha Hill from the statehouse, near Cass Gilbert Park. The legislators considered this uphill location to be unacceptable because the justices would be at an elevation higher than that of the members of the House and Senate. The legislators did agree, however, to allow the building of the Minnesota Historical Society, down the hill, to be renovated for the supreme court, which was done.

3. An exception is in the Alabama State House (not the State Capitol), where the House chamber is on the fifth floor and the Senate is on the seventh. The reason for the anomaly is that the building was converted from a former highway department building and did not lend itself to the traditional arrangement.

4. A larger community is also formed, of course, by being in the same building. While this seems obvious, it should be remembered that not all bicameral systems are brought together this way. Using France as an example, the Chamber of Deputies meets in the Palais Bourbon, while the Senate convenes in the Palais du Luxembourg, some distance away.

5. The Senate chambers are decorated in varieties of red in a disproportionate number of capitols. This also happens to be the dominant color of the British House of Lords. The lower houses are not predominantly any color, including the green of the House of Commons.

6. States whose capitols have legislative chambers in diametric opposition are Arizona, Arkansas, California, Delaware, Florida, Georgia, Hawaii, Idaho, Illinois, Indiana, Iowa, Kansas, Kentucky, Louisiana, Maine, Maryland, Michigan, Mississippi, Missouri, Nevada, New Jersey, New Mexico, New York, North Carolina, North Dakota, Ohio, Oklahoma, Oregon, Pennsylvania, Rhode Island, South Carolina, South Dakota, Texas, Virginia, Washington, West Virginia, and Wyoming.

7. States whose capitols have legislative chambers perpendicular to each other are Colorado, Minnesota, Utah, and Wisconsin.

8. Sine die, Latin for "without day," refers to adjournment without having fixed a day for reconvening; that is, the session is permanently concluded.

9. States whose capitols have the governor's office below the legislative chambers are Alabama, Arkansas, California, Colorado, Connecticut, Florida, Georgia, Idaho, Illinois, Indiana, Iowa, Kansas, Kentucky, Maine, Michigan, Minnesota, Missouri, Montana, Nevada, New York, North Carolina, Ohio, Oklahoma, Rhode Island, South Carolina, South Dakota, Tennessee, Texas, Utah, Washington, West Virginia, Wisconsin, and Wyoming.

10. States whose capitols have the governor's office and the legislative chambers on the same floor are Nebraska, Massachusetts, Michigan, Mississippi, New Hampshire, New Jersey, North Dakota, Oregon, Pennsylvania, Rhode Island, and Texas. States whose capitols have the governor's office above the legislative chambers are Alaska, Hawaii, Louisiana, Maryland, New Mexico, and Virginia. The governor has offices on the top floor of a nearby office tower in Arizona, Delaware, and Vermont . This is true in Ohio as well, but the governor of Ohio also maintains an active office on the ground floor of the statehouse.

11. States whose capitols have the governor's office in the front are Alabama (State Capitol), Arkansas, Colorado, Connecticut, Georgia, Idaho, Illinois, Indiana, Iowa, Massachusetts, Michigan, Minnesota, Mississippi, Montana, Nebraska, Nevada (State Capitol), New York, North Dakota, Ohio, Oklahoma, Pennsylvania, Rhode Island, South Dakota, Tennessee, Texas, Utah, Virginia, Washington, West Virginia, and Wyoming.

12. Massachusetts also has an Executive Council, but its role is nominal and not policymaking, as in New Hampshire. In West Virginia, the Board of Public Works, composed of elected state constitutional officers, shares executive power with the governor. In neither Massachusetts nor West Virginia does this body have its own chamber, unlike the Executive Council in New Hampshire.

13. The eight states without an executive mansion are Arizona, California, Massachusetts, Michigan, Oregon, Rhode Island, Vermont, and Wyoming.

14. Thus achieving, to an extent, what the supreme court could not. See note 2 above.

15. Julia E. Robinson, "The Role of the Independent Political Executive in State Governance," *Public Administration Review* 58 (1998): 119–28.

16. In an unusual arrangement, the secretary of state of Georgia serves as Keeper of the State Capitol Building and Grounds. It is a coincidence that the office has been occupied by two indefatigable wheelchair-bound extroverts: Ben W. Fortson (1955–1971) and Max Cleland (1983–1996), both of whom took great pride in maintaining the building and showing it to visitors. Cleland was elected to the United States Senate in 1996.

7. FEATURES OF STATEHOUSE INTERIORS

1. Charles T. Goodsell, *The Social Meaning of Civic Space: Studying Political Authority through Architecture* (Lawrence: University Press of Kansas, 1988), 10–13.

2. Edward T. Hall, *The Hidden Dimension* (London: Bodley Head, 1969), chap. 9; Fred I. Steele, "Problem Solving in the Spatial Environment," in *EDRA* 1 (1970): 127–36.

3. The unicameral system was adopted after the Nebraska State Capitol was completed, so it has two legislative chambers. The "Uni" meets in the room intended for the House, while the chamber constructed for the Senate is used for hearings or as an auditorium. Contrary to the logic of this choice, members of the unicameral body refer to themselves as senators.

4. Examples are the proscription against "adjourning to any other place" without the consent of the other house and the prescription that the "doors of each house" shall remain open except in certain circumstances.

5. The lower house is called the General Assembly in New Jersey and simply the Assembly in California, Nevada, New York, and Wisconsin. In Maryland, Virginia, and West Virginia, the name of the lower legislative body is the House of Delegates.

6. Different arrangements of parliamentary seating are discussed in Paul Goodman, *Utopian Essays and Practical Proposals* (New York: Random House, 1952), 168–72.

7. Round council chambers containing a circular dais are quite common in city halls built after 1960, as discussed in Goodsell, *Social Meaning of Civic Space*, 160–66.

8. Even though the statehouses of California and Louisiana had courtrooms for their supreme courts, the justices never used them, preferring quarters in San Francisco and New Orleans, rather than Sacramento and Baton Rouge. The exceptions where capitols never had supreme court chambers are Alaska, Delaware, Hawaii, Maine, Massachusetts, Michigan,

Missouri, New Mexico, Oregon, Rhode Island, and Washington.

9. William J. Metzger, the artisan who had carved the original Iowa Supreme Court bench in the 1880s, was called back in 1928 to add room for additional justices. Visitors find it difficult to distinguish the original and the later parts of Metzger's handiwork.

10. In comparing the furniture of Anglo-American and European courtrooms, John N. Hazard found that European prosecutors often sit in the judge's zone, contrary to the prosecution–defense equivalence seen in Great Britain and the United States: see "Furniture Arrangement as a Symbol of Judicial Roles," *ETC: A Review of General Semantics* 19 (1962): 181–88.

11. An associated point is that the money committees sometimes garner space of unusual quality, such as the top floor of the Alaska State Capitol, a spacious room below the Senate chamber in the Maine State House, and a paneled chamber near the entrance hallway in the New Hampshire State House. When supreme courts leave the statehouse and thereby abandon their courtrooms, they often fall into the hands of a money committee, as in Georgia, Idaho, and Michigan.

12. When I visited the office of the governor of Indiana, displayed on the chief executive's desk were footballs and basketballs from professional teams in the Hoosier State. It was explained that game balls from colleges and universities could not be accepted, since it would spawn cries of gubernatorial favoritism.

13. For a description of space-assignment politics in California, see Robert Sommer and Katherine Steiner, "Office Politics in a State Legislature," *Environment and Behavior* 20, no. 5 (1988): 550–75.

14. An unusually stark architectural manifestation of the significance of legislative staff obtains in New Jersey. The rear door of a recent staff addition to the building has been placed off center, creating a long facade distance on one side of the door and a short one on the other. Offices for the majority party are accommodated on the roomier side of the entrance, while minority offices are confined to the smaller side.

15. National Legislative Services and Security Association, *Services and Security Inside the Legislature* (Denver: National Conference of State Legislatures, 1992), 32, 43.

16. Michael McQueen, "Overcoming Tradition," *Washington Post,* 9 December 1986. It might be noted that a woman's restroom was being built just off the floor of the United States Senate in 1992.

Helen Dewar, "11 Incoming Senators Discover School's In," *Washington Post,* 10 November 1992.

8. CONDUCT IN AND AROUND THE STATEHOUSE

1. Roger G. Barker, *Ecological Psychology: Concepts and Methods for Studying the Environment of Human Behavior* (Stanford, Calif.: Stanford University Press, 1968). See also Phil Schoggen, *Behavior Settings* (Stanford, Calif.: Stanford University Press, 1989).

2. The only exception is the Nevada Legislative Building, where a black marble barrier was placed in front of the main door after a car rammed it.

3. According to a survey conducted in 1991, fourteen states were using walk-through or hand-held metal detectors within the statehouse, as reported in National Legislative Services and Security Association, *Services and Security Inside the Legislature* (Denver: National Conference of State Legislatures, 1992), 45. Yet in eight years of field research for this book, I passed through airport-style security systems at the main entrances of the capitols of only three states: Georgia, New York, and South Carolina.

4. These patterns were first brought to my attention by Peter Lucas of the Office of the Speaker for the Massachusetts House and M. Allen McCree, at the time Architect of the Texas Capitol.

5. Grady Clay, *Close-Up: How to Read the American City* (New York: Praeger, 1973), 52–61.

6. Just to the south of the New York State Capitol, a venturi-type crossroads exists in an underground space, beneath Rockefeller Plaza. Known as "Times Square," it is the common point from which is reached the statehouse to the north, the legislative office building to the west, the justice building to the east, and the buildings on the plaza to the south.

7. It should be kept in mind that when the Louisiana State Capitol was opened, Huey Long was no longer governor, but he still ruled the state with an iron hand.

8. Desk debate can also be sequenced, using an electronic system that allows members to signal when they want to speak by pushing a desk-mounted button.

9. The front lectern was removed from the Texas House during the restoration undertaken in 1995, but the back one remains.

10. States whose House chambers are divided by party are Connecticut, Indiana, Minnesota, and Missouri. States whose Senate chambers are divided by party are Iowa, New Jersey, and Tennessee.

States in which both chambers are divided by party are Colorado, Delaware, Idaho, Michigan, New Mexico, New York, Oklahoma, Pennsylvania, South Dakota, Utah, Virginia, Washington, and West Virginia. There are tendencies for partisan seating, although it is not obligatory, in the House chambers of California, New Hampshire, and Vermont, and the Senate chamber in North Dakota. It should be kept in mind that my data do not cover all fifty states.

11. For an extensive discussion of partisan seating arrangements, see J. A. Laponce, *Left and Right: The Topography of Political Perceptions* (Toronto: University of Toronto Press, 1981).

12. States whose House chambers are divided permanently by party are Indiana and Missouri. States in which both chambers are divided permanently by party are Delaware, Maine, and New York.

13. Samuel C. Patterson, "Party Opposition in the Legislature: The Ecology of Legislative Institutionalization," *Polity* 4 (1972): 344–66.

14. Lonis Oliff was formally honored by the Virginia Senate for her decades of service on March 13, 1992. Just four days later, she died of a stroke. A worthy successor carries on the tradition: Linda S. Bannister.

15. On the role of boarding houses in early Washington, D.C., see James Sterling Young, *The Washington Community, 1800–1828* (New York: Columbia University Press, 1966), 98–106.

9. THE STATEHOUSE SOCIALLY INTERPRETED

1. Henry-Russell Hitchcock and William Seale, *Temples of Democracy: The State Capitols of the USA* (New York: Harcourt Brace Jovanovich, 1976), 3.

2. This distinction originated with the nineteenth-century German sociologist Ferdinand Julius Tonnies. See *Community and Society* (*Gemeinschaft und Gesellschaft*), ed. Charles P. Loomis (East Lansing: Michigan State University Press, 1957).

Bibliography

Aylesworth, Thomas G. *State Capitals*. New York: Smith, 1990.

Daniel, Jean Houston, and Price Daniel. *Executive Mansions and Capitols of America*. New York: Putnam, 1969.

The Democratic Icon: A Look at State Capitol Restoration. Washington, D.C.: American Institute of Architects, 1994.

Ehlert, Willis J. *America's Heritage: Capitols of the United States*, 3rd ed. Madison, Wis.: State House Publishing, 1994.

Goodsell, Charles T. "Political Meanings of the American State Capitol." *Journal of Architectural and Planning Research* 10, no. 4 (1993): 294–307.

Goodsell, Charles T. "The Statehouse: Elite Space in Conflict." *Journal of Architectural and Planning Research* 15, no. 1 (1998): 6–23.

Hauck, Eldon. *American Capitols: An Encyclopedia of the State, National and Territorial Capital Edifices of the United States*. Jefferson, N.C.: McFarland, 1991.

Hitchcock, Henry-Russell, and William Seale. *Temples of Democracy: The State Capitols of the U.S.A.* New York: Harcourt Brace Jovanovich, 1976.

Oxendorf, Eric, and William Seale. *Domes of America*. San Francisco: Archetype Press, 1994.

Severin, Donald. *The Encyclopedia of State Capitols and Capitals*. Cove, Ore.: Mt. Fanny Publishing, 1999.

ALABAMA

Alabama Building Commission. *Alabama Capitol Complex Master Planning Study* [report], 1982.

Gamble, Robert S., and Thomas W. Dolan. *The Alabama State Capitol: Architectural History of the Capitol Interiors* [report for the Alabama Historical Commission], 1984.

Holmes, Nicholas H., Jr. "The Capitols of the State of Alabama." *Alabama Architect Handbook* (1980): 1–4.

Holmes, Nicholas H., Jr. "Charles Follen McKim and the Capitol of Alabama." *Alabama Review: A Quarterly Journal of Alabama History* 42, no. 1 (1989): 4–31.

Montgomery Area Chamber of Commerce. *A Self-*

Guided Tour of the Alabama State Capitol [brochure], n.d.

Sweeney, Thomas W. "Power of Place." *Historic Preservation News*, January 1993, 16–17.

ALASKA

"Alaska State Capitol." In *Alaska Blue Book*. Juneau: Division of State Libraries and Archives, 1991–1992, 239.

Legislative Affairs Agency. *Alaska's State Capitol* [brochure], n.d.

ARIZONA

Arizona Department of Library, Archives and Public Records. *Arizona State Capitol Museum* [brochure], n.d.

"The Capitol." *Arizona*, n.d., 3–9.

Wright, Frank Lloyd. *Oasis: Plan for Arizona State Capitol* [report], 1957.

ARKANSAS

Arkansas State Planning Board. *Capitol Grounds* [report], 1936.

Department of State. *The Arkansas State Capitol Plan, 1968–2000* [report], 1968.

Donaghey, George W. *Building a State Capitol*. Little Rock: Parke-Harper, 1937.

The Old State House: A Visitor's Guide [brochure], n.d.

Ross, Margaret. "The Hinderliter House: Its Place in Arkansas History." *Arkansas Historical Quarterly* 30, no. 3 (1971): 181–92.

Treon, John Alfred. "The Building of the Arkansas State Capitol, 1899–1915." M.A. thesis, University of Arkansas, 1964.

Walters, Dixie. "Time Is on Her Side," *Construction*, 22 March 1993, 25–27.

CALIFORNIA

Arts and Antiques of the State Capitol. Sacramento: Joint Committee on Rules, California State Legislature, 1984.

The California State Capitol: Self-Guided Tour [brochure], n.d.

Donnelly, Loraine B., and Evelyn T. Cray. *California's Historic Capitol*. Davis: Craydon, 1989.

Joint Committee on Rules, California State Legislature. *Restoration and Development of the Capitol* [report], 1975.

Marlowe, Lynn G. *California State Capitol Restoration: A Pictorial History*. Sacramento: Joint Committee on Rules, California State Legislature, 1988.

Pietro Mezzara, First California Sculptor. Sacramento: Senate Rules Committee, California State Legislature, 1982.

ROMA Design Group. *Capitol View Protection Plan* [report], 1991.

Sommer, Robert, and Katherine Steiner. "Office Politics in a State Legislature." *Environment and Behavior* 20, no. 5 (1988): 550–75.

COLORADO

Coel, Margaret. *Pride of Our People: The Colorado State Capitol*. Denver: Colorado General Assembly, 1992.

Colorado House of Representatives. *Art of the House* [brochure], 1990.

Memorials and Art in and Around the Colorado State Capitol. Denver: Colorado Legislative Council, 1992.

Pyle, William R. "History of the Colorado State Capitol Complex." M.A. thesis, University of Denver, 1962.

Visitor's Guide to Colorado's Capitol [brochure], n.d.

CONNECTICUT

Branch, Mark Alden. "Church and State." *Progressive Architecture*, May 1992, 110–18.

Cimino, D.C. *Development Plan: Connecticut State Capitol* [report], 1983.

Curry, David Park, and Patricia Dawes Pierce, eds. *Monument: The Connecticut State Capitol*. Hartford: Old State House Association, 1979.

Smith, Jennifer Whitley. "Politics and Professionalism: The Making of the Connecticut Capitol, 1872–1879." M.A. thesis, School of Architecture, Yale University, 1988.

The State Capitol: Hartford, Connecticut, 1879–1988. Hartford: Connecticut General Assembly, 1988.

DELAWARE

Delaware's Legislative Hall [brochure], 1990.

The Delaware State House: A Preservation Report.

Dover: Department of State, Division of Historical and Cultural Affairs, 1976.

FLORIDA

Capitol: A Guide for Visitors. Tallahassee: Historic Tallahassee Preservation Board, 1982.

Historic Tallahassee Preservation Board. *Florida Capitol Center* [brochure], 1983.

Morris, Allen. "The Seat of Government." In *The Florida Handbook, 1991–1992*, 251–68. Tallahassee: Peninsular, 1992.

State Museum of Florida History. *The Old Capitol* [brochure], n.d.

GEORGIA

Fortson, Ben W. *The State Capitol of Georgia*. Atlanta: Secretary of State, n.d.

Georgia Secretary of State. *A Capitol Idea!* [brochure], n.d.

Georgia's Capitol. Atlanta: Secretary of State, n.d.

Make Georgia a Shining Example. Atlanta: Georgia Building Authority, 1979.

HAWAII

Hawaii's State Capitol & Government. Honolulu: Office of the Governor and Hawaii Legislature, n.d.

The Resoration of Ali'iolani Hale. Honolulu: Office of the Administrative Director of the Courts, 1980.

IDAHO

"Capitol Tour Guide." In *Idaho Blue Book, 1993–1994*, 15–21. Boise: Idaho Secretary of State, 1994.

Idaho Centennial Commission and Department of Commerce. *Welcome to Idaho's State Capitol* [brochure], n.d.

ILLINOIS

Anderson, Lowell E. *A Guide to the Illinois Old State Capitol*. Springfield: Illinois State Historical Library, 1974.

Henderson, Earl W., Jr. "Sleuthing the Mid-1900s." *AIA Journal*, November 1967.

A History of the Demolition and Reconstruction of the Illinois Old State Capitol. Springfield: Illinois State Journal and Illinois State Register, 1968.

Illinois Capitol Guide. Springfield: Illinois Secretary of State, 1988.

Illinois Historic Preservation Agency. *Old State Capitol: State Historic Site* [brochure], n.d.

Illinois Secretary of State. *Illinois State Capitol* [brochure], n.d.

Sorensen, Mark W., ed. *Capitol Centennial Papers.* Springfield: Illinois State Archives, 1988.

Temple, Sunderine, and Wayne C. Temple. *Illinois' Fifth Capitol.* Springfield: Phillips Brothers, 1988.

INDIANA

Description of the New State House for the State of Indiana to Be Erected at Indianapolis, 1878.

The Indiana State Capitol Building: A Centennial Restoration, 1888–1988, n.d.

IOWA

Bussard/Dikis Associates. *Strategy for the Completion of the Iowa State Capitol Restoration Project* [reports], 1988, 1989.

Bussard/Dikis Associates and BRW Architects. *Iowa State Capitol Expansion* [report], 1989.

Iowa Legislative Public Information Office. *Welcome to the Iowa State Capitol* [brochure], n.d.

Johnson, Linda Nelson, and Jerry C. Miller. *The Iowa Capitol: A Harvest of Design.* Des Moines: Plain Talk, 1989.

Keyes, Margaret N. *Old Capitol: Portrait of an Iowa Landmark.* Iowa City: University of Iowa Press, 1988.

McClure, Judith Ann. "Iowa State Capitol Restoration." *Iowa Architect,* Spring 1992, 10–13.

Public Information Office, *Iowa Capitol Guide* [brochure], n.d.

KANSAS

Office of Secretary of State. *Kansas Capitol Square* [brochure], n.d.

Richmond, Robert W. "Kansas Builds a Capitol." *Kansas Historical Quarterly* 38, no. 3 (1972): 249–67.

KENTUCKY

Field, Elizabeth S. "Gideon Shryock: His Life and His Work." *Register of the Kentucky Historical Society* 50 (1952): 110–29.

Fleenor, C. M. *A Brief History of Kentucky's New Capitol,* 1910. Reprint, Frankfort, Commonwealth Historical Services, 1985.

Hardin, Bayless E. "The Capitols of Kentucky." *Register of the Kentucky State Historical Society* 43, no. 144 (1945): 173–200.

Kentucky Historical Society. *An Introduction to Kentucky's Old State Capitol* [brochure], n.d.

Kentucky Historical Society. *Kentucky's Historic Capitols* [brochure], n.d.

Kentucky Historical Society. *The Old State Capitol* [brochure], n.d.

Kentucky Office of Historic Properties. *The Governor's Mansion* [brochure], n.d.

Lewis, George A. *Kentucky's New State Capitol,* 1910.

Newcomb, Rexford. "Gideon Shryock—Pioneer Greek Revivalist of the Middlewest." *Register of the Kentucky State Historical Society* 26, no. 78 (1928): 220–35.

LOUISIANA

Hair, William Ivy. *The Kingfish and His Realm: The Life and Times of Huey P. Long.* Baton Rouge: Louisiana State University Press, 1991.

International Paper. *The Louisiana State Capitol* [brochure], n.d.

Jolly, Ellen Roy, and James Calhoun. *The Louisiana Capitol.* Gretna: Pelican, 1980.

Kubly, Vincent F. *The Louisiana Capitol: Its Art and Architecture.* Gretna: Pelican, 1977.

Louisiana Secretary of State, *The Old State Capitol* [brochure], n.d.

MAINE

Shettleworth, Earle G., Jr., and Frank A. Beard. *The Maine State House: A Brief History and Guide.* Augusta: Maine Historic Preservation Commission, 1981.

MARYLAND

Hanan, Sara B., and Edward C. Papenfuse. *The Maryland State House, Annapolis.* Annapolis: Maryland Commission on Artistic Property of the State Archives and Hall of Records Commission, 1984.

Maryland Office of Tourism Development, *Maryland State House* [brochure], n.d.

Radoff, Morris L. *The State House at Annapolis.* Annapolis: Maryland Hall of Records Commission, 1972.

MASSACHUSETTS

Ann Beha Associates. *The State House Historic Structure Report* [report], 1985.

Art in the Massachusetts State House. Boston: Massachusetts Art Commission, 1986.

Bostonian Society. *Old State House* [brochure], n.d.

Chase, Sara B. "A Brief Survey of the Architectural History of the Old State House, Boston, Massachusetts." *Old-Time New England* 68, nos. 3–4 (1978). [Reprinted as brochure by Bostonian Society, n.d.]

Dalton, Cornelius, John Wirkkala, and Anne Thomas. *Leading the Way: A History of the Massachusetts General Court, 1629–1980.* Boston: Massachusetts Secretary of State, 1984.

Hitchings, Sinclair H., and Catherine H. Farlow. *A New Guide to the Massachusetts State House.* Boston: John Hancock Mutual Life Insurance, 1964.

Massachusetts Secretary of State. *The Massachusetts State House: A Guide to a Walking Tour and a Short but Interesting History of the Building* [brochure], n.d.

MICHIGAN

Chartkoff, Kerry. "Michigan's 'Atomic Age' Capitol." *Michigan History* 74, no. 4 (1990): 28–31.

Chartkoff, Kerry. "Unveiling a Masterpiece: A Walking Tour Through the Restoration Process." *Michigan History* 74, no. 4 (1990): 20–27.

Eckert, Kathryn B. "Elijah Would Be Proud!" *Michigan History* 74, no. 4 (1990): 16–19.

Michigan Capitol Committee. *Restoration of the Capitol Building: The Restoration Process* [report], 1991.

Michigan Department of Management and Budget, Office of Facilities. *Preservation Master Plan, Michigan State Capitol, Lansing, Michigan* [report], 1987.

Office of the Senate Majority Leader. *The Michigan Senate* [brochure], n.d.

Seale, William. *Michigan's Capitol: Construction and Restoration.* Ann Arbor: University of Michigan Press, 1995.

MINNESOTA

Blatti, Jo. *The Minnesota State Capitol Complex, the 1940s to the 1980s.* St. Paul: Minnesota Office of the Governor, 1987.

Capitol Area Architectural and Planning Board. *Capitol Area Development* [report], 1986.

Capitol Area Architectural and Planning Board. *Competition Conditions and the Urban Design Framework* [report], 1986.

Capitol Area Architectural and Planning Board. *East Capitol Area: Design Framework Study for Urban Development* [report], 1990.

Capitol Area Architectural and Planning Board. *Minnesota's State Capitol Mall: Minnesota's Front Yard* [report], 1990.

Kompelien, Carolyn, Kendra Dillard, and Sherri Gebert Fuller. *Attention to Detail: 1905 Furniture of the Minnesota State Capitol.* St. Paul: Minnesota Historical Society, 1989.

Lawrence, Wade Alan. "Herter Brothers and the Furniture of the Minnesota State Capitol, 1903–1905." M.A. thesis, University of Delaware, 1987.

Minnesota Historical Society. *Minnesota State Capitol* [brochure], n.d.

Phelps, Gary. *History of the Minnesota State Capitol Area.* St. Paul: Capitol Area Architectural and Planning Board, 1985.

Thompson, Neil B. *Minnesota's State Capitol: The Art and Politics of a Public Building.* St. Paul: Minnesota Historical Society, 1974.

MISSISSIPPI

Mississippi Department of Archives and History. *Mississippi State Historical Museum* [brochure], n.d.

State Capitol Commission. *The New Capitol* [brochure], n.d.

Skates, John Ray. *Mississippi's Old Capitol: Biography of A Building.* Jackson: Mississippi Department of Archives and History, 1990.

MISSOURI

Edelman, Nancy. *The Thomas Hart Benton Murals in the Missouri State Capitol.* Jefferson City: Missouri State Council on the Arts, 1975.

Missouri Department of Natural Resources. *First Missouri State Capitol* [brochure], n.d.

Missouri Department of Natural Resources. *State Capitol and Missouri State Museum* [brochure], n.d.

The Missouri State Capitol: A Collection of Historic Information About Its Architectural Design. Jefferson City: Missouri Senate, 1979.

Ohman, Marian M. *The History of Missouri Capitols.* Columbia: University of Missouri Extension Division, 1982.

Parker, Lester Shepard. "Missouri's New State Capitol." *Scottish Rite Progress*, May 1925, 2–4, 7.

"Selecting Plans for New Capitol." In *Official Manual of the State of Missouri*, 19–31. Jefferson City: Missouri Secretary of State, 1914.

Souvenir Guide to Missouri's Capitol. Jefferson City: Missouri Department of Natural Resources, n.d.

Swartwout, Egerton. "A Description of the Plans Submitted by Tracy and Swartwout, Architects, in the Missouri State Capitol Competition." *American Architect* 102, no. 1922 (1912): 147–52.

Swartwout, Egerton. "The Missouri State Capitol." *Architectural Record* 61 (1927): 105–20.

Viles, Jonas. "Missouri Capitals and Capitols." *Missouri Historical Review* 13 (1918–1919): 232–49.

MONTANA

"The Graft That Failed." *Montana*, October 1959, 2–11.

McDonald, James R. *Historic Structure Report: Montana State Capitol Building* [report], 1981.

Montana Historical Society. *The Montana Capitol: A Self-Guided Tour* [brochure], n.d.

NEBRASKA

Breckenridge, Adam C. "Innovation in State Government: Origin and Development of the Nebraska Nonpartisan Unicameral Legislature." *Nebraska History* 59, no. 1 (1978): 31–46.

Brown, Elinor L. *Architectural Wonder of the World: Nebraska's State Capitol Building*. Lincoln: Nebraska State Building Division, 1978.

Crosby, Robert B. "Dedication of the George W. Norris West Legislative Chamber." *Nebraska History* 66, no. 1 (1965): 1–6.

Fowler, Charles F. *Building a Landmark: The Capitol of Nebraska*. Lincoln: Nebraska State Building Division, 1981.

Luebke, Frederick C., ed. *A Harmony of the Arts: The Nebraska State Capitol*. Lincoln: University of Nebraska Press, 1990.

Nebraska State Building Division. *Tower on the Plains: The Nebraska State Capitol* [brochure], 1978.

Nebraska State Capitol Commission. *The Nebraska Capitol* [brochure], 1926.

Sittig, Robert. "The Nebraska Legislature: Policy Implications of Its Organization and Operation." In *Nebraska Policy Choices*, ed. Russell Smith,

273–95. Omaha: University of Nebraska Center of Applied Urban Research, 1987.

Sittig, Robert. "The Nebraska Unicameral After Fifty Years." In *Nebraska Blue Book*, 41–60. Lincoln: Nebraska Legislative Council, 1986–1987.

Wesser, Robert F. "George W. Norris: The Unicameral Legislature and the Progressive Ideal." *Nebraska History* 45, no. 1 (1964): 309–21.

NEVADA

"The Capitol Story." *Nevada Highways and Parks* 19, no. 1 (1959): 3–9.

Nevada Department of Economic Development. *The History of the Capitol Building* [brochure], n.d.

Nevada Department of Museums, Library and Arts. *Nevada's State Capitol, Monument to Democracy* [brochure], n.d.

"Nevada State Capitol." In *Nevada*, 3–16. Carson City: Commission on Tourism and the 125th Anniversary Commission, 1991.

Nylen, Robert A. *The Architecture of the Nevada State Capitol*. Carson City: Nevada State Museum, n.d.

NEW HAMPSHIRE

Anderson, Leon W. *To This Day: The 300 Years of the New Hampshire Legislature*. Canaan: Phoenix, 1981.

New Hampshire's State House, A Visitor's Guide [brochure], n.d.

The State House of New Hampshire, Old and New. Concord: New Hampshire State Senate, 1943.

Welcome to the New Hampshire House of Representatives [brochure], n.d.

Welcome to the New Hampshire State House [brochure], n.d.

NEW JERSEY

Chalifoux, Matthew S. "The Architectural Evolution of the Legislative Chambers of the New Jersey State House, 1872–1905" (Paper presented at symposium on public art in New Jersey, 1988).

Short and Ford, Architects. *Legislative Space Study* [report], 1981.

NEW MEXICO

Shishkin, J. K. *The Palace of the Governors*. Santa Fe: Museum of New Mexico, 1972.

NEW YORK

Abrams, Jonathan K., ed. *Empire State Plaza: Design for the Future.* Albany: New York State Office of General Services, 1976.

Bleecker, Samuel E. *The Politics of Architecture: A Perspective on Nelson A. Rockefeller.* New York: Rutledge, 1981.

The Empire State Collection: Art for the Public. Albany: Empire State Plaza Art Commission, 1987.

New York State Office of General Services and State Commission on the Restoration of the Capitol. *Visitor's Guide to the New York State Capitol* [brochure], 1989.

Roseberry, C. R. *Capitol Story.* Albany: New York State Office of General Services, 1982.

Zdunczyk, David. *200 Years of the New York State Legislature.* Albany: Albany Institute of History and Art, 1978.

NORTH CAROLINA

"Legislating in the Old Capitol." *Popular Government* 43, no. 2 (1977): 11–27.

North Carolina Department of Cultural Resources. *The Capitol of North Carolina* [brochure], n.d.

North Carolina State Legislative Building [brochure], n.d.

Sanders, John L. "The North Carolina State Capitol of 1840." *Antiques* 128, no. 3 (1985): 474–84.

Sanders, John L. "This Political Temple, the Capitol of North Carolina." *Popular Government* 43, no. 2 (1977): 1–10.

State Capitol Foundation. *Heroes and Heroines on Union Square* [brochure], n.d.

NORTH DAKOTA

Biek, Robert F. *A Visitor's Guide to the North Dakota Capitol Grounds.* Bismarck: State Historical Society of North Dakota, 1995.

Green, Sheldon. "The Capitol: A Tale of Trickery, Flames and Good Fortune." *Horizons,* n.d., 16–30.

North Dakota State Capitol and Grounds [brochure], n.d.

Remele, Larry, ed. *The North Dakota State Capitol: Architecture and History.* Bismarck: State Historical Society of North Dakota, 1989.

Simons, Kenneth W. *North Dakota's Capitol.* Bismarck: State Historical Society of North Dakota, 1934.

OHIO

Berke, Arnold. "This Is Their Jewel." *Preservation* 48, no. 5 (1996): 76–85.

Capitol Square Renovation Foundation. *Ohio's Capitol: A Self-Guided Tour* [brochure], 1992.

Schooley Caldwell Associates, *The Ohio Statehouse Master Plan* [report], 1989.

OKLAHOMA

"Art Treasures of the Oklahoma State Capitol Complex." *Oklahoma Business,* September–October 1989, 13–18.

Oklahoma Tourism and Recreation Department. *Oklahoma Capitol Complex* [brochure], 1988.

Wade, Henry F. *Ship of State on a Sea of Oil.* Oklahoma City: Oklahoma Historical Society, 1975.

OREGON

Bentson, William Allen. *Historic Capitols of Oregon: An Illustrated Chronology.* Salem: Oregon Library Foundation, 1987.

Department of General Services, *A Framework Plan for Capitol Mall Development* [report], 1986.

The Pioneer Spirit: Oregon Capitol Souvenir Booklet. Salem: Oregon Legislative Administration Committee, 1988.

Welcome to Oregon's State Capitol [brochure], n.d.

PENNSYLVANIA

Department of General Services, *Welcome to Pennsylvania's Capitol* [brochure], n.d.

The Pennsylvania Capitol: A Documentary History. 4 vols. Harrisburg: Heritage Studies for Pennsylvania Capitol Preservation Committee, 1987.

Pennsylvania House of Representatives [brochure], n.d.

Projects of the Pennsylvania Capitol Preservation Committee [brochure], n.d.

The Senate of Pennsylvania [brochure], n.d.

The Supreme Court of Pennsylvania [brochure], 1986.

Welcome to Pennsylvania's Capitol and General Assembly [brochure], 1990.

RHODE ISLAND

Conley, Patrick T., Robert Owen Jones, and William McKenzie Woodward. *The State Houses of*

Rhode Island: An Architectural and Historical Legacy. Providence: Rhode Island Historical Society and Rhode Island Historical Preservation Commission, 1988.

Kempler, George. *A Self Guided Tour of the Rhode Island State House.* Cumberland: Colony Books, 1991.

Rhode Island Secretary of State, *The Rhode Island State House* [brochure], n.d.

SOUTH CAROLINA

Bryan, John M. *Creating the South Carolina State House.* Columbia: University of South Carolina Press, 1999.

Fant, Christie Zimmerman. *The State House of South Carolina: An Illustrated Historic Guide.* Columbia: Bryan, 1970.

Historic Documentation Report on South Carolina State House. Columbia: Ford Farewell Mills and Gatsch, 1993.

Maxey, Russell. *South Carolina's Historic Columbia: Yesterday and Today in Photographs,* 64–70. Columbia: Bryan, 1980.

The State House Committee Report. Columbia: Stevens and Wilkinson of South Carolina, 1993.

SOUTH DAKOTA

"Decoration of South Dakota Capitol." *Western Architect* 17, no. 4 (1911): 40–43.

Schuler, Harold H. *A Bridge Apart: History of Early Pierre and Fort Pierre.* Pierre: State Publishing, 1987.

Schuler, Harold H. *The South Dakota Capitol in Pierre.* Pierre: State Publishing, 1985.

South Dakota State Capitol [brochure], n.d.

TENNESSEE

Dekle, Clayton B. "The Tennessee State Capitol." *Tennessee Historical Quarterly* 25, no. 3 (1966): 3–28.

Gadski, Mary Ellen. "The Tennessee State Capitol: An Architectural History." *Tennessee Historical Quarterly* 47, no. 2 (1988): 67–120.

The History of the State Capitol Building [brochure], n.d.

Hoobler, James A. "William Strickland, Architect." *Tennessee Historical Quarterly* 45, no. 1 (1986): 3–17.

Mahoney, Nell Savage. "William Strickland's Introduction to Nashville, 1845." *Tennessee Historical Quarterly* 8 (1949): 46–63.

Tennessee State Museum. *The Tennessee State Capitol: A Self-Guided Walking Tour* [brochure], 1991.

TEXAS

Cutrer, Emily Fourmy. "'The Hardy, Stalwart Son of Texas': Art and Mythology at the Capitol." *Southwestern Historical Quarterly* 22 (1988): 288–322.

Fowler, Mike, and Jack Maguire. *The Capitol Story: Statehouse in Texas.* Austin: Eakin Press, 1988.

Freeman, Allen. "Thinking Big." *Historic Preservation,* January–February 1995, 52–59.

Robinson, Willard B. "Pride of Texas: The State Capitol." *Southwestern Historical Quarterly* 22 (1988): 227–87.

State Department of Highways and Public Transportation, *Texas Capitol Guide* [brochure], n.d.

The Texas Capitol: Symbol of Accomplishment, 4th ed. Austin: Texas Legislative Council, 1986.

3D/International and Ford, Powell and Carson. *Texas Capitol Preservation and Extension* [master plan and historic structures report], 1989.

Ward, Michael, *The Capitol of Texas: A Legend Is Reborn.* Atlanta: Longstreet Press, 1995.

UTAH

Cooley, Everett L. "Utah's Capitols." *Utah Historical Quarterly* 27 (1959): 258–73.

Historic Buildings On Capitol Hill. Salt Lake City: Utah Heritage Foundation, 1981.

Utah: A Guide to Capitol Hill [brochure], n.d.

Utah Travel Council, *Welcome to the Utah State Capitol Building* [brochure], n.d.

VERMONT

Robert Burley Associates. *State of Vermont Capitol Complex* [reports], 1968, 1974.

Robbins, Daniel. *The Vermont State House: A History and Guide.* Montpelier: Vermont Council on the Arts and Vermont State House Preservation Committee, 1980.

Sergeant-at-Arms Office and Friends of the Vermont State House. *The Vermont State House* [brochure], 1988.

VIRGINIA

Brownell, Charles E., Calder Loth, William M. S. Rasmussen, and Richard Guy Wilson. *The Making of Virginia Architecture*. Richmond: Virginia Museum of Fine Arts and University Press of Virginia, 1992.

Dodson, E. Griffith. *The Capitol of the Commonwealth of Virginia at Richmond: Portraits, Statuary, Inscriptions, and Biographical Sketches*, 2nd ed. Richmond: Dodson, 1938.

Kimball, Fiske. *The Capitol of Virginia*. Richmond: Virginia State Library and Archives, 1989.

Kummer, Karen Lang. "The Evolution of the Virginia State Capitol, 1779–1965." M.A. thesis, School of Architecture, University of Virginia, 1981.

Marcellus Wright Cox and Smith. *Master Plan and Study Report: Capitol Square Complex and Broad Street Station Site* [report], 1992.

Seale, William. *Virginia's Executive Mansion: A History of the Governor's House*. Richmond: Virginia State Library and Archives, 1988.

The Virginia State Capitol [brochure], n.d.

WASHINGTON

Department of General Administration. *Interior Completion and Renovation Program, Capitol Campus, Olympia, Washington* [brochure], n.d.

Governor's Mansion Foundation. *Washington State's Executive Mansion* [brochure], n.d.

Johnston, Norman J. *Washington's Audacious State Capitol and Its Builders*. Seattle: University of Washington Press, 1988.

Southwest Washington Chapter of American Institute of Architects, comp. *Legislative Building, State Capitol Group, Olympia, Washington* (Historic documents compiled for meeting of AIA chapter, 26 April 1978).

The State Reception Room [brochure], 1986.

Superintendent of Public Instruction. *Stalwart Stone* [brochure], 1997.

A Tour of the Washington State Legislative Building [brochure], n.d.

Washington State Capitol, Olympia [brochure], 1989.

WEST VIRGINIA

Cohen, Stan, and Richard Andre. *Capitols of West Virginia: A Pictorial History*. Charleston: Pictorial Histories, 1989.

"Come and See Your Capitol." *Charleston Daily Mail*, 19 June 1932.

The Supreme Court of Appeals of West Virginia [brochure], n.d.

The West Virginia Capitol: A Commemorative History. Charleston: Senate of West Virginia, 1995.

The West Virginia Governor's Mansion [brochure], n.d.

WISCONSIN

Cook, Diana. *Wisconsin Capitol: Fascinating Facts*. Madison: Prairie Oak Press, 1991.

Cravens, Stanley H. "Capitals and Capitols in Early Wisconsin." In *State of Wisconsin Blue Book, 1983–1984*, 103–68. Madison: Wisconsin Legislative Reference Bureau, 1983.

Rajer, Anton. *Wisconsin State Capitol Coloring Book*. Madison: Art Conservation Press, 1991.

Rajer, Anton. "Working Chronology of the Wisconsin State Capitol." Typescript, 1990.

"The Wisconsin Capitol: Official Guide and History." In *Wisconsin Blue Book*, 451–86. Madison: Democrat, 1917.

Wisconsin State Capitol [brochure], n.d.

Wisconsin State Capitol: Guide and History, 33rd ed. Madison: Department of Administration, Division of Buildings and Grounds, 1991.

WYOMING

Wyoming Capitol Tour Guide [brochure], n.d.

Wyoming's Capitol. Cheyenne: Wyoming State Press, 1987.

INTERVIEWS

Alabama. October 9–10, 1992. Don Drablos, McDowell Lee, Larry Oaks, William G. Pappas, William Woodsmall

Arizona. October 21–23, 1991. James Duke Cameron, Michael D. Carman, Tricia Daly, George C. Leiphart, Jane Richards, Polly Rosenbaum, Shirley Wheaton, Sharon G. Womack

Arkansas. May 5–6, 1993. Steve Barns, Swannee Bennett, Ann Pryor Clements, Christopher Dimon, Joan I. Duffy, William Lancaster, Tim Massanelli, Judy Thompson

California. December 19–20, 1991. Robert Connelly, Richard Gable, Dan Walters, Robert Wood

Colorado. July 20–21, 1992. Joan M. Albi, Lee Bahrych, Betty M. Chronic, Cole Finegan, David Hite, Lyle Kyle, Robert G. H. Pahl, Marie Sanborn, John Sanko, James C. Wilson, Jr.

Connecticut. June 23–24, 1992. Patricia Christiana, Marion F. Delaney, Joseph A. Devine, Eunice Groark, Joan Hall, David B. Ogle, Irving J. Stolberg

Delaware. August 2, 1993. Bernard Brady, McDonald T. Coker, Jo Ann M. Hedrick, Howard E. Row, Madeline D. Thomas

Florida. March 24–25, 1992. Joseph Brown, David Coburn, Terrie Corbett, Peter A. Cowdrey, Charles Frier, Mary V. Goodman, Allen Morris, Thomas Wheaton

Georgia. April 28–29, 1993. Max Cleland, Frank Eldridge, Jr., Lounell R. Jones, Luther C. Lewis, Jr., Cicero Lucas, Elizabeth A. Lyon, Dorothy Olson, Carolyn Pettus, Robert E. Rivers, Jr., Alan Spring

Hawaii. July 15–16, 1998. Kevin M. Ebata, Brenda Lei Foster, Renwick Joe Tassill, Marian E. Tsuji

Idaho. July 14, 1995. Kimberly Bigelow, Michael Despot, Kenneth J. Swanson, Merle Wells

Illinois. April 15–16, 1992. Jenny Aiello, Carol A. Andrews, Linda Hawker, John F. O'Brian, Robert Orr, Mark W. Sorensen, Wayne C. Temple, Jack Van Der Slik

Indiana. June 10–11, 1992. David E. Dawson, David J. Dixon, Barbara D. Fistrovich, John C. Fleck, J. Mack Huston, Betty L. Masariu, Donald Perry, Carolyn J. Tinkle

Iowa. July 8–9, 1992. William Dikis, John F. Dwyer, William Maloney, Jerry C. Miller, Susan Wallace, Mark Willemssen

Kansas. October 7, 1991. William D. Groth, Patrick J. Hurley

Kentucky. September 28–29, 1995. T. Rexford Cecil, Lewis N. Hughes, Rex Lyons, Tony McVeigh, William L. Phelps, Sherri Murphy Smith, James E. Wallace

Louisiana. March 22–23, 1992. Michael Baer, Donald Chaney, Mary Durusau, Kevin Harris, Murphy Kinchen, Pat Pickens, Mary Louise Prudhomme, Catherine Wohlert

Maine. May 19, 1998. Joseph W. Mayo, Rita Brochu Melendy, Earle G. Shettleworth, Jr.

Maryland. July 29–30, 1993. Nancy M. German, Susan E. McCahan, Welford L. McClellan, Gregory A. Stiverson, Kristin B. Thompson

Massachusetts. November 13–15, 1991. Leonard C. Alkins, Leonard L. Desautelle, Peter Lucas, Mary McLellan, Ronald J. Norton, Thomas Pizzuto, Lisa Simonetti, Jordan St. John

Michigan. June 8–9, 1992. John Beutler, Kerry Chartkoff, David H. Evans, Richard C. Frank, Jerry Lawler, Jeffrey McElvey, Marty Selfridge, Willis H. Snow

Minnesota. July 6–7, 1992. Edward A. Burdick, Marilyn Cathcart, Zona De Witt, Patrick E. Flahaven, Gary Grefenberg, Peter Isaacs, Carolyn Kompelien, Paul Mandell, Val Michelson, Mary Murphy

Mississippi. May 3–4, 1993. Irb Benjamin, Charles J. Jackson, Jr., Kenneth H. P'Pool, Ermea J. Russell, Nan Watkins

Missouri. November 30, December 1–2, 1995. Mary Pat Abele, Mark N. Allen, Russell B. Coy, John Cunning, Ronald K. Kirchoff, Booker H. Rucker, Keith Sappington, Jerry Wilson, Kenneth H. Winn

Montana. July 7, 1995. Mike Cooney, Debra M. Fulton, Betti Christie Hill, Dallas O. Miller

Nebraska. October 6, 8–10, 1991. Dennis Baack, Richard Brown, Andrew F. Cunningham, Charles DeVries, Robert C. Ripley, Robert Sittig, Jerome Warner

Nevada. July 14, 1998. Gordon Absher, Jeffrey M. Kintop, Lorne J. Malkiewich, Robert Nylen

New Hampshire. November 12, 1991. James L. Garvin, Kenneth Leidner, Robert Raiche, Donn Tibbetts

New Jersey. February 1–2, 1993. Matthew S. Chalifoux, Donna Frangakis, Dolores A. Kirk, Karen Poling, Karen Wightman

New Mexico. July 23, 1992. Stephen Ray Arias, Susan Campbell, Molly G. Chavez, Margaret Larragoite, Cynthia Sanchez, Scott Seymour

New York. September 23–27, 1991. Dennis R. Anderson, John Ewashko, Thomas Maloney, John Nealon, William F. O'Connor, Stephen F. Sloan, Thomas Tipple, Richard H. Van Patten, Larry Wayne

North Carolina. October 18, 1993, June 26, 1994. Sylvia Fink, John L. Sanders, Denise G. Weeks

North Dakota. June 30, 1995. Donald D. Mund, Keith Nelson, John D. Olsrud, Beverly Schlenker

Ohio. September 16–18, 1991, May 29–30, 1992. Fern V. Conte, Richard L. Fickenworth, Richard H. Finan, Dean Johnson, Lee Leonard, Robert D. Loversidge, Jr., Dan W. McCalla, Brian McMahon, Edward D. Schirtzinger, Roberta Steinbacher, David Sweet

Oklahoma. November 2–3, 1995. Bob L. Blackburn, Carol Boone Gwin, Wayne Hager, Paul B. Meyer, Jolane Rimer, Lance Ward, Larry Warden

Oregon. December 18, 1991. Cecil L. Edwards, Dea Knickerbocker, Elisabeth Walton Potter, Dan Simmons

Pennsylvania. May 26–27, 1992. Mark R. Corrigan, Robert L. Glenn, Irving Hand, Ruthann Hubbert-Kemper, Clancy Meyer, Jeremy F. Plant, Tomas H. Spiers, Jr.

Rhode Island. June 25–26, 1992. Libby Arron, Joseph A. Cirillo, Elmer E. Cornwell, Jr., Brian Coyne, James Craemer, George Kempler, Al Klyberg, Laurence K. Walsh, William McKenzie Woodward

South Carolina. April 26–27, 1993. Lisa Addison, Frank B. Caggiano, Michael M. Frick, Ann Martin, Sandra K. McKinney, D. Ray Sigmon

South Dakota. June 28, 1995. Terry Anderson, Duane Eckert, Stephanie Ellenbecker, John G. Moisan, Jay Vogt

Tennessee. October 12–13, 1995. Burney Durham, Bud Gangwer, Ted Guillaum, James A. Hoobler, William R. Snodgrass

Texas. May 5–6, 1992, July 26, 1995. Dealey Herndon, John E. Hodges, Betty King, Bekki Lammert, Ron Lindsey, M. Allen McCree, Clare Scherz

Utah. July 5, 1995. Solveig J. Coles, Joseph B. Ligori, Carole E. Peterson, Joan B. Thomas

Vermont. July 2, 1993. Robert H. Gibson, Robert L. Picher, David Schutz, Jane Williams, John J. Zampieri

Virginia. August 9–10, 1993. Lonnie E. Craig, Joseph H. Holleman, Jr., Bruce F. Jamerson, Nancy M. Maupin, Hugh C. Miller, Susan Clarke Schaar, Charlotte S. Toxell, Mary Ellen Verdu

Washington. December 16–17, 1991. James M. Dolliver, Dee R. Hooper, William C. Jacobs, Roberta Perry, Jeanne Smith, Alan Thompson, Ross Young

West Virginia. July 12–13, 1993. Louise Burke, Daniel E. Gilchrist, Gregory M. Gray, Darrell E. Holmes, Paul D. Marshall, Sam Sutton, Pat Wendell

Wisconson. July 10–11, 1992. Dale Dumbleton, Joyce Inman, Charles Quagliana, Anton Rajer, Donald J. Schneider, Gerilyn Schneider

Wyoming. June 26, 1995. Paul Galeotos, Judy Sergeant

Index